OPERATION
SWALLOW

ALSO BY MARK FELTON

Zero Night: The Untold Story of World War Two's Greatest Escape

*The Sea Devils: Operation Struggle and
the Last Great Raid of World War Two*

Castle of the Eagles: Escape from Mussolini's Colditz

*Ghost Riders: Operation Cowboy, the World War Two Mission to
Save the World's Finest Horses*

OPERATION SWALLOW

AMERICAN SOLDIERS' REMARKABLE
ESCAPE FROM BERGA CONCENTRATION CAMP

MON

ICON

Published in the UK in 2019
by Icon Books Ltd, Omnibus Business Centre,
39–41 North Road, London N7 9DP
email: info@iconbooks.com
www.iconbooks.com

Sold in the UK, Europe and Asia
by Faber & Faber Ltd, Bloomsbury House,
74–77 Great Russell Street,
London WC1B 3DA or their agents

Distributed in the UK, Europe and Asia
by Grantham Book Services, Trent Road,
Grantham NG31 7XQ

Distributed in Australia and New Zealand
by Allen & Unwin Pty Ltd, PO Box 8500,
83 Alexander Street, Crows Nest, NSW 2065

Distributed in South Africa
by Jonathan Ball, Office B4, The District,
41 Sir Lowry Road, Woodstock 7925

Distributed in India by Penguin Books India,
7th Floor, Infinity Tower – C, DLF Cyber City,
Gurgaon 122002, Haryana

ISBN 978-178578-577-1 (hardcover)
ISBN 978-178578-599-3 (paperback)

Text copyright © 2019 Mark Felton

Typeset in Janson Text

Printed and bound in Great Britain by
Clays Ltd, Elcograf S.p.A.

To Fang Fang, with love

Contents

CONTENTS

CHAPTER 1

Hold the Line!

Remember your orders are to hold at all costs. No retreat, nobody comes back.

Maj. Gen. Norman Cota

Take cover!" was the first order of the day on the morning of December 16, 1944. Hans Kasten had been asleep in his bivouac not far from the hamlet of Nachtmanderscheid, on the road to the strategically vital town of Clervaux in the northern tip of Luxembourg. The veteran Twenty-Eighth Infantry Division was guarding the border between Luxembourg and Germany in a heavily forested, hilly part of Europe called the Ardennes. Since landing in Normandy in June 1944, the Allied armies had pushed the Germans back to the very borders of the Reich, and were preparing to break into Germany itself in the coming spring. Roads through the Ardennes were few and the terrain considered unsuitable for offensive actions, so the Americans were satisfied to hold the region with the minimum of troops while concentrating their forces on more vulnerable sectors in France. Indeed, the area was considered so quiet that green units were sent there to acclimatize to conditions at the front, and battle-weary divisions rested.

Kasten's unit, the 110th Infantry Regiment, was a part of the Twenty-Eight, one of these American divisions that had seen extensive action and had been sent to the Ardennes to rest and refit. Originally hailing from Pennsylvania, the men wore a red keystone patch on their shoulders to commemorate the Keystone State. The Germans had christened this symbol the "Bloody Bucket" for the punishment the Germans had dealt out to the American division in the Hürtgen Forest, and the death and mayhem that they had dealt out in kind.[1] The Battle of the Hürtgen Forest had been an American attempt to break into Germany in late 1944 that had turned into a slaughter against a well-prepared enemy and ended in stalemate. After the breakout from Normandy in August 1944, it had looked as though the Germans were beaten, but now, in December, they had managed to stabilize their front line and could still give the Allies a bloody nose. What no one in the Allied high command expected was a full-scale offensive from the Germans so late in the war, and certainly not in the depths of winter in the unsuitable Ardennes.

To the north of the Twenty-Eighth Division's position was the Belgian part of the Ardennes, garrisoned by more American divisions. With more than twenty inches of snow on the ground, Kasten, exhausted after coming off watch, had been huddled beneath sparse army blankets trying to catch some shut-eye when all hell had broken loose.

Kasten involuntarily reached up and touched a livid-looking scar that ran in a jagged line like a lightning bolt across his forehead. He had seen the sharp end of war long before the Ardennes, on the other side of the world. The scar was a memento of a white-hot shard of shrapnel that had struck him while he was aboard a troop transport in December 1941. Only instead of being German, this particular fragment of bomb casing had come courtesy of the Japanese. Kasten's background and life journey had been complex and surprising.

He was born in Honolulu in August 1916 to well-to-do

German parents who immigrated from Bremen. He had been raised in Milwaukee, Wisconsin, graduating with a degree in art history from the University of Wisconsin.[2] But his freethinking and defiant attitude led him to take the unusual step of "retiring" straight out of college and go "off to the South Seas."[3] He'd joined the Merchant Marine and shipped out to the Philippines in the pay of a dredging company.

"The best thing I did was that I retired after college," Kasten said. "Everybody talks about what they're going to do after they retire but when they finally do retire, they're too old to do anything and they've lost all their dreams."[4]

At sea when Pearl Harbor was attacked by the Japanese on December 7, 1941, his ship put in to Fiji and then headed to Brisbane, Australia, arriving on Christmas Eve.

America needed young men, and after listening to a rousing speech from the US ambassador, Kasten volunteered to return to the States to help the war effort. He and many other young Americans boarded a returning troop transport bound for San Diego. Shorthanded, the captain asked for volunteers to man the vessel's antiaircraft guns. Kasten found himself operating the port aft gun.

It wasn't long before Kasten, still a civilian, was in the thick of the action. A lone Japanese aircraft bombed his ship while they were steaming through the Tasman Sea. One minute Kasten was hammering away at the enemy aircraft, the next he was waking up in the ship's sick bay with one hell of a headache and sixteen stitches holding together a nasty gash across his forehead.[5]

After arriving at Fort Sheridan, north of Chicago, Kasten had been assigned to the Transportation Corps. But due to his high intelligence and varied life experience, his superiors attempted to have him reassigned as a teacher at an Officer Candidate School. Kasten refused the transfer, stating clearly that he had joined the US Army to fight, not teach.[6] Shipped over to England, Kasten found himself part of a unit that was tasked with unloading and distributing military supplies in the great port of Liverpool. Disgusted with the level of corruption and thieving that he witnessed, he volunteered for the infantry. Retrained at Tidworth Barracks, Kasten was the best marksman in his company.[7]

*

Now England was but a distant memory as Kasten's company sector was subjected to an intense German mortar barrage in the Ardennes Forest. The GIs tumbled into dugouts and foxholes, trying to make themselves as small as possible as the bombs detonated all across the position, blowing down trees and throwing up clumps of frozen dirt and ice high into the overcast sky. White-hot shards of shrapnel scythed down on those too slow to reach cover. Kasten, a veteran of D-Day and the terrible Battle of the Hürtgen Forest—where tens of thousands of Americans and Germans had fought themselves to a stalemate through fifty square miles of dense, soggy woodland near the German city of Aachen—knew what was coming next. All the veterans in the unit knew. When the artillery fire slackened, an infantry attack would usually follow. The veterans in the Twenty-Eighth had witnessed this happen so many times, their reactions were almost automatic.

Kasten was his rifle squad's Browning Automatic Rifle (BAR) gunner. John Kopczinski, his best friend since basic training in Tidworth, volunteered to be Kasten's assistant gunner—his job was to carry the weapon's stack of magazines and help Kasten keep the gun in action.[8]

Running uphill in a crouch, Kasten, a tall, lean man with his distinctive Vandyke moustache and beard and piercing blue eyes, lugged the heavy BAR with him while Pfc. Kopczinski followed with the ammunition. Both men charged forward, almost oblivious to the occasional mortar bomb that still landed around them, before they flung themselves into a small bunker constructed out of a hole in the ground covered with tree trunks for rudimentary overhead protection.

All along the line other riflemen and machine gunners jumped into foxholes and dugouts, ready for anything the Germans could fling at them. Charging up the slope close to Kasten was nineteen-year-old Pfc. William Shapiro, a combat medic from the East Bronx in New York City. Like Kasten, Shapiro was the product of immigrant parents who had moved to the United States for a better life, in Shapiro's case escaping anti-Jewish pogroms in Russia. Now, these same families had sent their sons back to Europe to fight Nazism. Drafted at eighteen, Shapiro had trained at Walter Reed General Hospital before landing on Omaha Beach in Normandy that summer.

Shapiro's green steel helmet displayed red crosses inside white circles, marking him as a noncombatant; he also wore a Red Cross brassard. But artillery and mortars do not differentiate, and before he reached cover a shell exploded close by with a blinding flash. Shapiro was blown several feet by the blast and landed in the snow nearby, unconscious. Other medics and riflemen managed to drag his limp body to cover before he was evacuated back to the regimental aid station at the castle town of Clervaux.

Hans Kasten slammed a twenty-round magazine into the BAR and cocked the weapon, hastily setting up its bipod on the bunker's lip. He glanced at Kopczinski, who propped his M1 carbine against the frozen side of the bunker. His friend smiled grimly before both men turned to stare out of the fire slit, awaiting the attack that they knew must come at any second.

Kasten was older than the average dogface, and so much more experienced in life, so many of the young GIs in the outfit looked to this fiercely independent, unorthodox man for guidance or advice. But perhaps his independent style and strong opinions were not to everyone's taste, particularly those of his superiors, because Kasten hadn't been promoted beyond private first class. There wasn't much call for enlisted men with free-thinking, defiant attitudes. He even looked different from the average GI, with the ends of his moustache waxed and turned up "German-style."[9] He was, put simply, a man of the world, and older than his twenty-seven years suggested.

The Twenty-Eighth Infantry Division, a part of the US VIII Corps, had a simple task—conduct aggressive defense within the Corps zone. The Corps units consisted of, from north to south, the 106th Infantry Division, the Twenty-Eighth Division, the Ninth Armored Division (minus two-thirds of its strength), and the Fourth Infantry Division. The Twenty-Eighth was assigned a portion of the Schnee Eifel, a heavily wooded extension of the Ardennes running along the Belgian-German frontier that consisted of high, windswept plateaus, deep, snow-filled ravines, and ghostly, fog-shrouded forest valleys. The Twenty-Eighth Division's three regiments, with Kasten's 110th Infantry in the center, guarded a twenty-five-mile-long bow-shaped front covering the Our and Sauer Rivers. Maj. Gen. Norman "Dutch" Cota's headquarters were located twelve miles back at the small town of Wiltz, with VIII Corps HQ a farther twelve miles west at the strategically vital crossroads town of Bastogne.[10]

Prior to the morning of December 16, 1944, the Ardennes had been a sector of the US lines where no serious fighting was expected. It was very thinly held. The assigned divisions were either "green" units, like the 106th Division, learning on the job by undertaking small patrol actions against the Germans, or shattered and exhausted units like the Twenty-Eighth that had been pulled out of the Hürtgen Forest meat grinder after suffering crippling casualties, their surviving veterans stiffened by the arrival of plenty of replacements. Either way, the Ardennes was a low priority for the Americans. The Allies were gearing up to break into Germany and cross the Rhine—and the last thing they expected was a massive German offensive. The Battle of the Hürtgen Forest had surprised the Allies—German resistance had been fierce and skillful, but surely overwhelming American and British pressure would be brought to bear somewhere else along the Siegfried Line and the hastily reassembled German defenses overcome.

This Allied belief in an imminent German military collapse unexpectedly changed in December. American divisions found themselves assailed by Adolf Hitler's last desperate gamble to wrest back the strategic initiative on the Western Front—the well-named Operation Herbstnebel (Autumn Fog). In an extraordinarily short period of time since the German Army had been defeated in Normandy, retreated through France, and crossed the Siegfried Line into Germany, Hitler had managed to assemble 250,000 men and more than one thousand tanks and assault guns. He was intent on slashing through the thinly held Ardennes, where he had surprised the French and British so memorably in the summer of 1940, and strike across the Meuse River to capture the strategically vital Allied supply port of Antwerp. In one stroke, Hitler believed that he would split the Americans from their British allies and cut off supplies to three Allied armies, with disastrous results. The entire plan depended upon surprise, speed, and bad weather. Two great tank armies would cross the rivers that bordered Belgium and Luxembourg in the Ardennes and surge forward to take the vitally important road junctions at St. Vith, blocked by the 106th Division, and Bastogne, the approaches via the towns of Marnach and Clervaux controlled by Cota's Twenty-Eighth. From there, the roads to the Meuse would be wide open. The operation was timed for December, when the area would be deep under snow and bad weather would ground the Allied air forces, which had aerial superiority over the battlefield and made any offensive operations nearly impossible.

The Allies had also lost the advantage of Ultra, the top-secret decrypts of German signals traffic generated by the Enigma code that had been broken by British scientists at Bletchley Park in England. Though they were usually fully aware of Hitler's plans before he launched them, because the Germans had been forced back behind their own border, they had stopped using radios and instead reverted to the telephone network, which the Allies could not penetrate. Therefore, Hitler achieved complete tactical surprise on the morning of December 16.

*

Hans Kasten let out a loud curse as he peered over the lip of his position downslope toward the Our River. It looked like half the German Army was surging across, gray-and-white-clad figures in the hundreds fanning out on the American side of the river, many firing as they ran or hurling stick grenades. The Germans had crossed using rubber boats under a smokescreen, while bridge-building units went to work trying to create crossings of the following heavy armor and supply vehicles.

Kasten quickly shouldered his BAR and zeroed in on the nearest running figures. He began working through magazines at a prodigious rate, his rounds peppering the ground all around the advancing Germans, knocking them down in clumps.[11] Return fire thudded into the hillside, kicking up spurts of snow all around Kasten or cracking past his head as the Germans dashed from cover to cover, firing rifles and machine guns in an effort to suppress the deadly American return fire.

Every few seconds Kasten would release another empty magazine, the BAR's muzzle steaming in the cold air, then turn and yell at Kopczinski for more ammo. Riflemen in foxholes to his left and right hammered away with their M1 Garands, the sounds of shooting constantly interspersed with metallic pings as empty ammo clips automatically ejected from their weapons. In this manner, the 110th Regiment would stand firm against all comers till the following day, severely disrupting the German timetable for reaching the Meuse.

*

At Company I, 422nd Infantry Regiment, 106th Infantry Division, Pfc. Joseph F. "Mish Kid" Littell and his comrades had been strangely left alone by the Germans since their great offensive had broken. Littell, a good-looking, clean-cut twenty-year-old with neat, side-parted dark brown hair, had acquired his unusual nickname because he had been born in Hankow, China, to American missionary parents in 1924.[12] He shared something in common with Hans Kasten, though the two had yet to meet: Littell's father was appointed bishop of Honolulu in 1930, fourteen years after Kasten was born there.

Joe Littell had had an unsettled early childhood, common in missionary families, changing schools and countries often. Then, at age twelve, he had been sent to boarding school in Delaware. Unlike many of the other grunts in the 422nd foxholes, Littell had already savored Europe before the war. In 1938, he had been selected by his headmaster as one of thirty young boys from thirty American schools who would be sent to Germany on an exchange program with the Nazi government. The idea was to foster greater understanding between Germany and the

United States, and the visits were organized by American-German friendship societies. A reluctant Littell had attended an elite National Socialist Education Academy at Köslin, two hundred miles east of Berlin on the Baltic Sea between January and June 1939, shortly after Hitler had annexed Czechoslovakia and Austria and not long before he invaded Poland and started World War II. Littell, who was repulsed by the politics of Nazi Germany, reluctantly wore the Hitler Youth uniform, complete with swastika armband, and got plenty of practice "Heiling the Führer of the Third Reich." Even more incredibly, his graduation diploma was personally signed by no less a dignitary than Reichsführer-SS Heinrich Himmler, the second most powerful man in Germany.[13]

Now, more than five years later, he was facing his former school chums across the battlefield, his time in prewar Germany giving him an excellent grasp of the language and an abhorrence of Nazism. It was something that Littell would share with Hans Kasten, who had also studied in Germany before the war, and had memorably even met Hitler while staying at a youth hostel. Kasten had briefly spoken to Hitler, and formed the opinion that the Führer was already quite mad.

The 422nd Infantry's frontage faced wide, snowy fields with tall stands of dense, gloomy fir trees beyond. Commanded by one of the youngest colonels in the US Army, George Descheneaux, the 422nd's regimental headquarters was located in a *gasthaus* in the town of Schlausenbach just behind the lines. The 106th Division commander, Maj. Gen. Alan W. Jones, was forty minutes by jeep behind the front at the crossroads town of St. Vith, which, along with Bastogne, was to be held at all costs by the Americans in order to prevent German armored forces from exploiting the road network toward the Meuse River and beyond.

German artillery fire had erupted quite suddenly at 0530 hours on December 16. Several dozen men from various 106th Division companies were caught out of cover. Pfc. Peter Iosso had been making his way wearily back to his position when the barrage went up. An Italian American from Newark, New Jersey, Iosso had turned nineteen just two months before. He was serving in the 422nd Infantry, assigned to the Company E weapons platoon, where he manned a .30-caliber medium machine gun. Normally he would have been with his weapon, nicely ensconced inside a log bunker covering the ridge, but he had been detailed to a combat patrol ordered to insert itself into the ground in front of the American position the night before. Iosso, a little guy, was wading through deep snow back toward his position, thoroughly worn out and soaking wet, his boots sodden, a pair of spare socks drying in his armpits, when a shell from the German's opening barrage exploded close by, knocking him unconscious.

For an hour Joe Littell and his comrades had pressed themselves into their holes beside their bivouac positions behind the ridge; the ridgeline was only thinly held when there was no alert on. German artillery rounds had whined overhead, sounding like freight trains ripping through the heavens before landing somewhere behind them with booming explosions. The ground had shaken continuously like an earthquake; the American soldiers covered their heads with their arms or gritted their teeth and huddled lower in their holes. More than one man prayed out loud as the firestorm of metal and explosives grew in intensity. Occasionally, a shell dropped short, throwing up a geyser of snow, mud, and rock close by. In the distance, the reports of the German guns rumbled like summer thunder, and soon a new and far more frightening sound had joined the cacophony—a high-pitched screaming that was enough to curdle blood. German

Nebelwerfer rocket batteries added their peculiar projectiles to the opening barrage of the great German offensive. The GIs soon had a name for them—"screaming meemies."[14]

Close behind Littell's position, the Company I commander, Capt. David Ormiston, slammed down the field telephone receiver he had been holding to his ear while trying to hear the voice on the other end over the whine and crash of incoming shells. The line had suddenly gone dead while he had been talking to battalion headquarters. The artillery fire had probably severed the line. But a few minutes later a runner arrived from headquarters. The messenger quickly dismounted from a snow-and-mud-splattered jeep and rushed into Ormiston's command post, a stone farmhouse hidden among the trees. The messenger ducked through the house's doorway, flinching when another shell landed close by, and quickly handed the note to one of the sergeants who was crouched near Ormiston.

"Message from Regiment, sir," the NCO yelled after glancing at the paper in his hand. Ormiston glanced up from a tactical map that he had been examining.

"Read it, Sergeant," he yelled back, ducking when a shell landed close enough to spray the roof of the house with falling debris.

"Go on combat alert for a German ground attack and await further orders," the sergeant called.[15] His eyes locked with Ormiston's. The news was electrifying, but also ominous. Ormiston knew that his regiment, the 422nd Infantry, like every other American unit, was spread mightily thin along this section of the line.

The 422nd was one of three regiments that constituted the 106th Infantry Division, a fresh unit that had arrived from England and been sent to the "quiet" Ardennes sector to gain some experience. Arriving at St. Vith, six miles behind the front on December 10 after an exhausting 470-mile journey in unheated trucks, the division's three regiments had settled into prepared positions vacated by other units.

They were deployed abreast with the 422nd Infantry covering the northern sector, two thousand yards west of the Siegfried Line on the western slopes of the Schnee Eifel. The regiment's left flank touched the village of Schlausenbach, the right meeting the 423rd Infantry at Oberlascheid. The 423rd's lines extended southwest to the town of Bleialf. Meanwhile, the 424th Infantry covered the south, from Bleialf to around Winterspelt, tying in with Hans Kasten's veteran 28th "Bloody Bucket" Division.

Division HQ was at St. Vith, where Major General Jones had his 106th headquarters inside a large convent school. The town was a vital crossroads that the Germans were determined to capture and exploit quickly.[16]

In the five days that the 422nd was in the line before the German assault, cases of trench foot had skyrocketed. The special snow overboots issued to the troops had been mistakenly left behind in England, so the GIs endured wet feet in the deep snow as their ordinary combat boots struggled to cope. Sick men taken off the line were not replaced, as no fresh troops were available, further thinning the already threadbare American positions. The GIs shivered in the frigid air, as no proper winter uniforms had been issued, either—the men simply wore every item of clothing they possessed beneath their long green great-coats or combat jackets and further wrapped themselves up in green blankets like Victorian old ladies. But the cold was bone-chilling and constant, with the men rotating from their bivouacs in warmer farmhouses and barns up to the ridgeline bunkers and foxholes for guard duty. Morale was low. Even more ominously, the units were short of mortar ammunition, and they possessed no tank support, which would later prove critical.

Captain Ormiston glanced back at the tactical map with its colored transparent overlays indicating the positions occupied by his platoons and the other companies and battalions in the regiment. Like elsewhere along the Ardennes front, the units were holding three or four times as much territory with the normal complement of men. A German push could roll right over them.

"Have the platoon commanders report to me at once," Ormiston shouted, ducking involuntarily as another German shell landed close to the house, rocking it to its foundations and bringing down plaster from the ceiling like falling snow. Atop the ridgeline outside, the men of the 422nd gritted their teeth and braced themselves for a German assault.

*

Pfc. Peter Iosso came around to find that it was now fully light and his chin was bleeding. His feet were frozen and painful. Pulling himself up, he made his way to his company positions, where he reported for sick call. Iosso was sent immediately to the battalion aid station, where a medic patched up his lacerated chin.[17] But things were starting to look grim when Iosso was told that he would not be evacuated back to the regimental hospital—it was too dangerous, because the Germans had started to press around behind the 106th Division's position. Iosso and his comrades all along the snowy ridgeline and the occupied villages behind began to realize that they were in a very hazardous situation. The Germans—who, Iosso and his friends had been told repeatedly, were a spent, defeated force—were apparently advancing in huge numbers right through the American lines, and no one appeared to be able to stop them.

This thought had already occurred to Pfc. Joseph Markowitz, who was manning a field telephone switchboard at the Third

Battalion, 122nd Infantry's headquarters, established inside a captured German pillbox right on the much-vaunted Siegfried Line. The pillbox, one of many the Americans had taken near the Schnee Eifel, actually faced the wrong way, but they made excellent and well-protected command bunkers. The son of Hungarian Jewish immigrants, Markowitz, twenty-four, was from the South Bronx in New York City. A college graduate, he had been almost overwhelmed by a stream of fire missions being routed through his switchboard from forward artillery observers up on the ridge, sending coordinates back to the artillery batteries to fire on German positions. Markowitz thought the situation so bad that he decided to put on every single item of clothing that he possessed—he had a dreadful feeling that soon he was going to find himself outside in the snow and ice. His premonition was completely correct.

CHAPTER 2

Surrounded!

Death was an every hour occurrence in those days. Life was cheap.

Pfc. Hans Kasten

The German artillery and mortar fire stopped abruptly after ninety punishing minutes. There was an eerie, pregnant silence broken only by snow falling from trees. Then, away to the north and south, Joe Littell and his comrades started hearing the sounds of heavy fighting. German panzer and Volksgrenadier divisions were attempting to smash their way through the American lines and capture vital river crossings and, most important, the road junctions farther west at St. Vith and Bastogne.

Littell and his platoon, along with most of Company I, had joined the regiment's other companies up on the exposed ridge, leaving their warmer bivouacs on the reverse slope, following another order from Regiment: "Enemy action reported on our northern flank and south of us, on the 423rd's southern flank. Dig in along the ridge and, in the event of an attack, hold the ridge at all costs."[1]

The 422nd's job, like the other units holding the line, was to absorb the initial German assault and try and hold them up long enough for proper reinforcements to arrive.

For the rest of the day their sector remained quiet as the German force opposing them attempted to encircle the 106th Division. The German commander had deployed two of his three regiments at either end of the high ground, intending to move forward and take St. Vith with his third once the 106th's flanks had been pushed in and infiltrated.[2] Littell's regiment was the one blocking the middle route to St. Vith, hence the delay in the German assault.

Based in an old schoolhouse in St. Vith, the 106th Division's commander, Maj. Gen. Alan W. Jones, knew his regiments were vulnerable, but felt he had no choice but to put them into the line owing to the length of front he was being asked to garrison. The real danger was a three-mile gap between the two regiments up on the Schnee Eifel ridge and Jones's third regiment, the 424th, that tied in with Hans Kasten's neighboring Twenty-Eighth Infantry Division. This massive gap was virtually undefended, save for the town of Bleialf, which was garrisoned by a hodgepodge of antiaircraft, tank destroyer, and cavalry reconnaissance units. If the Germans took Bleialf they could drive west to Schönberg and cut the 422nd and 423rd Regiments off. And this was exactly what the Germans intended to do—hence no direct assault on Littell's or the neighboring regiments' positions.

Littell and his twelve-man squad had been detached down into the valley below the ridgeline to patrol, sweeping the area for enemy combatants, but nary a German had been heard, let alone seen. But in the meantime, the Germans were hammering the neighboring American units, including the adjoining Twenty-Eighth Division, mercilessly.

*

By nightfall on December 16, the regiments in Hans Kasten's Twenty-Eighth Infantry Division were just managing to hold on to their positions. The 424th Regiment was exhausted but had not given up its foxholes and bunkers. In the 423rd's sector, violent hand-to-hand fights had erupted in hastily defended villages behind the ridgeline. The regiment held, but its seam with the 424th was now under direct threat. How much longer these thinly manned positions could hold against such a massive enemy thrust was unknown, but it would certainly not be for long if they were not quickly reinforced and resupplied.

*

Littell's outfit, the 422nd Infantry, had so far been spared a direct German assault, with US artillery fire managing to hold off the attack on the regiment's northern shoulder. But German infantry had managed to penetrate on the left flank and move into some of the rear areas, including assaulting the village of Schlausenbach, the location of Colonel Descheneaux's regimental headquarters. A strong German spearhead had also penetrated the three-mile gap, assaulting the town of Bleialf, which was holding but under intense pressure. Many officers in the 106th's three regiments were casting nervous glances rearward. They were wondering how long VIII Corps HQ would wait before ordering a general withdrawal west. If they left it too long, the regiments would soon become surrounded.

*

For Hans Kasten and the men of the 110th Infantry Regiment, the battle had been deadly serious all day and night of the sixteenth and into the morning of the seventeenth. Stubbornly, the American lines held. The GIs inflicted massive casualties on the white-clad Volksgrenadiers who were trying to secure the ridgeline so that German tanks could cross the Our in safety.

The tanks' target was the vital crossroads town of Bastogne, and the Germans needed to capture it quickly.

Eventually, German numbers and firepower began to overwhelm the thin line of defenders on the ridge. Kasten had kept his BAR in action for hours, his bunker almost ankle deep in spent brass cartridges, with Pfc. Kopczinski passing him fresh magazines or running back down the hill to fetch more supplies when the ammunition began to run short. But soon there were no more crates of ammunition to distribute, and as American casualties mounted and German units began to penetrate the line, the end was rapidly approaching.[3]

For what seemed like the thousandth time, a grim Kasten rammed another magazine into his BAR, cocked it, and then ran a hand over his dirty face. He was exhausted and existing purely on adrenaline. There had been hardly a moment to eat or drink anything for hours. Suddenly, a German rifle round ricocheted off a log close by his head and he was instantly back in action, the deafening hammering of the BAR filling the little bunker where he crouched with his friend, adding to the roar of battle all along the snowy ridge. With the coming dawn, the Germans were making a renewed and frenzied assault on the stubborn American positions, their leaders acutely aware that the offensive was already badly behind schedule.

Behind Kasten's regimental position, German forces had started to move into the rear areas, not only with infantry but also tracked assault guns. At the ancient Luxembourg town of Clervaux, which dominated the Clerve River crossings and the road to Bastogne, US troops who had been on rest and relaxation leave were hastily gathered together for a defense of the vital settlement, overlooked by a medieval white castle, its towers topped by pointed black witch's hat–style roofs. But many chose to flee instead of fight, joined by stragglers from smashed units retreating from the front in considerable disorder.

German artillery was already falling on Clervaux, adding to the confusion as reluctant rear area personnel were suddenly finding themselves being issued weapons and ammunition and told to take up defensive positions.[4] A concerned Col. Hurley Fuller, commanding the 110th Regiment, was monitoring the deteriorating position from his headquarters in the Hotel Claravallis in Clervaux. He pushed up what reserves he still possessed to try and reinforce his companies defending the ridgeline and the villages behind, his face a mask of anguish as he issued a stream of orders to his harried junior officers.[5]

*

"Jesus!" exclaimed Joe Littell, his eyes narrowing beneath the brim of his helmet, his gloved hands tightening automatically around the butt of his M1 Garand rifle.

His stomach contracted, butterflies whirling through his guts as a dozen German soldiers suddenly emerged from a stand of tall fir trees some five hundred yards down a snowy slope from Littell's platoon position atop the ridge.[6] It was the morning of December 17, and the 422nd sector, in contrast to everywhere else, was still eerily quiet. A low mist hung in the canopy of trees like smoke against the gray overcast sky that was heavily pregnant with snow. Littell glanced to his right, licking his lips in excitement and astonishment. He could see American helmets spaced out at regular intervals, their owners hunkered down in shallow foxholes, rifles balanced on the lips of their earthen scrapings. Many of the helmets had been given a rough coating of whitewash or had ripped-up bedsheets turned into ersatz snow covers to help the GIs blend in to the winter landscape.

"Here they come!" Littell exclaimed in a loud hiss to the GI in the next foxhole a few yards to his left.

Pvt. Art Kranz turned his unshaven, grimy face toward Littell, his eyes wide like saucers, his face unhealthily pale and drawn. "I see 'em, Mish," Kranz muttered, before his head whipped back toward the approaching Germans.[7]

To Littell's right, Pvt. Ben Kruger swore quietly, pressing his rifle into his shoulder. The Germans kept coming. Some wore long gray greatcoats under their equipment that had already turned white to the waist as they plunged through the thick snow, loping along like wolves, while others had white covers on their helmets or snowsuits over their uniforms. They carried rifles and machine pistols held across their chests, and some had stick grenades tucked into their belts. They moved forward confidently, widely spread out but seemingly oblivious to the presence of Littell and his buddies hundreds of yards away atop the ridge. All along the line, M1 helmets bobbed as the GIs took a bead on individual German soldiers.

S.Sgt. J. B. Parish ran over at a half crouch to Littell's squad and knelt on one knee, cradling his Thompson submachine gun in his arms. He adjusted his helmet with one gloved hand and grimaced as he stared at the Germans.

"Hold your fire," Parish hissed curtly, his breath pluming in the thirty-degree air. The platoon sergeant, who was only in his early twenties, sounded out of breath, whether from rushing between positions or from nerves, Littell and the others didn't know. Parish glanced at Littell.

"Wait till they get closer. I'll tell you when to fire."[8]

Some of the other GIs looked up at their platoon sergeant, hardly seeming to comprehend the order, their faces blank or their expressions anxious. Everyone on the gun line was as green as fresh grass, including the officers and NCOs. As soon as he spoke, Parish was off to the next squad, running in that crouched way all soldiers soon developed on the front line, his tommy gun at the ready.

Littell pressed his right cheek against the cold wooden butt of his rifle and peered along the sights, trying to line up on the moving Germans. It seemed unreal. Time seemed to slow down.

How could they not see us?

He flicked off the safety catch with a reassuring snap, his finger wrapping around the weapon's trigger, taking first pressure. The only noise was the loud crashing and thuds of German and American artillery and mortars away to the north and south. Someone somewhere was catching hell from the Krauts.

Littell and the other Company I GIs settled their rifles on the Germans, every man faithfully following Staff Sergeant Parish's order to not fire until he gave the signal. It was unreal, seeing German soldiers so close. For most of the men in this inexperienced regiment, this was their first view of a real live German soldier. They had known that the Germans were close since the regiment took up its position a week earlier, though they hadn't seen any. The Germans sometimes tried to spook them, knowing that they had replaced experienced troops. They occasionally drew swastikas on trees.

Now, out in the open, the German patrol that Littell and his comrades stared at looked capable and determined as they pushed on up the hill toward the position. Probably a reconnaissance squad sent to locate or probe the American positions. There were undoubtedly many more waiting out of sight in the tree line.

Littell and the others focused on the advancing Germans, eyes squinting along rifle sights, breath pluming in the chill air, totally concentrated on what must inevitably happen next.

Throats and mouths were dry with excitement and fear and expectation. But then when it seemed that firing must erupt at any second, suddenly most of the Germans stopped in their tracks, abruptly about-faced, and started loping back toward the tree line. One or two of the GIs exclaimed in confusion or glanced furtively at their pals in the next foxholes. The Germans must have realized they were running straight into the arms of their enemies. But two of the Germans didn't hear the order to retire, probably lost in the noise of artillery fire and swishing snow and ice. These two still came on, now just three hundred feet from the American gun line.

Littell sensed movement behind him and saw Staff Sergeant Parish return and crouch down close to his foxhole. Littell shifted his gaze back to the pair of Germans, taking a fresh bead on the leading man. He was close enough now to make out his features clearly beneath his coalscuttle helmet. Littell was only twenty, but this German appeared even younger.

"Fire!" Parish shouted close by, and Private Kruger, on Littell's left, pulled his trigger, followed a split second later by Littell. The bullets punched into the leading German, throwing up brief sprays of red. The enemy soldier suddenly straightened up and crashed face-first into the snow, his Mauser rifle bouncing off his steel helmet as he fell. Private Kranz fired a split second later, along with others in the squad, and the second German went down soundlessly, a round striking him in the face and turning his head into jellied pulp.[9] Both enemy soldiers lay still in the snow, apart from a few twitches.

Littell let out a long breath.

I've killed a man! was Littell's first shocked thought. *I've shot and killed a man! I've snuffed out the life of another human being![10]*

Littell's body went limp and he started to shake. He groggily clambered out of his foxhole, feeling light-headed, and moved behind the ridge. He had to move; he couldn't stay looking at the corpses of the men that he and his friends had just killed. No one noticed—they were all having similar thoughts, trying to process the couple of seconds of extreme violence that they had just perpetrated. It had been unlike anything in their short lives before—it was unreal. Many, like Littell, raised in a religious household, felt a terrible guilt at having killed for the first time. One second those two Germans had been powering through the snow toward them, rifles held purposefully across their chests, the next they were just bleeding lumps in the virgin snow. And Littell had done this. He tried to pull himself together. Hands shaking, he shouldered his rifle and took out a cracker and an army chocolate bar from his pocket and quickly ate them. But seconds later he was leaning against a tree trunk, quietly heaving out his guts into the snow.[11] When he finished he felt a little better. He returned to his foxhole, avoiding eye contact with his buddies, who said nothing as they, too, mulled over their first taste of action.

"Littell," a voice said close by.

He turned. It was Staff Sergeant Parish.

"Heads up. Combat patrol, ten minutes."[12]

Littell sighed and nodded. The platoon was sending out a small patrol into the valley to see if any Germans remained in the vicinity. It wasn't the first time Littell had performed this task, but since his first clash with the enemy, the war had suddenly become fearfully real—and deadly.

*

In Pfc. Kasten's 110th Infantry position, the Germans were not running away—they were attacking uphill relentlessly in huge numbers despite their massive casualties, and they were starting to win. Unlike Littell and the 106th, Kasten and his comrades had long ago lost their fear and fascination with the taking of human life—the Hürtgen battle had seen to that. And now they were knee-deep in German corpses, but enough of the enemy was still alive to decide the issue. The Germans had successfully penetrated the boundary between the 110th and its neighboring regiment, the 109th, at the village of Hoscheid. German engineers had also managed to throw makeshift bridges across the Our River, and panzers and assault guns were starting to rumble across and join in the fight—the American infantry had little with which to stop them, just a handful of supporting Sherman tanks and their own bazookas, for which there was a shortage of rockets. The 110th's positions were becoming increasingly untenable in the face of the massive German attack, and the regiment was being progressively surrounded.[13]

Kasten fought on without hesitation or relief. Suddenly, Pfc. Kopczinski, Kasten's assistant gunner, cried out and Kasten turned. His friend lay still, unconscious and bleeding in the bottom of the bunker. He'd been struck twice by bullets and was completely paralyzed.[14]

"John!" Kasten yelled above the din of firing, exploding hand grenades, and shouting American and German soldiers. He reached out and shook his friend, but there was no response.

"Medic!" Kasten yelled, looking up and down the ridgeline. "Medic, we got a man down here, medic!" He quickly turned back to the BAR and loosed off a long burst at the nearest Germans before turning back to his friend, who still appeared to be breathing.

"Hang in there, John," shouted Kasten. "Hang on, buddy, help's coming."

A few seconds later one of the company medics, his helmet marked on four sides with a red cross inside a white circle, flopped down beside Kopczinski and started to go to work on him.

"Doc, is he alive?" Kasten asked breathlessly in between firing the BAR.

"He's alive," replied the grim-faced medic, adding, "watch yer front" as he administered a shot of morphine to Kopczinski.

A few minutes later, his wounds wrapped in field dressings, Kopczinski was evacuated by stretcher off of the line. He was the last one who was taken out to the battalion aid station behind the position before the final surrender.[15]

The fighting continued for a few more minutes after Kopczinski had been taken to the rear, but Germans were now all around them. With casualties mounting and with communications back to divisional headquarters cut, the surviving American officers gave the order to cease fire and surrender. Word was quickly passed from position to position. Kasten was incredulous when he first heard. At no point during the war had he ever thought that he might be taken prisoner—killed, yes, but not forced to surrender.

Within a few minutes, a strange silence settled over the battle-field, which was littered with dead Germans lying in the snow like bloody bundles of dirty laundry. Tree trunks were chipped and riddled with bullets. In and around American positions lay dead or wounded GIs, the white earth here and there scorched black by grenade explosions. The wounded groaned or screamed, while the medics moved resolutely among them, ministering with what little equipment and drugs they had remaining. Here and there shell-shocked men sat cradling their heads in their hands or laughing hysterically. Then Kasten heard the guttural calls of German soldiers moving along the line. "*Raus, raus*," they yelled, ordering the GIs who could still stand to climb out of their foxholes and dugouts at gunpoint, while others violently wrenched rifles and machine guns out of their hands and stacked them in piles on the frozen ground.

One man shouted, "Hands up, Chicago gangsters!" over and over in heavily accented English.[16] It was a ridiculous refrain, borne of watching too many prewar Hollywood movies, and it would have been funny under other circumstances, but not now.

Soon hundreds of German soldiers swarmed over the ridgeline, pushing and shoving the disarmed and confused GIs into rough groups. Many men took the opportunity to dispose of weapons or personal possessions before the Germans got to them. One man deliberately removed his wristwatch and smashed it against a rock, declaring loudly, "Those bastards don't get this!"[17] Others whacked their rifles against tree trunks to break off the wooden butts, or tossed vital mechanical parts from machine guns deep into the woods.

Kasten and one group of about two dozen dazed and exhausted survivors were herded into a rough line beside a snowy track, and stood silently with their hands up while several German soldiers started working their way down the column. Germans wrenched back GIs' greatcoat sleeves and ordered them to take off their watches. They were told to remove their combat webbing, which was placed in a pile near their confiscated weapons. This meant not only the loss of their ammunition pouches, bayonets, and gas masks but, vitally for prisoners of war, their water bottles and medical packs.[18] Other Germans roughly frisked each GI, taking any items that they fancied, including gold rings, any medical supplies or rations, cigarettes, and their useful little combination eating tools.

When they had finished, the Germans left Kasten and his comrades with only the uniforms they stood in and their M1 steel helmets. Everything else was shared out among the Germans, whose supply situation was precarious at best. With nothing to eat, drink, or smoke—and in some cases minus mittens after

Germans had snatched them off frozen hands—the GIs were ordered to fall in and start walking east.

"*Raus, raus!*" yelled their German guards. "*Amerikanische Schweinehunden!*" With the occasional encouragement of a rifle butt, fist, or boot, the survivors of Kasten's decimated company trudged wearily through the snow along tracks and roads whose surfaces had been churned up by passing German vehicles.

Kasten soon realized that the column of prisoners was only lightly guarded; the Germans needed every man they could get up at the front, fighting the remaining Americans. And each time a German vehicle came slipping and sliding along the muddy, snowy road, the guards yelled at the prisoners to scatter onto the high banks, then reform in the roadway once it was clear. Kasten was determined to escape, and escape quickly before he had been marched miles into the German rear areas.[19]

As he trudged along, he glanced ahead. He was midway up the column of prisoners. A young German soldier was a few yards ahead; an MP40 machine pistol slung over one shoulder and a cocked Walther P .38 pistol in his right hand. He was smoking a liberated American Lucky Strike with his other hand. Kasten glanced behind him. Some distance back another German, a Mauser rifle slung over his shoulder, shadowed the column, while farther back still were several more armed guards. They were calling to each other, laughing, and smoking, obviously pleased at their haul of prisoners. Kasten glanced to his right, where the roadway met a high snow-covered, mud-splattered bank several feet tall. Beyond was thick fir forest, and with the snow hanging heavily in the branches and the overcast sky giving little light at ground level, it was not possible to see more than a dozen yards into the timber.

Kasten was considering his options when he heard the sound of approaching engines from behind a corner up ahead. The guards began to shout at the prisoners to move to the bank, using their weapons to push the GIs roughly. Kasten followed the order, and partly clambered up onto the bank as a Kübelwagen field car and a couple of Opel Blitz trucks slowly rumbled around the corner, the vehicles packed with German troops. As the vehicles passed, some of the soldiers on board shouted insults at the Americans or exchanged jokes with their guards, momentarily distracting them. Kasten didn't hesitate—he pushed backward up and over the snow bank and quickly burrowed down into the ditch on the other side, pulling fresh snow over himself and lay still, trying to control his violently shivering body and chattering teeth.

Suddenly, from close by, he heard German voices. They were getting closer.

CHAPTER 3

Go West!

I'm worried about some of my people.

Maj. Gen. Alan W. Jones

Hans Kasten screwed his eyes shut tight and tried to regulate his breathing, but the deep cold made it difficult and he was shivering uncontrollably. The German voices came closer and closer, and he could hear their boots crunching through the frozen snow. Kasten braced himself for a shout and the sound of a rifle bolt being pulled back. But the footsteps continued on their way, their owners not paying any heed to the silent American figure lying prostrate in the ditch behind the snow bank. The German vehicles rumbled noisily by and then the guards started hollering at the long column of prisoners, herding them back onto the road to resume their march east, deep into the German rear.

Kasten opened his eyes. All he could see were snow-laden tree branches and patches of overcast slate-gray sky. It was becoming dark. After a while, the sounds of the column receded and he was alone, save for the rumble of faraway artillery or mortar fire and the occasional burp of a machine gun or crack of a rifle somewhere in the thick woods. After a few more seconds, he sat up, his greatcoat white with clinging snow. He looked about—nothing, just trees and snow. Gingerly, he got to his feet and crouched, shivering, like a dog that was sniffing the air for trouble.

Kasten didn't have much of a plan save for heading west toward the American lines. And he had only a sketchy idea of where his company headquarters was located, having never been back far from his own frontline positions since arrival.[1] But he was an experienced soldier and a resourceful man. He would find his way regardless. He was unarmed, but that didn't matter. He would try and steer well clear of any Germans, using darkness and the trees to cloak his movements.

The 110th Regiment's command post (CP) was in the pretty little town of Clervaux, about three miles behind the Our River. Clervaux, which lies in a hollow between two steep, tree-covered ridges, is in the very northern tip of the Grand Duchy of Luxembourg and is dominated by its medieval castle and the ancient twin-spired Abbey of St. Maurice and St. Maur. The 110th Regiment's First Battalion had companies billeted in little villages between Clervaux and the river, with platoons rotating up to the ridge above the river to watch the front line. Company A's command post was at Heinerscheid; Company B's— Hans Kasten's outfit—at Marnach, a tiny Luxembourg town of a couple of hundred residents; Company C's at Munshausen; and Company D's at Grindhausen. Support Company and Cannon Company were at Clervaux.

Kasten decided to try and reach the closest American position at Marnach, which was some two miles from where he judged himself to be. His plan was to skirt the main road, still busy with German supply vehicles and armor, keeping to the thick trees to try and pass through the enemy lines, which were extremely porous as their infantry and tanks fanned out against the 110th Regiment's remaining positions. Of course, there was the possibility that Company B's CP had been overrun or had hastily bugged out to the rear by now, but that was a chance Kasten would have to take.

Rubbing his frozen hands together, Kasten set off through the trees, trying to keep the road in view as he moved along, heading roughly west. It became more difficult once night fell. The country was quite hilly, and the thick fir trees made the going slow and exhausting. Kasten was glad of his steel helmet because branches constantly whacked him as he pushed through the undergrowth. He pressed on, his uniform soon almost completely white with snow, his nose and cheeks red with cold, his body frozen to the bone, and his boots damp. He was lucky; the fighting seemed to have shifted elsewhere, but Kasten hid several times to rest during the night, exhausted by the earlier combat and the tough, nerve-racking hike to Marnach. Other times, he was forced to seek a hiding place when the lights of German vehicles moving on the nearby road threatened to illuminate him, or when he encountered groups of enemy troops or supply units moving behind the front, many of them using horse-drawn wagons.

In the early hours he came upon the town of Marnach. He crept closer until he could make out the collection of stone houses huddled on both sides of the road to Clervaux. No lights were in evidence and the town looked deserted; the roofs were snow laden, the windows black and empty. No Germans were seen, either. Kasten watched for a while, but saw neither friend nor foe. Eventually, the cold eating into him, he could stand it no longer—he had to find shelter or run the risk of dying of exposure. He took a final look about and then started down the main street.

Bits and pieces of American kit were lying discarded in the street, but the buildings were largely intact, with little evidence of fighting. It looked as though Kasten was too late—his company command post was long gone. They had bugged out after all.

*

As Hans Kasten was making his way slowly back to the American lines, a tense conversation had occurred between Maj. Gen. Alan W. Jones, commanding Joe Littell's beleaguered 106th Infantry Division, and the VIII Corps commander, Lt. Gen. Troy Middleton. The line from Jones's command post in St. Josef's Convent School in St. Vith to Middleton in Bastogne was crackly and cut out frequently, and both men had to revert to shouting into their receivers in order to be heard.

"I'm worried about some of my people," yelled Jones, his pencil-thin moustache giving the fifty-one-year-old the look of film star Clark Gable. He was referring to Littell's 422nd Regiment and its sister unit, the 423rd, still up on the Schnee Eifel. No unit numbers or details would be given over the phone in case the Germans had tapped into the line.

"I know," came Middleton's muffled voice. "How are they?"

"Not well," shouted Jones, stuffing a finger into his other ear so that he could hear more clearly, pressing the cold receiver against his right ear until it almost hurt. "And very lonely," he added.

"I'm sending up a big friend, 'Workshop,'" came Middleton's reply, referring to the Seventh Armored Division. "It should be with you about oh-seven-hundred tomorrow."

Jones winced at the news—there was no way on earth that the Seventh Armored could make it to him so quickly. His overriding concern was whether the two regiments atop the Schnee Eifel should be withdrawn.

"Now, about my people," shouted Jones, making no comment on Middleton's news about the armored division coming to his aid. "Don't you think I should call them out?"

But Middleton didn't hear this last sentence as the line temporarily cut out.

"You know how things are up there better than I do," replied Middleton when the static cleared. "But don't you think your troops should be withdrawn?"

Tragically for Littell and his comrades, Jones didn't hear this last sentence either, as the line failed again. "I want to know how it looks from where you are," shouted a frustrated Jones, several staff officers hovering nervously nearby. "Shall I wait?"[2]

The call ended on a note of confusion as the line finally failed— Jones thought that Middleton wanted him to keep the regiments in position on the Schnee Eifel, while Middleton thought that Jones was going to withdraw them to safety before it was too late. Jones put down the receiver and turned to Col. Malin Craig, one of his artillery officers, his face ashen and drawn.

"Well, that's it," he said, referring to the Schnee Eifel regiments. "Middleton says we should leave them."[3]

Jones's depression was not helped by reports that arrived at 2240 hours indicating that the neighboring Twenty-Eighth Division units were now mostly cut off and isolated. Clervaux and Marnach were both reported to still be in US hands for now, but the situation was extremely fluid and changing rapidly by the hour.

*

"Hey soldier!" yelled a voice with the unmistakable growl of a senior noncom.

Hans Kasten, half crouched over as he crept along the street, stopped in his tracks and looked around. Across the street stood an American first sergeant, his uniform grimy and boots and pants spattered with mud. In the darkness Kasten had not seen the handful of GIs in position to defend the road. Now he was challenged and ordered to report.

"Get your ass over here," said the first sergeant, beckoning impatiently with one gloved hand. Kasten saw that he had a Thompson submachine gun slung over his right shoulder.

Kasten hastened across the road.

"Top," Kasten said, touching his helmet brim in salute. A first sergeant, known as "top kick" to the men, was a company's senior noncommissioned officer (or noncom) and based with headquarters. Several nervous-looking privates were occupying house fronts facing the street. Kasten assumed that others must be deployed farther out beyond the town, and he had somehow managed to stumble through the outpost line unseen and unchallenged. But due to the state of the American lines, it was clear that other stragglers had already passed through Marnach, fleeing the debacle that had engulfed Kasten's company up on the ridge.

"Who are you?" barked the first sergeant impatiently, looking him up and down with narrowed eyes.

Kasten explained where he had come from and what had happened to him. "I'm looking for my company CP," he finished.[4]

"Well, you're in luck, soldier," replied the first sergeant. "Follow me."

The first sergeant turned and strode down the street to a three-story house. Kasten followed him inside. He was immediately aware of other GIs in rooms leading off the hallway, busily hunched over tables or typewriters, while others sat nursing steaming hot tin mugs of coffee or smoking Luckies. Most barely glanced at him as he followed the first sergeant through a door under the stairs that led to the cellar.

"CO's down yonder," the first sergeant said, jerking a thumb, before starting down the stairs. Kasten descended, boots noisy on the wooden risers. The burble of radio static and chat came from a large wireless set manned by an operator, while the company commander stood behind him, smoking a cigarette, his steel helmet resting on the edge of a table across which several situation maps were laid. Sacks of potatoes were piled up along one wall.

The officer, a green-looking second lieutenant, turned when he heard Kasten and the first sergeant enter the room.[5] He looked barely out of his teens; his face was smooth and clean-cut, but his eyes were those of a deeply worried individual.

"Found this one wandering the street outside, sir," the first sergeant said, giving Kasten's name, rank, and company.

"My entire gang has been marched away, sir," announced Kasten.[6]

This statement didn't seem to register with the young officer. "Can you speak German?" he asked, most probably because of Kasten's surname.

"Fluently," replied Kasten.

The officer looked relieved by Kasten's reply. "Okay then," he said, "you stay here so when the Germans capture us you can talk to them."

Kasten was flabbergasted by the officer's demand, and the first sergeant's eyes had grown wide, too, as he listened. "Begging your pardon, sir," he said, "I've only just escaped from them. Staying here just to be captured again is *not* my intention."[7]

"You'll do as you're damn well told, Private!" snapped the overstressed lieutenant, his eyes flashing. "That's an order!"

Kasten glanced at the first sergeant. He didn't look happy, either. The officer soon lost interest in Kasten and turned back to the radio operator, where another report had come through.

"Come on, let's go upstairs," the first sergeant said to Kasten, and the two of them returned to the first floor. But just as they reached it, they heard a commotion outside, followed by some shots and shouting.

"Kraut infantry!" yelled one of the other GIs after glancing out the window. "They're right outside!"

Kasten turned to the first sergeant. "I'm getting out of here, Top."

The noncom hesitated, opening his mouth to say something, but then there was an almighty crash and the front door to the house slammed open. Germans entered brandishing rifles and machine pistols, and they yelled for everyone to get their hands in the air.

Kasten ducked into a back room, the first sergeant right behind him, his Thompson in his hands.

American shouts of "Don't shoot!" and "We surrender!" joined the cacophony of guttural German orders punctuated by occasional shots.[8]

"You coming?" Kasten asked, looking toward a window that led to the rear of the property.

"Damn straight…let's move!" hissed the first sergeant, his eyes slightly wild. Together, they wrenched open the window and dropped to the snow outside, breaking into a sprint as their legs powered them away from the house. Dawn was just breaking. As they fled, each expected a bullet between his shoulder blades at any moment.

*

For Joe Littell and his comrades in the 422nd and 423rd Regiments still occupying positions atop the two-thousand-foot-high Schnee Eifel ridge, their fate had been finally sealed in the early hours of December 17, when the village of Bleialf, dominating the three-mile-wide gap between the two immobile regiments and their sister 424th Regiment, had fallen.[9] German armor was now heading straight toward the town of Schönberg, where it would meet more panzers and infantry that had slipped around the north of the 422nd. Once a junction was accomplished between the two German pincers, Littell and his eight thousand comrades would be completely surrounded, trapped like rats in a barrel.

*

Hans Kasten and the first sergeant managed to stay one step ahead of the advancing Germans, cutting cross-country. They had decided to head for the 110th Regiment's command post located in Clervaux, almost three miles west of Marnach. This was where Lt. Col. James Rudder had established his headquarters.

Its ancient castle dominated the town, sitting atop a rocky spur, surrounded on three sides by the meandering River Clerve. The main approach to the settlement was down a snaking road from a high ridge above, a series of three steep hairpin bends presenting any defenders with ample opportunity to make the Germans pay dearly.

Colonel Rudder had been receiving a stream of increasingly desperate reports from his forward companies throughout the sixteenth and into the early hours of December 17, and it was obvious that the American line was buckling or even disintegrating in places. Units of the German Second Panzer Division had taken Marnach and driven headlong down the road toward Clervaux. Capture of the town opened the way for a dash to Bastogne and its vital crossroads. It was absolutely imperative that Clervaux not fall to the enemy.

But the news from the front continued to deteriorate. Rudder received reports that the Germans had penetrated the northern boundary between the 109th and 110th Infantry at the town of Hoscheid—this cut him off from his parent Twenty-Eighth Infantry Division. German engineers had managed to complete the first major bridge across the Our River, enabling heavy armor to cross in strength and begin to engage US defenders.[10]

38

When Hans Kasten and the Company B first sergeant made it to Clervaux after escaping from the Germans at Marnach, they found the place was in an uproar. A scratch force of defenders was manning positions scattered around the town. The men were mostly from the 110th's First Battalion, primarily cooks, clerks, signalers, and other ancillary troops from Headquarters and Support Companies, with some gunners from Cannon Company. Also present was the 103rd Engineer Battalion and the guns of 109th Field Artillery Battalion. There were also doctors and medics from Companies B and D, 103rd Medical Battalion staffing an aid station that was already overwhelmed by wounded. Many stragglers from units smashed in the fighting hardly paused in Clervaux, despite the orders of senior officers, and continued to withdraw west in a routed panic.

To stop what was coming would require more than just infantry supplied with rifles and grenades. To fight tanks, tanks or tank destroyers were required. About thirty Shermans were operating in and around Clervaux, drawn from two units, Company A, 707th Tank Battalion attached to the 28th Infantry Division, and others from Company B, Second Tank Battalion, Ninth Armored Division.[11] But would they be enough to stop the German panzer juggernaut?

*

Kasten and his companion found 110th Regimental Headquarters inside the imposing Hotel Claravallis with little trouble. They immediately reported for duty. A harried officer briefly interviewed Kasten.

"My entire gang has been marched away," declared Kasten once again, stone-faced.[12] The officer ordered that Kasten be issued a fresh weapon and plenty of ammunition and told him to report to Capt. Clark Mackey of Headquarters Company, who was commanding the troops occupying the castle.

Mackey assigned Kasten a defensive position in one of the castle's tall white towers. In total, Mackey was able to assemble 102 officers and men and remained in contact with Fuller at the Hotel Claravallis by radio and telephone.[13]

Hardly able to catch his breath after his adventures, Kasten soon found himself crouching by an open window high up in the castle, a cold wind blowing in his face, his newly issued M1 Garand rifle locked and loaded and pointing south. Below, in the town, Kasten could see jeeps and ambulances jostling with one another on the muddy roads, all trying to evacuate west, while more stragglers were being rounded up and told to man positions. There would be no surrender this time—only a fight to the finish.

Kasten ducked impulsively as the whine of incoming ordnance cut through the rumble of vehicle engines.

"Incoming!" bellowed a sergeant's voice, and everyone in the vicinity ducked down or hit the deck. German shells began arriving like express trains, their booming detonations sounding across Clervaux as houses were blasted into smoking ruins and dirty black and yellow holes were gouged out of the white snowy fields nearby. The Germans were softening up the town before launching their assault. Kasten ducked with each shell, gripping his rifle tightly, before peeking back over the windowsill. The castle rocked at each near miss, and occasionally a shell struck its ancient walls with a deafening roar, plaster raining down like snow on the defenders huddled at their windows or doorways.

Then at 0930 hours word arrived that German armor was cautiously approaching Clervaux. The shelling stopped as abruptly as it had begun. The first German battle group from the Second Panzer Division arrived soon after and slowly began attempting to work its way down the set of three hairpin bends along a road descending from a ridge outside the town into Clervaux.[14] Two platoons of PzKpfw IV tanks from the Third Panzer Regiment were supported by about thirty halftracks carrying a battalion of the Second Panzer Grenadier Regiment dressed in whitewashed steel helmets and snowsuits. Also supporting the assault were squat little German StuG III assault guns from the Thirty-Eighth Panzerjäger Abteilung.[15]

From his position in the castle, Kasten and the other defenders could see something the Germans couldn't. Defending each of the hairpin bends was an M4 Sherman tank, its turret mounting a 75 mm gun, waiting for a German tank to come around the corner. They were under the command of Lt. Raymond E. Fleig, Second Platoon, Company A, 707th Tank Battalion.[16]

Fleig's first Sherman was parked in front of a large, gloomy Victorian sanatorium building located beside the first bend. There was a brief exchange of fire before the Sherman burst into flames. The German armor ground on past the sanatorium's cemetery and approached the second hairpin on the icy road. Here, low and well covered, sat the second American tank. A German tank was knocked out, but another nosed around, turning into the bend. The German fired a second after the American. The Sherman was hit and exploded, flames and debris arching away into the snow-laden trees. Now only the third US tank remained, guarding the third and final hairpin bend. It was all that stood between the advancing Germans and the town.[17]

CHAPTER 4

The Alamo

But I'm telling you, it's going to be the Alamo all over again!
Col. Hurley Fuller

Inside Clervaux Castle, Hans Kasten peered out of his window, watching with horrified fascination as the last Sherman tank defending the road into town engaged the advancing German armor. It was an unequal duel—the Sherman suddenly went up in flames, the boom of the explosion reaching Kasten and his companions a few seconds later.

German armor was pushing the burning German and American tank hulks aside and making a renewed effort to advance down the winding road from the south into Clervaux. The Americans still had tanks, but they were heavily outnumbered. A Sherman in the town and another on the approach ramp to the castle opened fire at the German panzers, their flat, high-velocity gun reports echoing down the streets as their first rounds pinged off the leading StuG with almighty metallic thuds before whining away into the trees. But a shot soon found its mark, and the StuG lurched to a halt, orange flames leaping from its engine deck. Tiny, gray-clad stick figures clambered out of the main hatch, one on fire. The Shermans' machine guns joined in, the noise heavy and hollow as the big thumb-sized .50-caliber rounds from the turret-mounted

42

gun shredded the ice-blown trees, and every so many rounds a red tracer would arc away like some slow-motion laser, allowing the gunner to see his fall of shot.[1]

The American tanks on the hairpin bends and outside the castle managed to knock out four German tanks and assault guns during the opening of the battle. With the burning vehicles blocking the road into town, the German advance ground to a halt—for now, at least.[2]

*

The town of Schönberg fell to the Germans around this time, dooming the 422nd and 423rd Regiments atop the Schnee Eifel. But Joe Littell and his comrades had little idea of the wider strategic picture. They still clung doggedly to their dugouts and trenches, but little fighting was taking place on their front. German armor now controlled the road from Auw to Schönberg, and it was bypassing the trapped American regiments and heading straight for the important crossroads at St. Vith—directly toward the 106th Division's commander, Major General Jones, and his schoolhouse headquarters. Jones knew the situation was dire, but communicating with the 422nd and 423rd was becoming increasingly difficult.[3]

As it had always been the intention of the Germans to isolate the American position atop the Schnee Eifel, rather than try and capture it, their artillery had first smashed the American artillery, then crept over regimental and company headquarters before finally landing in the front lines. The damage done to US command and control was significant. American communications were a mess. Field telephone lines were cut and radios were unreliable because of the bad atmospherics in this hilly, forested region, coupled with the cold, wet winter weather. The only hope for Littell and his comrades was to fight their way off the Schnee Eifel toward Schönberg and affect a link-up with the remains of the 106th Division and the advancing Seventh Armored. But time was not on their side.

*

Reports were soon reaching Colonel Fuller in Clervaux that though the German advance down the main road from Marnach had been temporarily stopped, a further force of panzers—this time including heavy forty-five-ton Panther tanks and more panzer grenadiers—was assaulting the Clervaux railroad station north of the town, where a platoon of five Shermans from Third Platoon, Company B, Second Tank Battalion were holding out.[4]

Inside the railroad depot, the Americans had set up a battalion aid station that was crammed with wounded. Among them was Pfc. Bill Shapiro from the East Bronx. A combat medic in the 110th Infantry, he'd been badly concussed by a German artillery shell the day before and was brought in for treatment.[5]

Colonel Fuller was, by midmorning, a very worried man. He called the Twenty-Eighth Division commander, wanting to speak to Maj. Gen. "Dutch" Cota. Instead, he had to go through Cota's chief of staff, Col. Jesse Gibney.

"It's hopeless here," shouted Fuller down the crackling line. "I want permission to pull back everything I can and defend along the high ground west of town."

"Impossible!" snapped back Gibney, horrified. "Your orders are to defend in place. Don't give up any ground, do you hear?"

"Let me speak to General Cota," demanded Fuller.

"The general's at dinner and can't be reached by phone," shot back Gibney.

At that point an officer burst into Fuller's room, his eyes wide.

"Colonel!" he cried. "Six Kraut tanks are coming down the street from the castle!"

This made up Fuller's mind. He pressed the telephone receiver back to his ear and spoke.

"All right, Gibney. You're transmitting the general's orders, and I've got to obey them. But I'm telling you, it's going to be the Alamo all over again!"[6] He had barely finished his sentence when the roar of tank fire from close by outside rocked the building.

*

The platoon of Shermans fighting around Clervaux railroad station held on grimly under intense German panzer and anti-tank fire. But it was an uneven fight. Fuller was called to the radio in his HQ at 1700 hours. The tank platoon commander, Lieutenant Scully, was yelling into his radio over the sounds of battle, sounds that Fuller could now hear for real, instead of just through his radio.

"We're surrounded, Colonel," screamed Scully, "and can't get out! They're closing in and we're fighting like hell." There was a particularly loud explosion and the radio hissed static.

"Lieutenant!" shouted Fuller into the microphone. "Lieutenant, do you read me, over?"

The static and whistles and moans coming from interference to the line suddenly cleared. Scully's voice came through load and clear. "Guess this is it!" yelled the young lieutenant. Then there was only static.

"God damn it!" cried Fuller, throwing down the microphone in frustration.

Reports of fresh German assaults reached him shortly afterward. A ring of Krupp steel was being squeezed around Fuller's remaining defensive positions in the center of town.

*

At the battalion aid station, panic had set in. The wounded were lying all over the floor inside the railroad depot buildings, small potbellied stoves providing little heat. Men were moaning or weeping as the remaining medical staff did what they could. Suddenly, the ranking officer, Maj. Clyde Collins, started to call out.

"Any of you men that are Jewish, get rid of your dog tags. There are SS outside."[7]

This order spread rapidly among the wounded. All American soldiers' tags were marked with a letter denoting their religion. Jewish American soldiers' tags were stamped with an *H* for "Hebrew." Many, like medic Bill Shapiro, had never even considered that their religion would have any bearing if they were taken prisoner.

"I wasn't a Jew when I went to war," he said later. "I was an American soldier."[8]

Some of the more farsighted Jewish American GIs, including Shapiro, pulled off their tags and stuffed them into the stoves to destroy them. They had no idea what kind of treatment they could expect from the Germans, and largely assumed that as American soldiers, they would be afforded basic prisoner of war rights according to the Geneva Conventions.[9]

Shapiro struggled to his feet, his head aching as concussion set in, and staggered outside with those who could walk. Loud sounds of fighting continued from Clervaux, while German troops occasionally fired bursts of automatic fire or pistols into the air outside the aid station as they herded the Americans outside.

"*Raus! Raus! Raus!*" shouted the panzer grenadiers at the Americans.

The Germans were not SS, but it was an easy mistake to make. Either way, they were aggressive and twitchy after a hard fight into the town.

Pushing and shoving the Americans, many of whom were nursing bandaged wounds, the German soldiers began to relieve their prisoners of anything of use. Shapiro, as a medic, was still wearing his equipment when he was captured. A young panzer grenadier frisked him expertly, taking his watch, medical supply packs, cigarettes, steel helmet prominently marked with red crosses on white circles, and his combination eating tool. But the German didn't stop there. He pulled down one of Shapiro's raised hands and tapped a gold ring with his finger. Shapiro sighed heavily and struggled to pull the ring off of his frozen finger, before handing it to the German, his face like thunder. He didn't care about the military equipment, or even the cigarettes that the German had looted, but the ring was something else. His brother had given it to him for his bar mitzvah. He scowled as he watched the German turn the ring over in his fingers before depositing it in his tunic pocket, a beady little smile of triumph grazing his lips.[10]

With their hands raised above their heads, Shapiro and his comrades were marched a few hundred yards into Clervaux to one of its many hotels. As they walked they had a grandstand view of the fight still raging for the castle, where the roar of battle reverberated off the surrounding hills. Once at the hotel, the prisoners were crammed into a downstairs meeting room and left under guard for the night without food or water.[11] They were better off than some of the other wounded—in at least one place, Americans too badly injured to walk were finished off by their captors with a bullet to the back of the head.[12]

*

The Sherman tank by the entrance to the castle was rocked on its tracks as a high-velocity German tank shell penetrated its armor with an ear-splitting thump. It burst into flames, and the desperate crew tried to climb out of the inferno. German machine gunners raked the burning tank, hitting the first crewman who managed to bail out, and then striking a comrade who paused to try and help him.[13]

By now, more and more German vehicles were appearing on the ridge opposite the castle, driving down the road from Marnach, the obstructions pushed to one side. The castle was under long-range machine-gun fire, bullets peppering its façade, while heavier American weapons spat back at any Germans that could be seen; white, snow-suited panzergrenadiers flitted through the trees as they descended on the town in force.

*

Shortly after, German armor and infantry broke through into the center of Clervaux town. A Panzerfaust antitank launcher took out a Sherman that was guarding Colonel Fuller's headquarters. The explosion blew in the remaining windows in the hotel, rocking the building on its foundations. Men dove for cover as the ceilings cracked and fell. Then, above the rattle of small-arms fire came loud rumbling. A big German Panther tank crunched its way down the street toward the hotel, its coaxial machine gun spitting fire at American positions until it came to a halt right outside of the American headquarters. Its electrically powered turret whined as the long 75 mm high-velocity gun swung around until it pointed directly at the hotel's façade. The remaining headquarters personnel, who had watched this spectacle open-mouthed, suddenly realized what was going to happen and hit the deck as the Panther fired. The shell roared through several walls before detonating, collapsing half of the hotel. A huge, blinding, and choking pall of dust, smoke, and debris billowed over the ruined building.

In the radio room, Fuller knew that the end had now come.

He telephoned General Cota's headquarters at 1830 hours, coughing as he spoke to Colonel Gibney again, the air in the basement thick with dust and smoke.

"German armor is outside," yelled Fuller, the sounds of battle noisy from above. "I'm evacuating my headquarters."

Fuller didn't discuss this decision any further—he and his staff were in a desperate situation. If they were going to avoid capture they had to move now. Grabbing their personal weapons, Fuller led a couple dozen headquarters staff out of a back window and began scaling a rocky cliff behind the hotel.

*

With the 110th Regiment's headquarters overrun, the only remaining active defensive position in Clervaux was the castle, where Kasten and 109 other GIs were firing down at the approaching German infantry. It was now down to Captain Mackey and his collection of rear echelon personnel and infantry stragglers to fulfill General Cota's order: "Hold at all costs. No retreat, nobody comes back."

German tanks and assault guns began to open heavy fire directly on the castle, which was already being raked by automatic fire. The longer that Mackey's unit could hold the castle, the longer the delay imposed on the advancing Second Panzer Division and the greater the chance that vital crossroads farther west could be denied to the Germans. The Germans had to subdue the castle, or the Americans could shoot at convoys moving past on the road west.

One of the senior noncoms shouted up a staircase from the floor below after seeing Colonel Fuller's headquarters overwhelmed.

"We're next, boys!" he called.

The men manning the window positions exchanged glances.

Hans Kasten and the gallant defenders of the castle were about to take part in the 110th Regiment's very own Alamo.

*

The night of December 17–18, 1944, proved to be a living hell for Hans Kasten and the defenders of Clervaux Castle. The German fire was continuous and heavy as tanks and infantry pounded the ancient fortress with guns, mortars, and machine-gun fire. Captain Mackey's gallant men fought back with everything at their disposal, but the volume of fire soon thinned their ranks considerably. Incredibly, they had even managed to take some German prisoners during the fighting in the grounds of the castle, and these bemused panzergrenadiers sat huddled in the cellar under guard waiting patiently for release by their comrades. They knew it wouldn't be long in coming.

The castle's façade was scorched, peppered with bullet hits, its windows largely blown in, and the roofs, shaped like black witches' hats, were holed. But the defenders still spat fire and death at the advancing Germans, desperately trying to hold on for one more hour. Ammunition, food, and water were dwindling fast, but men like Kasten, their faces blackened by smoke, uniforms filthy and torn, managed to keep their weapons in action. In the streets and fields that surrounded the castle dozens of Germans lay dead, their white snowsuits stained dark crimson.

Sometime before daybreak on the eighteenth, the last operational Sherman tank took up position in the castle's outer courtyard. It was a final line of defense against the massed German panzers that every man in the castle could hear descending on their lonely position.

For Hans Kasten and his comrades, they all knew that no relief was coming to their aid. They were fighting a last-stand action, and there were only two outcomes for them: death or capture.

Captain Mackey had made it clear that the latter option would not be considered until the ammunition was expended and the defenders were down to knives, fists, and boots. He knew that every hour he and his company managed to cling on to the castle was another hour that the Germans lost from their plan to surge west. And indeed the stubborn American defense of Clervaux had put a serious dent in the Fifth Panzer Army's carefully planned timetable of advance. The Second Panzer Division and other units sucked into the fight were becoming impatient at the delays in snuffing out American resistance. Units were slowly bypassing the burning, ruined town, but the castle had to be subdued quickly to release the rest of the units to continue on their way west.

As light began to brighten the sky, the intensity of German fire directed at the castle increased. Bullets constantly slammed into its stout walls, or ricocheted around its interior, while heavy tank shells blew out great chunks of masonry that fell into the snowy courtyards.[14] Wounded Americans lay in the basements screaming or moaning, the couple of medics doing what they could for them with their dwindling supply of morphine and bandages.

Hans Kasten popped up at the sill of the window he'd been defending since the day before and loosed off a couple of rounds at some German panzergrenadiers he could see moving a few hundred yards yonder, ducking back down as machine-gun bullets stitched a neat row of holes into the stonework just above his head. Then he heard the sound of a tank gun nearby. He took a quick look. The Sherman in the front courtyard had moved out from cover and fired. Its big diesel grunted noisily as it reversed back into cover to reload. Kasten looked toward the winding road that led into Clervaux from the ridge above, where the Americans had managed to stop the German advance the day before. More German assault guns were passing the wrecked American and German armor and descending the hill.[15]

The Sherman pulled forward again and quickly fired at the mass of enemy tanks and assault guns that were carefully nego-tiating the snowy, icy hairpin bends, the flat report of its high velocity gun echoing in the courtyard. But the tank had been spotted. Before it had time to reverse into cover, a German tank shell bounced off the front armor plates with a metallic thud and whined away over the castle like a burning white missile. The Sherman took cover, and then it pulled back out to fire on the Germans. This time its luck ran out. A German shell impacted the Sherman between the turret and the hull, blowing off part of its gun. Now there was nothing to stop the German armor from pouring into the town and joining their comrades who had attacked from the north, via the railroad station.

*

For Joe Littell and the men of the 422nd and 423rd Regiments trapped up on the Schnee Eifel, attempts had been made through-out the night of December 17–18 to formulate a plan. Lieutenant General Middleton at VIII Corps had spoken again to the 106th Division's commander, Major General Jones, promising an air-drop of supplies until the Seventh Armored Division could break through to their relief. However, due to the continuing poor weather, as the eighteenth broke cold and foggy, this was quickly scrubbed, and the necessary aircraft were grounded.

Jones decided early on the eighteenth that the 422nd and 423rd Regiments would have to save themselves. Orders were issued that the regiments should break out west and assault the occupied town of Schönberg, and then hopefully affect a linkup with the Seventh Armored.[16] It was a plan born of utter desperation, requiring much luck to succeed.

CHAPTER 5

Give Us This Day Our Daily Bread

It looks as if we'll have to pack it in.
Col. George L. Descheneaux, 422nd Infantry
Regiment

On the morning of December 18, 1944, Maj. Gen. Alan W. Jones finally gave permission for his two beleaguered regiments to attempt a breakout. The 422nd and 423rd Infantry still occupied positions on the Schnee Eifel and numbered more than eight thousand men,[1] including Pfc. Joe Littell. Though the German forces that were pressing on toward the vital crossroads town of St. Vith now surrounded them, Jones felt sure that the two regiments, still well supplied with ammunition, transport, and sufficient food for twenty-four hours, could force their way through the German lines and withdraw west more or less intact. Simply remaining static would doom them to a slow death and, ultimately, the surrender of the survivors.

The attempt was to be made at daybreak on the nineteenth, when the regiments would assault the German-occupied town of Schönberg, opening the way for their withdrawal to St. Vith. But for the men who would actually have to attempt this feat of arms, morale was at rock bottom. They shivered and complained in their snow-covered positions, where they tried to keep warm inside dugouts and shell scrapings. Snow fell incessantly, the forest floor buried deep, the fir trees heavy with thick drifts.

Almost every soldier's boots were wet, their feet and toes slowly losing a crippling battle with trench foot and frostbite. They were also hungry. No hot food had reached them since the morning of December 16. Nothing raised a man's morale like some hot food in his belly, and the young soldiers had to make do with cold K rations and cigarettes. Then the snow increased, a frigid wind blowing across the forest, whipping the snow into a storm that cut down visibility to just a few feet. The weather conditions caused confusion among the companies and their platoons as officers tried to keep some tactical control of the situation, radios refused to work properly, and runners became lost in the whiteout.[2] The hesitant leadership of Descheneaux and Charles C. Cavender, the two colonels commanding the beleaguered regiments, only added to the GIs' problems.[3]

*

At Clervaux Castle, the fighting had raged all night long. The fortress remained the only defended position in the town, a position that was still proving a costly and time-consuming thorn in the side of the Germans as they tried to move units and vehicles past it in order to continue their now-delayed advance on the crossroads town of Bastogne farther west. Hans Kasten and the 108 other men who constituted Captain Mackey's last-ditch defense force had been steadily whittled down through constant German shelling, and tank and machine-gun fire. But against all the odds, the Germans hadn't managed to penetrate the main building—the GIs, though now running short on ammunition, the castle's basements crammed with moaning wounded and dying men, had kept up a withering fire from the building's many windows and doorways, killing dozens of German panzer-grenadiers who got too close. But with no relief coming, it was only a matter of time before the defense folded.

By early morning, as the two regiments surrounded on the Schnee Eifel began to organize themselves for their attack on the town of Schönberg, Captain Mackey made his way from floor to floor of the shattered Clervaux Castle. He looked dead on his feet, his uniform filthy with plaster dust, and his exhaustion-ringed eyes slightly wild. A head count revealed that sixty-two men were still alive. Mackey made his way down to the basement and attempted to contact Colonel Fuller's headquarters at the Hotel Claravallis on the telephone, but there was no reply. As the ranking officer it was down to Mackey to decide what to do.

"Ammo is nearly exhausted, sir," reported one of his few remaining officers.

"What about water?" asked Mackey, his face sullen.

The young lieutenant shook his head, ignoring the sounds of battle that raged above him. "It's broken down, sir," he replied, running a filthy hand across his smoke-blackened forehead.[4]

The lieutenant ran through the ammunition and supply situation in detail—at best, with the remaining men, they could hold on for only a few more hours. Mackey sighed.

"I can't contact the colonel," he said. "Looks like his HQ has bugged out or already folded."

He made his decision. He and the defenders had done their duty. Now it was his duty to try and save the survivors' lives. Resistance from now on would be a futile gesture. He would surrender. They had imposed a serious disruption to the careful German timetable, perhaps long enough to enable reserves to be brought forward to stop the Germans before they reached St. Vith.

"What shall we do about the command car, sir?" one of the senior noncoms asked as Mackey was organizing the surrender. Out in the castle's courtyard stood an M3 command carrier, a half-track fitted with extra radios.

"Torch it," ordered Mackey curtly.

Shortly afterward the noncom tossed a white phosphorous grenade into the carrier, which immediately burst into flames.[5] At the same time, a cease-fire was arranged with the Germans, and some prisoners that the Americans had taken were released. Then, under a white flag made from a dirty and torn tablecloth tied to a curtain pole,[6] the bloodied and battered survivors of the castle battle filed out of the building with their hands high in the air. They staggered, bearded faces almost black with filth and cordite stains, uniforms torn and in many cases bloody from flesh wounds, eyes staring and fearful as they threw down their personal weapons into a pile as German troops held them at gunpoint.

Soon the castle was on fire, as the blaze from the burning M3 spread to the ruined main buildings. Hans Kasten felt dejected as he was marched from the burning ruins of the once majestic castle. For the third time in three days he had fallen into German hands.[7] But this time, it didn't look as though he would be given a chance to escape.

German panzergrenadiers, themselves filthy and weary from the protracted fight for Clervaux Castle, lined Mackey and his sixty-one surviving soldiers up in the grounds and forced them to take off their equipment before searching them thoroughly for valuables and cigarettes. This was the second time that Kasten had been frisked. The GIs, hollow eyed and shell-shocked, were forced to sit on the snowy ground under guard, denied water or food, while the Germans decided what to do with them. By now, the castle was well alight, flames roaring out of the doorways and windows where Mackey's brave men had held off all comers for two days, or arching through the roofs, a great black pall of smoke rising thousands of feet into the air over the town.

*

In the snow atop the Schnee Eifel, Joe Littell and his cold, hungry comrades formed up in their platoons to begin the march through the blizzard to the assembly point preparatory to launching their attack on the town of Schönberg. Leaving the positions that had been their homes for some time seemed strange to many of the men, especially as they had witnessed almost none of the fighting that had overwhelmed the other divisions on the front line since December 16. But every man knew that they were nonetheless surrounded, even though they hadn't seen any Germans.

Once assembled into their battalions, the 422nd Infantry began to walk through the forested landscape, their officers trying to orient themselves in a landscape lacking identifiable features and with limited visibility. Soon, the battalions were lost, as trails branched off along yet more snow-filled forest tracks.[8] By the late afternoon, the officers decided to halt. They ended up a mile from where they were supposed to be, cold, wet, and increasingly fed up.

*

In Clervaux, Hans Kasten and his comrades from the castle were herded into an apple orchard, the tree branches bare of leaves or fruit.[9] The bodies of dead German soldiers were laid out on the snowy grass, their white uniforms stained with their blood. They were panzergrenadiers killed by the Americans as they attempted to storm the castle. A German truck stood nearby. A couple of guards walked over and unhitched the tailgate, revealing a pile of shovels and picks.

A German officer, his visor cap set at a rakish angle on his head, his own snowsuit stained and torn from intense combat, walked over to the exhausted and dejected Americans. He was smoking an American cigarette, his young face haggard with fatigue. He pointed at the truck with one gloved hand.

"You collect tools," he said in good English. Then he pointed at the bodies lying in a disordered row on the ground. "You bury my men, understand?"

Captain Mackey stood up and nodded. He spoke briefly to a noncom, who got the men unwillingly to their feet. Several of the panzergrenadiers guarding the Americans were in an ugly mood, and one or two of the prisoners were shoved roughly toward the truck or struck with a rifle butt to encourage them.

The ground was frozen hard, and Kasten and the other prisoners labored until night fell, digging shallow graves and interring the Germans. There were a lot of German bodies, which gave Kasten some consolation.[10] The corpses were a testament to the incredible fight that he and the others had made at the castle. Rough wooden crosses were mocked up by the prisoners and their guards and hammered into the earth at the head of each cold grave, with the owner's steel helmet and dog tag hung over the marker.

When the grim business of burying the dead was finished, the Germans brought up a large metal tub full of what they called coffee. They could afford to be a little magnanimous—for the first time since D-Day, the Germans were winning in the west. Despite their exhaustion, the German soldiers were ecstatic and a little in shock at their victories against the seemingly invincible Americans.

The wearied prisoners, their hands and backs sore from labor, and some nursing wounds from the battle, were each given a tin mug into which a ladle of brown watery liquid was doled out. It wasn't real coffee, but the ersatz kind made from acorns. Not for the first time, the American prisoners questioned how an army that couldn't even provide real coffee to its soldiers, and still relied on horse-drawn wagons to bring up supplies to the front, had managed to defeat the best equipped Allied force in Europe.

Kasten, who hated coffee, drank the disgusting substitute out of pure thirst.[11] When Captain Mackey asked for some food for his men, the Germans laughed in his face. The state of the refreshments was actually a warning of what was to come. Germany had been at war now for more than five years, and caring for prisoners of war, particularly now that the Americans and British were busy reducing Germany's cities and transport infrastructure to ashes, was no longer something they much worried about. Kasten and his comrades would spend an uncomfortable night in the orchard next to the graves of their fallen enemies, shivering, hungry, confused, and, above all, scared.

*

As dawn broke on December 19, Kasten and his comrades were roused from lying on the frozen ground by shouting German guards and roughly pushed into a ragged line. No food or water was provided. Instead, the Americans started to march. Urged along by aggressive and often gloating guards, the GIs marched through the battle-torn town and out into the countryside along the road back toward the Our River and deep into the German rear areas.[12]

If any of the Americans expected to ride into captivity, they were mistaken. Every German vehicle was tied up trying to supply the advancing panzer and infantry units, and American POWs were not a priority cargo. Instead, the prisoners would walk east.[13] It was the beginning of a nightmare journey into an uncertain captivity that many of the men would not survive.

*

On the Schnee Eifel, the 422nd and 423rd Infantry Regiments had managed to sort themselves out among the fog-and-snow-shrouded trees and moved up to prepare to assault the town of Schönberg. The regiments were no longer in contact with each

59

other, but they knew the objective and what was at stake. Failure to break through at Schönberg would probably mean capture.

The men, after a freezing night in the open, were even more dispirited than before. In long, snaking platoons they tramped wearily through the thick, blowing snow, exhausting them even before the assault was delivered. They would be attacking without the benefit of artillery preparation, as they had been ordered to destroy the guns to avoid capture. Instead, they would have only their personal weapons with a few machine guns in support. The attack was scheduled for 1000 hours.[14]

As the 423rd assembled atop the snowy ridge above Schönberg they were spotted. They emerged from the tree line and advanced down the long white slope toward the town in company-sized formations. The Germans reacted quickly, plastering the area with fire from 20 mm antiaircraft guns used in the ground role. Some platoons didn't even manage to get clear of the ridge. Pvt. Ernest B. Valmont's platoon was pinned down on the hill from withering German fire, the men hugging the frozen earth as cannon shells, mortars, and artillery detonated all around them, killing and maiming many.[15] Complete confusion reigned.

The long approach toward the town was soon littered with ugly shell craters and dead and wounded Americans. German small-arms fire blasted across the ranks of exposed GIs, as American officers tried to urge their men on. Without cover, the Americans took terrible casualties, but nevertheless the First and Third Battalions grimly pressed their attacks as ordered. The survivors would retreat then rally in the woods, and the whole bloody process would be attempted again. Over several hours of carnage, the 423rd tried to close on the town, but it was hopeless. After suffering heavy casualties, the survivors pulled back into the woods in disordered groups and tried to link up and reorganize themselves.[16]

For Colonel Descheneaux's 422nd Infantry, the attack that day soon degenerated into a slaughter. Unfortunately, as the companies blundered about the gloomy woods they ran into elements of the Führer Begleit Brigade, an elite German Army unit that normally provided a special heavily armed escort for Hitler himself. The 422nd had been moving west along a forest road when German tanks emerged out of the mist to their front and immediately opened fire. The PzKpfw IV panzers raked the trees with machine-gun fire, and their main guns opened up with 75 mm high explosive shells that scattered lethal shrapnel through the forest, while the unit's antiaircraft battery unleashed a murderous fire from its halftrack-mounted 20 mm cannons. Against this, the 422nd had only their rifles, machine guns, and a few bazookas.[17]

As the American GIs pulled back, German panzergrenadiers followed them, firing as they came on.

"Take that, you Kraut sons of bitches!" screamed Joe Littell as he unleashed an eight-round clip from his M1 Garand at the nearest Germans, who were moving through the trees like gray-and-white-clad wraiths.[18]

He had no idea if he'd hit any of them, but his blood was up. Suddenly, fresh firing broke out from the flank—more German infantry, this time from the Eighteenth Volksgrenadier Division, were moving up to support the Führer Begleit Brigade. Littell, crouched behind a tree trunk fumbling to reload his rifle with frozen fingers, watched as German bullets struck a GI close by— he crumpled and slumped soundlessly to the ground.[19] Then another man almost within touching distance screamed out and fell dead as intense enemy fire peppered the trunks and ground all around the American soldiers, many of who were starting to withdraw.

"Pull back!" yelled a voice from behind Littell.

He turned and saw an American officer gesturing madly from behind another stump.

"Let's get outta here!"

The men within earshot needed no encouragement, and Littell and the others quickly loosed off a few rounds toward the Germans and started to run. Littell ran at a half crouch, ecstatic to be leaving the trap, when suddenly he was struck by a great and powerful force and thrown violently to the ground. He passed out.[20]

*

Hans Kasten tramped along a muddy road through the snowy forest toward the German frontier, one of hundreds of GIs all heading east in a ragged column of human despair. There was hardly any talking among the exhausted and dispirited prisoners, who marched with their frozen hands thrust into the pockets of their thin combat jackets or grimy greatcoats, or else hugged themselves for warmth. The Germans had mostly stolen their gloves. Many had green blankets thrown over their shoulders like shawls. Nearly every man still wore his steel helmet.

The road was busy, and the prisoners were constantly shunted to the side as lines of German vehicles—everything from lumbering Panther tanks to horse-drawn supply wagons—dragged by, often splattering the dejected prisoners with more mud. German guards tramped along beside their charges, one every thirty yards, a rifle or machine pistol slung over their shoulders.

Kasten and the others noticed that the Germans were having supply problems. Almost every truck they saw heading west was towing another vehicle, indicating that the enemy was short of fuel. Some of the vehicles coughed and belched acrid smoke as they passed—burning charcoal fueled these hastily modified contraptions.[21] The GIs were also surprised at how many horses and wagons the Germans were using. Yet, regardless of the US Army's own superiority in vehicles and equipment, their massive supplies of fuel, and everything else that kept the world's most mechanical army on the move, the Germans had dealt them a great blow. And Kasten and thousands of other Americans who were being herded into grimy, sullen columns to be marched to the Fatherland had paid the price for their leaders' underestimation of the Germans. But these thoughts were largely left for later. What Kasten and his comrades cared about most at this point was the cold, which was eating into their bones, the empty feeling in their bellies from lack of food, and the fearsome thirst they felt from having been denied water since capture. Many men resorted to stuffing dirty snow into their mouths in an effort to get something to drink, but this only made them colder and risked a beating, or worse, from a guard for breaking ranks.

*

Pfc. Joseph Markowitz was at that moment sitting in a jeep that was going nowhere. The 106th Division's scattered transport was trying to follow the assaulting troops and escape toward St. Vith. But the failure of the attacks to open a way through at Schönberg soon doomed this endeavor. Within a short while the convoy of trucks and jeeps loaded with support personnel and combat soldiers trying to escape the pocket came under German fire.

Markowitz grabbed his personal weapon and abandoned his jeep, leaving the engine still running, and took to the woods. Loping forward through the snow, and hardly able to see because of the storm, Markowitz soon heard the bark of German infantry weapons up ahead. Quickly changing direction, the young American dashed off and witnessed hundreds of GIs giving up to the enemy. Germans were collecting their prisoners in a frozen field. Markowitz knew that the game was up. He smashed his rifle against a tree until the wooden butt broke off and then gingerly emerged into the open with his hands above his head.[22]

The 106th Division's supporting artillery units were next. Pvt. Pete House of Battery A, 590th Field Artillery was driving a weapon carrier that was towing a 105 mm howitzer on the morning of December 19. The battery was attempting to relocate to a fresh position as the pocket started to fold. It all seemed pointless, as House knew that the entire battery possessed only three unfired artillery rounds.

As soon as the guns were unhitched at their new position, they came under tremendous German fire.[23] When the shelling lifted, the survivors emerged to find several of the guns and vehicles had been destroyed or badly damaged and many men were dead or wounded. The battery had no ammunition left, so continuing the fight was out of the question.

*

When Joe Littell came to he was lying on a blanket in the snow. A medic with red crosses in white circles on his helmet was leaning over him. Pain shot up and down his left leg. He struggled to look and saw that his leg was bandaged below the knee.

"You're going to be fine, soldier," the grimy-faced medic said. "I pulled a pretty good shell fragment out of your leg at midcalf, cleaned the wound, and treated it with sulfa. You're going to be okay. What you need to do is lie here and rest for a while."

"I appreciate what you did for me," replied Littell groggily. "Where am I?"

"You're at the battalion aid station," the medic responded matter-of-factly, before he stood and moved on to another casualty.[24]

Littell looked about and saw dozens of other GIs milling about between some tents that had been erected among the trees. Several ambulances and jeeps were parked about, while spread around outside the tents were many more wounded men, some being attended to by medics and doctors.[25] Stacked against the side of one large tent was a pile of corpses several feet high, with frozen arms and legs sticking out at crazy angles. Littell could hear the rumble of artillery fire in the distance. He lay back and closed his eyes.

*

What was left of the 422nd Infantry was inside a pocket that now measured barely two square miles in the woods above Schönberg. The Germans had the area under constant artillery fire. The 423rd had already started to surrender when the 422nd's Colonel Descheneaux came to the same realization— resistance was pointless.

"I don't believe in fighting for glory if it doesn't accomplish anything," Descheneaux announced to his surviving officers inside his makeshift command post in the woods.[26] The officers looked back at their commander with stony, impassive faces.

"It looks as if we'll have to pack it in," continued Descheneaux. Several of the other officers started at their colonel's words, shocked and angered.

"Jesus, Desh," said Lt. Col. Thomas Kelly, commander of the regiment's attached artillery component, "you can't surrender!"

"As far as I'm concerned, I'm going to save the lives of as many as I can," replied Descheneaux, meeting Kelly's furious eyes with his own.

"And I don't give a damn if I am court-martialed!" he added angrily.[27]

There was nothing more to say. The end had come.

CHAPTER 6

The Long March

On these marches, there was no laughter. Not a smile, not
a joke, for there was nothing to smile at and nothing but
hunger and weakness was in our minds.
Pfc. Theodore Rosenberg, 106th Infantry Division

Pvt. Pete House of the 590th Field Artillery was astounded
and shocked when the order to surrender was received by
radio. Everything had gone eerily quiet following the devastating German shelling that had smashed his battery's position.
The survivors had held a quick meeting. It was decided that they
would spike the remaining functional 105 mm howitzers and vehicles, then try to break out of the German encirclement on
foot.[1]

House and his comrades worked with feverish speed to destroy
their guns, acts that to trained soldiers seemed almost sacrilegious. Then they formed up into a ragged column armed with a
few rifles and pistols, and headed off deeper into the woods.[2]

*

When the German fire slackened over Pvt. Ernest Valmont's
position in the woods atop the ridge above Schönberg, he
started to hear an order being shouted by officers and noncoms.
It began in the distance and rapidly traveled from position to
position, the same refrain over and over.

"Destroy your weapons!"[3]

Valmont watched, horrified, as his platoon leader calmly stood up and walked over to a tree. He reversed his M1 carbine and smashed the butt against the trunk until it broke. With tears in his eyes he told his platoon to do likewise.

"This was the worst thing I ever did in my life," wrote Valmont.[4] It was a feeling shared by every soldier in the 422nd and 423rd Regiments that day.

*

S.Sgt. J. B. Parish stood looking down at Joe Littell, who lay sleeping on a dirty army blanket in the snow outside his battalion aid station, one calf wrapped in a fresh shell dressing. The light was already draining from the sky, yet it was only 1600 hours. Littell's eyes fluttered open and he stared up at the familiar face of his platoon sergeant.

"Littell, how're you doing?" Parish asked gently, his face strained and grubby.

"I'm okay," Littell croaked.

Parish looked nervously about himself, and then glanced back at Littell.

"Can you walk?" he asked, his voice concerned.

"Yep, I think so," Littell replied, moving his wounded leg, which throbbed with pain.

"Well, you better get up then, 'cause the order came down for us to surrender."[5]

At first Littell thought he was hearing things, but before he could question Parish, the sergeant had stalked off to round up the other members of his platoon who were still alive. Littell raised himself up on his elbows and looked around for his rifle, but it was gone. Then he saw a half-track standing nearby—it was packed with Garands, machine guns, bazookas, and mortars.

Littell's company had already gathered all their weapons together. He decided that remaining on his blanket was probably
not a good idea, considering the circumstances, so he awkwardly
clambered to his feet, pain shooting up his leg from the calf
wound. But he found that he could stand unaided. He started
to limp toward regimental headquarters, located close by. One
thing he noticed was the silence—there were none of the sounds
of violence that had been the background noise to his life since
December 16—no rattle of machine guns, thump of mortars,
or wild crash of artillery. There was just a rather eerie silence
broken only by the revving of truck engines and the burble of
muted conversations among the snow-laden trees.

*

For Hans Kasten and the men of the 28th Division who had
surrendered at Clervaux, their lives had become an unending
struggle against fatigue, hunger, and thirst. The Germans intended to move the prisoners east on foot for several days
until they reached Gerolstein, a small town just inside Germany
where rail transport was waiting to take the GIs to a prisoner
of war camp. But the Germans had not expected to capture so
many prisoners, and their system for dealing with such numbers
was rudimentary at best. Short on most types of supplies themselves, and in many cases feeding their soldiers and fueling their
advancing vehicles on stocks captured from the US Army, there
was little to spare for prisoners. And that included food and fresh
water. Unfortunately for the prisoners, they had been stripped of
most of their portable rations when they surrendered, including
their water bottles, leaving them in a very precarious situation.

The distance from Clervaux to Gerolstein was almost forty
miles, a short drive in vehicles, but made on foot over snowy,
muddy roads with wounded and exhausted men, it would take

several days. It didn't help trying to point out to the Germans what the Geneva Conventions stipulated regarding prisoner of war rights; more than one troublesome American who tried to argue with his captors was simply disposed of. At this point the Germans were advancing and riding high on an unexpected wave of victory. They felt bitterness toward the Americans for bombing German cities, and also harbored a feeling of superiority as soldiers over an enemy that they did not yet respect. When they saw how lavishly equipped and well supplied American units were, and yet they had still surrendered, this engendered ill treatment and contempt among German troops, many of them veterans of the terrible battles on the Eastern Front, where little quarter was given by either side.

As the column of prisoners continued east, more and more Americans joined its ranks; the Germans collected together men from many different units and divisions and sent them all toward Germany.

*

Joe Littell realized that Staff Sergeant Parish was telling him the truth about surrendering once he had hobbled over to his regimental headquarters, a collection of tents and vehicles in a small clearing. He could see plenty of American officers, but disturbingly they were talking to several German officers. The Germans were dressed in steel helmets and field-gray greatcoats, or special white winter snowsuits with pistol holsters around their waists or machine guns slung across their backs. They looked young and capable. Littell stared, fascinated, as some kind of agreement was reached between the American and German officers. One of the Germans suddenly broke from the huddle and ran over to the top of the ridgeline, signaling vigorously with one arm.[6] Within seconds, German troops were loping up the snowy hillside, grinning fiercely beneath their helmets and hoods, weapons at the ready. They wasted no time in starting to push the Americans into lines to be carefully searched.

Littell was shoved into one such group of prisoners, who held their hands up. A young panzergrenadier covered the party with his MP44 assault rifle while a colleague started to move down the line, patting each man down and tossing any "contraband" onto the dirty snow. As usual, watches, cigarettes, wedding rings, and useful pieces of kit were quickly seized. After patting Littell down and relieving him of his watch and a pack of cigarettes, the German soldier pulled out the American's wallet. He quickly rifled through it, while Littell looked on with growing alarm and anger. When the German glanced at a photograph of Littell's parents taken outside their New York apartment building, and another of his sister holding her pet cat, Littell spoke up.

"May I please keep the photographs?" he asked in fluent German.[7]

The enemy soldier glanced up in surprise on hearing his own language spoken. He stared at Littell for a few seconds, then down at the wallet in his hands. Then, without a word, he tossed the wallet back at Littell, who caught it with his gloved hands. The German moved on down the line.

The column of prisoners trudged wearily over the ridgeline and down toward the German positions, over the same ground that the 422nd and 423rd Regiments had tried to cross in their failed assaults on Schönberg. The dispirited Americans reassembled on the main road, which was nose to tail with every type of German vehicle heading west.

Once organized, the men began to march east, enduring the jeers and jibes of every passing German convoy, a great mass of nine thousand dirty, dazed, and disheveled men. The surrender of the 422nd and 423rd Infantry Regiments was one of the greatest defeats ever suffered by American arms, surpassed only by the surrender to the Japanese at Bataan in April 1942, when fifteen thousand Americans had passed into a cruel captivity in the Philippines.

*

Pvt. Ernest Valmont and the surviving members of his platoon lined up to be frisked by German soldiers. Several of the GIs were spat on by the aggressive Germans, and more than a few cuffed around the head for showing any signs of pride or resisting having their personal possessions stolen from them.[8]

The treatment meted out to captured GIs varied depending on the mood of the unit that they surrendered to. Some Germans treated their captives according to the law, though all German soldiers stole watches, rations, rings, cash, and other valuables from their prisoners. But sometimes the arrogance of the enemy, now riding unexpectedly high on victory, led to terrible scenes.

When Pvt. Pete House surrendered, after blundering around the woods for a few hours with a large number of other men from Battery A, 590th Field Artillery, they were lined up by the German antiaircraft battery that had turned their 20 mm cannons onto the woods to flush out the Americans.[9] The Germans were preparing their weapons for transport, and they were shorthanded. An officer turned to the long line of American prisoners who were under guard beside the icy road.

"You," bellowed the officer, pointing to one of the Americans, "you help." The German officer pointed at one of the 20 mm guns, which was being hastily made ready to move.

"No, I ain't helpin'," replied the American prisoner, shaking his head. "It's against the Geneva Convention, see."

The German officer smiled and nodded.

"*Ja*, Geneva Convention." Then he pulled out his Luger pistol and shot the American right between the eyes.[10]

The other prisoners reeled back in horror as the man's brains splattered across the road's high bank and his body lay twitching in the mud. They had all heard about the Malmedy Massacre, when elements of the Second SS Panzer Division, known as Das Reich, had shot more than eighty American prisoners in a field in cold blood on December 17. The story had been widely disseminated among US forces before the surrender. It was clear that the Germans were not too interested in the law regarding POWs at this point. No further dissenting opinions were voiced when the German officer picked another GI at gunpoint to help his men pack up their equipment.

*

Pvt. Troy H. Kimmel had received a hip wound during the fighting on December 19. There were no surviving aid men with his platoon, but his buddies had patched Kimmel up themselves. When his unit from the 106th Division surrendered, Kimmel and the rest of his company were shoved into a roofless, gutted building. German soldiers carefully searched them, stealing anything they fancied, including, unfortunately for many of the prisoners, their field jackets and snow overshoes.[11]

Early on the morning of December 20 a German officer entered the shattered building. He ordered that all seriously wounded men were to be left behind—they would be taken to a hospital and properly cared for. Kimmel tried to join this party, but was refused. He was lucky, for the wounded were never heard from again. The German officer addressed the room in excellent English.

"You are to be marched into Germany," he announced. "Anyone who tries to escape will be shot. Anyone who does not keep up will be shot." If any of the prisoners thought that the Germans were bluffing, they were soon cruelly disabused of this notion.

*

Hans Kasten's column, like all the columns of Americans shuffling into the Reich, was suffering badly through lack of food and water. The Germans simply didn't care. Men could be shot for grabbing handfuls of snow to stuff into their parched mouths or for stealing frozen turnips piled in the corners of fields beside the road. But the same offenses might cause only a beating with a rifle butt[12]—still enough to kill weakened and often wounded or sick men.

The Germans organized the thousands of American prisoners into hundred-man columns that marched in five ranks of twenty prisoners each. In this manner, just a handful of guards could easily control them. Every twelve miles the guards would be relieved. Not so the prisoners, who had to keep shuffling along in the freezing, snowy weather. The Germans gave the prisoners occasional rest stops, but normally because the guards wanted to relieve themselves. When the sentries wanted to eat they would reach into their bread bags and pull out some cheese, sausage, or a piece of bread and eat it while they marched, much to the chagrin of the prisoners, who were soon very hungry.[13]

*

"American prisoners!" shouted a German soldier who stood high up on the bank of the road as Joe Littell's column trudged by. "The war now goes in Germany's favor! American and British forces are thrown back in a catastrophic defeat until they reach the North Sea! Germany will therefore win the war after all!"[14] For Littell and thousands of other GIs heading toward the

Reich, the German soldier's boasts, delivered in a phony serious voice, didn't sound as ridiculous as they would have three days earlier. Littell tried not to think about it, and he concentrated on putting one foot in front of the other, his wounded calf still giving him plenty of pain as he struggled along.

*

Pete House's column was constantly forced off the road by passing German armor and vehicles. The desperately tired GIs scrambled up the road's snowy banks to avoid the vehicles, some of which, including tanks, took a perverse pleasure in deliberately trying to run the Americans down. A German sergeant who had a Kübelwagen field car was in charge of several of these hundred-man columns. Each time the traffic cleared, he would race along the lines of prisoners, tooting his horn, forcing them to climb the banks once again. House was so tired that he was beyond caring and refused to move from the roadway when the Kübelwagen came powering up behind him. The other prisoners on the bank looked on with exhaustion-ringed dead eyes as the German vehicle screeched to a halt and the sergeant stood up in the passenger seat. A column of German tanks was temporarily halted on the other side of the road as well.[15]

House turned and watched as the German sergeant angrily pulled out his pistol and pointed it at him while he shouted something that House could not understand. But then they heard the loud cocking of a heavier weapon. House and the sergeant turned toward a huge Panther tank that was parked on the opposite side of the road. A crewman in the black uniform of the panzer arm had leveled an MG34 machine gun mounted on the tank's turret. But instead of pointing it at House, its muzzle was leveled menacingly at the German sergeant. The tank crewman shouted something. The sergeant hesitated, looking at the tanker and then at House before he cursed loudly, holstered his pistol, and ordered his driver to pull around the stubborn American.[16] House glanced up at his savior, who smiled and touched two fingers to his black forage cap in a casual salute, before the guards started yelling and shoving the prisoners back into line and moving them off.

*

As the American prisoners slogged along the roads toward Germany they saw plenty of evidence of the defeat that their nation had suffered. There were smashed and abandoned US vehicles everywhere, and plenty of dead. Pfc. John W. Reinfenrath of Company B, 423rd Infantry passed these gruesome sights throughout the whole of December 20. Some of the sights would stay with him for the rest of his life—a dead GI hanging half out of the hatch of a destroyed tank, the body already dusted with fresh snow, or the barefooted corpses of GIs that were piled in snowy ditches beside the road, their frozen flesh as white as alabaster, their superior quality footwear and socks stolen by passing Germans.[17]

*

On the second night of the march east, Hans Kasten's column halted at a small village, and the men were worried that they might be forced to spend another night out in the open. Fortunately, the Germans had made arrangements for the prisoners to stay in the only building large enough to accommodate several hundred men—the local parish church.[18]

Kasten and his comrades trailed into the tidy church, sitting in rows on the hard wooden pews and lying in any spare space that they could find, thankful to be out of the elements. The church was unheated and freezing cold, but it was infinitely superior to sleeping in the snow and cutting wind.

For the first time since the night spent digging graves in the Clervaux apple orchard, the Germans provided the prisoners with a hot drink. For men who had been surviving by eating snow, the large tubs of ersatz coffee were a godsend.

"Any men who can speak German, identify yourselves immediately," ordered a German sergeant in his own language. The prisoners mostly had no idea what the Kraut was bawling about, and cared even less, but Kasten stood up and raised his hand.

"You speak German?" demanded the sergeant impatiently. Kasten nodded and replied that he did.

"You will interpret for the prisoners," the sergeant said.[19]

The Germans organized small working parties—as they termed groups of prisoners used for menial labor—to collect hot drinks from some local civilians who had been dragooned into assisting the prisoners in their midst. Kasten took charge of a working party, and they made several trips to collect large pots of hot coffee. Kasten quickly fell into conversation with the civilians, trying to glean some information about where they were and what was happening at the front. The news was universally disappointing—Dr. Goebbels was feeding the German populace an unending stream of good news. The German spearheads were rapidly approaching the Meuse River. The Americans were in full retreat, et cetera, et cetera.[20]

On his last trip outside to collect coffee, an older woman sidled up to him when he was out of earshot of the bored-looking sentry.

"Take this," muttered the woman conspiratorially, slipping something into Kasten's greatcoat pocket.

He glanced down and saw it was a thick sandwich wrapped in a cloth.

The lady briefly placed a gloved hand on Kasten's arm, saying in German, "I have an uncle in Texas."

"That sandwich for a starving man was equivalent to a bar of gold today," Kasten said later.[21] That night he slept on the only spare space available inside the church—the altar. It didn't bother him. He had given up on God a long time before.

*

The first major stop on the road to Gerolstein was the small German town of Bleialf, on the Belgian-German border. Here, Kasten's column of prisoners coming from Clervaux met up with Littell's huge column from the Schönberg area. Here, too, the Germans ordered that all the wounded, who until now had been shuffling along with the help of their friends or carried on stretchers, were to be left behind. Together, the remnants of the 28th and 106th Infantry Divisions captured during the battle atop the Schnee Eifel would continue on to Gerolstein.

*

As the columns entered the bomb-and-shell-ravaged German frontier town of Prüm, trouble started. A large and very hostile crowd of local citizens lined both sides of the muddy road into town. Behind them were the stark reminders that until three days ago Germany had been losing, and losing badly. The shells of houses stood stark against the slate-gray sky, their windows devoid of glass, their roofs caved in, scorched wooden beams jutting out like broken ribs. Some houses had lost their fronts, revealing the interiors like a doll's house rudely flung open for inspection. Here a room with a bed still against an undamaged wall, there a bathroom with a sink hanging from its pipes. Outside the houses were piles of rubble, now buried under snowdrifts. The citizens hungrily clawed at these white piles, seizing up broken bricks and pieces of wood that they flung at the lines of American soldiers, or else used to lash out at their legs or heads as they shuffled past. The guards did little to stop this abuse. Young boys dressed in the black-and-brown uniforms of the Hitler Youth led the assaults, egged on by local Nazi Party leaders.[22] It was all good propaganda—those who had despoiled these communities had surrendered in their thousands to the mighty armies of the Reich, raged Joseph Goebbels's wireless broadcasts, who even in the sixth year of total war could deliver knockout blows to the hated Allies.

And woe betide any of their own that showed kindness or compassion to the young American soldiers. The woman who had given Hans Kasten a lifesaving sandwich was not the only person to see beyond the propaganda. As Troy Kimmel, his hip wound still bothering him, hobbled through bomb-damaged Prüm, an old woman tried to give the prisoners some bread. The German sergeant in charge of Kimmel's column bellowed with rage and beat her mercilessly with his rifle butt.[23]

*

Pvt. Joseph Markowitz stood with his hands up, along with the rest of the men in his column. They had already run the gauntlet into Prüm, and some German soldiers had decided to shake them down again, in their seemingly inexhaustible search for loot.

Markowitz still had his galoshes over his combat boots, but a German soldier ordered him to remove them. As he straightened up and handed over the precious boots, the German started frisking him. He felt something in one of Markowitz's pockets and roughly pulled it out. It was a small tin of aspirin. The maker's name was Bayer. The German's eyes widened and his face grew thunderous.

"Bayer," he said several times, "this is German name."

Markowitz said nothing—the pills were made in America. It was a famous company.

"You take from dead German soldier!" yelled the enemy panzergrenadier in thickly accented and hesitant English.

Markowitz was confused and denied any wrongdoing. The German was getting madder by the minute and called over his comrades, shouting in his own language and gesturing at Markowitz. The American understood German well enough to know that he was facing death—if found with German possessions it was assumed they had been pilfered from dead German soldiers. Swift retribution would be forthcoming. But just as Markowitz thought that his time was up, a German noncom snatched the tin from the young trooper, examined it, and told him that Bayer products were widely distributed all over the world and to forget it.[24] Markowitz let out a long breath as his German inquisitor moved on down the line, still turning the tin of aspirins over in his gloved hands, muttering under his breath.

*

Privates Ernest Valmont and Pete House were also herded into Prüm. Several hundred man columns were gathered together and placed in a local church for the night.

"They told us if we were quiet we would be fed," Valmont said. "This never happened. We did not eat."[25]

House's group slept on the floor of a shell-damaged college building. The Germans provided no food or drink for the famished and thirsty prisoners.[26] There would be nothing but cold comfort from these devastated frontier towns full of angry and embittered German civilians.

CHAPTER 7

Friendly Fire

*Oh my God—I am most sorry for having sinned against
you—because you are so good.*
1st Lt. Paul Cavanaugh, Army chaplain

Along line of wooden boxcars hitched up to a large black
German war locomotive sat idle in the rail yards at the German town of Diez, near Limburg. The train, hauling its special
cargo, had puffed into the crowded station hours before. Inside
each wagon dozens of American prisoners of war sat or stood, so
crowded in that movement was almost impossible. Walking
along on either side of the boxcars, which held in total a thousand GIs captured in the Ardennes, were bored-looking German
guards bundled up in greatcoats, gloves, scarves, and steel helmets, with Mauser rifles slung over their right shoulders. As they
walked, the guards stamped their feet to keep warm or blew on
their hands.

The human cargo had been imprisoned inside the wagons for
three days now, and largely denied food or water. Several white
faces pressed against little barbed wire–crossed windows at each
end of the boxcars, pleading feebly with the guards to be let out.
The guards mostly ignored these plaintive calls or waved a hand
at them dismissively. But then another sound cut in over the
calling and the sound of guards' boots crunching through snow

and ice beside the trains—the wail of a siren. It rose and rose until it reached an ear-splitting pitch before falling away and then climbing up again, a banshee wail that chilled the blood of the already frozen men locked inside the boxcars.

"*Alarm!*" yelled the German guards. Ignoring the violent hammering and the screaming of a thousand voices coming from within the boxcars, they fled toward air-raid shelters beside the station, abandoning their charges to their fate. Then, above the wail of the siren came a new sound—the drone of approaching aircraft, their engines reverberating across the night sky. Death was coming on swift wings.

*

Gerolstein was in as bad a mess as Prüm and the other German towns that the American prisoner columns had marched through since being captured; it had been badly damaged by Allied bombing. But it was also an important railhead for the German Army, and it was crowded with troops, vehicles, and horses unloading from trains and moving west toward the front in Belgium. The columns of defeated Americans were met for the first time by German military police that held snarling Alsatians on straining metal leashes, their breaths pluming in the air like smoke as they barked incessantly at the passing prisoners.

Hans Kasten walked purposefully at the head of his column, seemingly unaffected by the ordeal of the march. He had been kept busy interceding with the German guards on behalf of this or that POW who had taken a beating for eating snow or stealing turnips. Kasten was an imposing presence, and his eyes flashed with intelligence and strength, unlike the dull expressions of defeat and desperation that were worn on the faces of so many in the column. Men were already starting to lose the will to keep going, and people like Kasten, who were able to dig that little bit deeper into themselves, encouraged and cajoled those around them not to give up.

Joe Littell struggled into Gerolstein in pain. He should not have been standing, let alone marching, on his wounded leg, but he kept moving out of pure fear. He knew that if he fell out of the column he would probably freeze to death.[1] Gritting his teeth, he hobbled into Gerolstein with his comrades, hoping that the worst was now over.

As Kasten's column entered the town, other groups of prisoners who had arrived the night before were stirring from their freezing quarters and assembling outside for roll call.

Pete House's column had arrived in Gerolstein after dark on December 20, following another long and painful march, and was given some ersatz coffee before being herded into a bombed-out wire-basket factory near the railroad station. House considered himself very lucky to be indoors after the harrowing journey since capture. The large room he and several hundred other Americans were crowded into on the second floor was comparatively warm.[2] Pvt. John Reinfenrath's column had also arrived on the twentieth and was billeted in a large empty warehouse, where the men slept directly on the freezing concrete floor.[3]

Food remained everyone's primary focus. The Germans fed some groups and not others. Pfc. Theodore Rosenberg was one of the lucky ones to be fed—but it was no feast. The Germans distributed just twenty loaves of ersatz bread and two buckets of marmalade among the entire column. Each man received a piece of bread the size of a cigarette pack.[4]

At dawn on December 21, Pete House and his column walked out of the bombed factory where they had spent their most comfortable night since capture and formed up in the rubble-strewn yard. Their legs ached from so much marching and their feet were sore, many afflicted with frostbite. It was freezing cold as the men stood around hugging themselves, wishing for a cigarette or something to eat or drink. Surprisingly, the former wish was fulfilled when a truck clattered into the yard. German soldiers jumped down from the cab and unhitched the tailgate, revealing several cardboard boxes filled with tinned American corned beef captured from the front. The prisoners were hurriedly assembled into a queue and the meat was issued: one can per four prisoners.[5]

John Reinfenrath's column was mustered, and each man was issued two packets of American hardtack biscuits. The Germans then issued one can of cheese between five men, and they made it clear that this was to last for some days. But the Americans, famished to the extreme, their stomachs feeling as though they were stuck to their backbones, salivated like dogs at the sight and smell of food and most quickly consumed the lot.[6]

As Hans Kasten's column joined the others already gathering at the station, it was obvious that transport east was now the only option. The sheer number of prisoners that the Germans had taken meant that they had to be removed from the combat zone as quickly as possible. They were an encumbrance that the Germans could do without—their columns blocked roads to the front, and they required a considerable diversion of manpower to guard. Better that they were shipped to prisoner of war camps as soon as possible.

"*Raus, raus!*" shouted the sentries as they herded the first huge batch of weary prisoners onto the long platform at Gerolstein station. The men stood several rows deep staring at their transport east, and many, including Kasten and Littell, felt a terrible foreboding. If anyone thought that the worst was now over, they were quickly dissuaded of this notion when the German guards unrolled the wooden boxcars' sliding doors.

The smell that assailed Kasten was the first intimation of

trouble to come. It was the smell of horses after a long journey—dung, musty straw, and urine, the stench of a farmyard encapsulated inside each smallish boxcar. The horses had already been unloaded, but they were still present in spirit. All of the prisoners were repulsed and horrified.

"*Raus, schnell!*" yelled German guards, who began pushing the prisoners forward in front of the open boxcars, using their rifles to encourage the mass of disgruntled, tired, and hungry Americans into the hellish wooden boxes, sixty or so to each car.[7] Alsatians snarled and barked at the Americans' heels, further hurrying them to board. Several men balked after viewing the insides of the boxes, which were generally festooned with horse droppings and filthy straw. Kasten put up his hands to halt the men behind him and demanded to the guards in their own language that they be permitted a few minutes to clean out the mess before boarding, but he was told in no uncertain terms that there was no time—get on board now, or else.

Many of the Americans noticed that the boxcars were about half the size of those back in the States. They were designed to carry eight horses or a maximum of forty men. But the Germans pressed the prisoners inside until each boxcar was loaded with more than sixty gasping men. "There we were," recalled Theodore Rosenberg, "packed in so tightly in the most foul and stench that human beings ever stayed in."[8]

In Pete House's boxcar, a quick head count revealed that sixty-four Americans were crammed inside. The only way they could all sit down was to sit front to back in rows on the dung and straw. No one, including the lightly wounded and sick, could lie down in any of the boxcars without considerable reorganization.[9]

John Reinfenrath's party was slightly luckier than many of the other prisoners, for the straw inside their boxcar was clean. In order to improve the air quality, the prisoners opened the small, rectangular window high up at each end of the car. Barbed wire had been nailed haphazardly across these openings,[10] but the cold air that wafted inside, though freezing the men further, at least cleansed the atmosphere a little of dung and horses.

Combat medic William Shapiro, captured alongside Kasten, was still suffering from the lingering effects of concussion when he struggled aboard a crowded boxcar. The car was filled with moaning and groaning as wounded, exhausted, and frostbitten prisoners struggled to find a position to sit. Shapiro could do nothing for these men—the Germans had already stolen his medical kit, and he was only just keeping himself together after the long march from Clervaux.

Kasten himself was, as usual, seemingly tireless. Once the boxcar door had been hauled shut by the guards and locked, he realized that it was no good expecting the military chain of command to sort this appalling mess out. There were plenty of officers and noncoms on the trains, but many were wounded, sick, or past caring. Leadership now devolved upon the men with the greatest will to survive this ordeal, and the strength of character to help their comrades. It no longer mattered whether you had bars on your shoulders or the single chevron of a private first class on your upper sleeve; what mattered was whether other men would listen to you and do your bidding. And Hans Kasten, though just such a lowly Pfc, had already proven this in his intercessions with the Germans on behalf of his comrades during the long march to Gerolstein. He had saved many men from beatings that would have killed them.[11] And the men knew it. The others were looking to him in their moment of despair, and he didn't disappoint. In his loud and commanding voice, Kasten explained that if they wanted to get through this journey they had better do as he said. Being packed in so tightly meant the wounded and sick would suffer greatly over the coming days.

Kasten organized the car so that the men could take turns sitting and standing.[12] In this way, the men in Kasten's car managed to get some proper rest, whereas in many of the cars the law of the jungle had asserted itself as military discipline started to evaporate, or charismatic leaders were absent.

Everyone was suddenly hushed by the scream of the big black locomotive's steam whistle. Then, with wheels and bogeys clashing and squealing on the icy tracks, the train lurched violently forward. The prisoners grabbed each other or pressed against the wooden walls of the boxcars for balance as the train slowly pulled out of Gerolstein station, black smoke puffing furiously from its engine as it hauled the long line of tatty boxcars and their filthy, starving, and parched passengers east through a rolling countryside still buried under snow. Like slaves in the bowels of some wooden ship during the Middle Passage, most of the GIs had no idea of their destination or of the duration of their journey. All they knew for certain was that they were in a living hell.

One person who did know what was happening was Joe Littell. Just before the door had been slammed shut at Gerolstein, Littell had demonstrated his own emerging leadership potential when he had shouted out in perfect German to the guard.

"Where are we going?"

Surprisingly, the guard—a middle-aged man, like most guards dealing with prisoners—shouted back, "You are being taken to a POW camp near Frankfurt."[13]

In Littell's boxcar, at least, the men now knew the length of time they would have to endure those inhuman conditions. From his prewar geographical knowledge of Germany, Littell estimated that the distance to Frankfurt was about 125 miles. It would take the trains an average of five days to reach their destinations, as Allied bombing was causing terrible disruption to the railway system, and POW transports were considered to be low-priority cargo. Troop and ammunition trains were the most important movements on the system.

*

Throughout that first day, the cramps set in. Legs and feet were agony to move, with many men suffering from frostbite that caused their feet to swell in the daytime. Removing their boots, many found they couldn't put them back on. Toes were painful with sores like boils, and men constantly screamed out in the overcrowding as people trod on each other while jostling for space.[14]

Soon, men needed to go to the lavatory, but the Germans had provided no facilities of any kind, not even a bucket for each boxcar. In the worst ordered cars, men simply urinated or defecated in the corners, while in others some attempts were made to bring order to the chaos, with empty tins or boxes being utilized. Fortunately, the Germans had permitted many of the prisoners to retain their M1 combat helmets. Unlike other nations' helmets, the M1 was unique in actually being two helmets in one. An inner helmet liner, like a lightweight construction worker's headgear, nestled inside a steel outer shell. In combat, GIs had often used the outer shell as a receptacle to boil water or to shave in. Many of these steel shells were now pressed into service as rudimentary commodes.[15]

In one car, a prisoner perched uncomfortably atop one of these helmet shells, his pants around his ankles while other prisoners looked away or complained. There was no lavatory paper, just the filthy straw from the floor, and when that had been used, nothing at all. But there was one source of paper left to the prisoners. The GI reached inside his greatcoat pocket and carefully extracted an envelope. His eyes misty with tears, he extracted the thin sheets of foolscap and glanced at them with sorrow. A letter from a wife, a mother, or a sweetheart, perhaps. Then, with a heavy sigh, he used the letter to wipe himself clean, tears of shame and anger making furrows down his dirty, stubbly face. These connections to home and family were destroyed, and with their destruction went a little bit of each man that had been forced into this horror. They knew also that those selfsame wives and parents would shortly be receiving a letter from the War Department informing them that their husband or son was missing in action. The families they had left behind in the States would suffer the agony of not knowing, of fearing the worst, of a kind of grief held in limbo until the Germans got word of the captured to the Red Cross. Many feared that their families would never know what became of them.

*

The stench of human waste was added to the animal smells, creating an atmosphere inside the wagons that almost defied description. The contents of the toilet receptacles were emptied out through the little windows at each end of the cars.[16]

The little barbed wire–encrusted openings gave the only view the prisoners had of the outside. Thirst was tormenting the prisoners from the moment the doors to the cars had been slammed shut. Already denied proper hydration on the marches to Gerolstein, there at least had been opportunities to eat fresh snow from beside the roads. But on the trains the prisoners could see the snowy fields and white snow piled deep on station roofs as their locomotive slowly chugged through towns and villages on the journey east, but this snow was just out of reach. They were like thirsty men in a lifeboat at sea, surrounded by water but unable to drink.

Every so often, when the train slowed right down or came to a complete stop, some water might be distributed, but no food.[17] This was a serious problem for men who had received nothing substantial since December 15, the last day of normality before the German offensive had broken. The famished prisoners had quickly consumed any food that the Germans had issued on the morning of the departure from Gerolstein, including hardtack, cheese, or ersatz bread, during the first day of the journey.[18] Experiences varied from train to train, but very little or no food was distributed for days as the trains dragged deeper into Germany. The shock of going from being fed properly in the US Army—where even up on the line hot food was sometimes available or calorific intake could be maintained through a variety of good-quality ration packs—took a terrible toll on the prisoners. Morale and health sank appreciably. The uncertainty of how long they would have to remain on the hellish trains added to this low morale. After a few days, in subzero temperatures, without access to clean water, sanitation facilities, or proper food, men would start dying.

*

POW transports were supposed to be marked to prevent misidentification with troop and ammunition trains, which were legal targets under the Geneva Conventions. However, by this stage of the war, the Germans were not adhering properly to the rules.[19] The trains used to transport the American POWs out of Gerolstein had arrived bearing military supplies and animals. They had then been emptied and quickly refilled with POWs, who were shipped straight out. It is doubtful if the roofs of any of the wooden boxcars were painted with large white letters spelling "P.O.W.," and even if they had been, the continuous snowfalls would have quickly obscured these identifying marks. The price to be paid for this was a hefty toll in blood when one train arrived in the small town of Diez, near Limburg, on the afternoon of December 23, 1944.

The Royal Air Force had targeted railway marshaling yards and signal boxes since early 1940 in an attempt to disrupt German rail communications. Bombing tracks was largely a waste of time, as the German railways were extremely well prepared for this eventuality, and wood and spare rails were piled beside the tracks at intervals so that repairs could be made quickly. However, smashing up rail yards and the trains in them was a more productive use of aircraft and the results were often devastating.

When an air raid siren began its mournful wail at 1800 hours on December 23, and the German guards immediately took shelter, abandoning the prisoners to their fate, a terrible tragedy was about to be played out as fifty-two twin-engine Mosquito bombers from No. 8 Group RAF swung in to attack the crowded rail yard at Diez,[20] unaware that a huge number of American POWs were trapped in a train at the center of their target.

There was a barbed wire compound away from the trains where prisoners were supposed to be sent when the trains were stationary, but the compound was already so overcrowded that the authorities refused any more admittance.[21] This meant that the prisoners arriving on the new train could not get off.

The screaming of aircraft engines grew in intensity as the hundreds of prisoners crouched lower inside their wooden boxcars, their faces turned up to the grimy ceilings, many shouting and cursing as they realized what was about to happen.

"Lay down!" yelled Kasten above the din, "lay down on the floor, men!"

It was easier said than done, but it was the only thing they could do. The men pressed themselves into the filthy floor of the boxcar, or on top of one another, knowing full well that all that stood between them and a horrible death were the thin wooden walls and roof of the car.

The first group of Mosquitos hammered down toward the yard, lit by the baleful jaundiced glow of large parachute flares, and released their bombs. Huge detonations shook the POW transport, orange and red flames leaping skyward close by as the aircraft passed overhead, their engines deafening to the trapped men. Then they heard the sound of another aircraft diving in to attack. The screaming and shouting reached a new fever pitch of intensity as the British plane came closer and closer. In one carriage 1st Lt. Paul Cavanaugh stood up and yelled above the noise:

"Now everybody repeat after me these words!"

Sixty expectant faces turned to the Catholic chaplain, who had shared with them the ordeal of the march and the last three days of filth and squalor aboard the train.

"Oh my God—I am most sorry for having sinned against you—because you are so good…"

Voices began to join the Jesuit priest's loud call to prayer as the roar of the engines grew loader and German antiaircraft guns started to fire close by and the Americans prepared to die… "*ego te absolvo a peccatis tuis in nomine Patris, et Filii, et Spiritus Sancti*" (I absolve you of your sins in the name of the Father, and the Son, and the Holy Ghost).[22]

CHAPTER 8

A Christmas Story

Christmas still meant something to most of us—regardless of everything that had happened, we still remembered the day and what it stood for.
Pfc. Theodore Rosenberg, 106th Infantry Division

The detonation of the first bombs was so loud aboard the POW transport train that they momentarily shut out all the screaming, shouting, and praying. The cars felt as though they were a child's toy train that had been lifted bodily by a giant unseen hand and then dropped back onto the rails, where they shuddered and rocked violently.[1] The men could hear nothing for a few seconds, and lay on the floor, their heads buried in their arms, steel helmets firmly on if they still possessed them, muttering and moaning in their terror.

"Father, say some more prayers!" somebody in Chaplain Cavanaugh's car screamed.

The priest pulled himself up as the screaming descent of the next Mosquito began high above them.

"Oh God, have mercy on us!" shouted Cavanaugh, his hands on the backs of the two men crouching closest to him. "Mary, help us! St. Joseph, pray for us!"[2]

The next bombs landed, and everybody screamed and hugged the floor as debris and shrapnel rattled down on the roof like steel rain.

*

Hans Kasten continued to shout encouragement and instructions to the men in his boxcar throughout the bombardment. He didn't join in the prayers—he'd been a confirmed atheist since he was fifteen years old.[3] The sounds of the bomb detonations were getting closer and closer, and through the tiny cracks between the timber sides of the car, an orange glow could be seen. The town was on fire. The orange of the flames mixed with the yellow glare of the parachute flares the British were dropping to illuminate the rail yard,[4] the combination burning bright like the very fires of hell.

*

Farther down the train hysteria reigned. In one boxcar, the occupants smashed down the door in their desperation to be free and started to run out into the maelstrom of explosions and flying shrapnel. Another Mosquito passed overhead, dropping its stick of bombs. One landed close by the train, killing eight Americans as they ran around looking for cover.[5]

In Cavanaugh's car, the men started to hear American voices calling to each other outside the train—more men had broken loose.

"Let's get out of here!" yelled a young soldier close to Cavanaugh. "Come on, let's break the door down!" A dozen or so of the men nearest the door started to hammer at it until Father Cavanaugh yelled above the din.

"At ease! At ease!" he cried, waving his arms. "Stay where you are. We have protection here from all but a direct hit. Lie low and keep your heads covered."[6]

The priest's exhortation had the desired effect; the men resumed crouching on the floor.

In Kasten's car, he gave a similar order when men tried to break out. As a seasoned combat soldier, Kasten knew that any cover was better than none, and running around outside in the middle of an intense air raid would only get more men killed and wounded.

*

On and on went the raid, as the fifty-two Mosquitos bombed and strafed, eventually finding the POW transport. The end two boxcars were suddenly obliterated in a flash and booming detonation, which lifted the rest of the cars, the men screaming as they were thrown about. Everybody knew that the train had been hit, and there was pandemonium. The men in the last two boxcars hadn't stood a chance; a 250-pound bomb had blown up both cars, flinging body parts over a wide radius as the cars quickly burned down to their steel chassis and wheels.[7]

Then, as suddenly as the raid had begun, the drone of aircraft engines faded into the distance as the last parachute flare guttered out, and then there was a kind of silence. The prisoners slowly unfurled themselves from their protective positions on the floor and raised their heads like furtive animals, listening in case the bombing should suddenly resume. The only sounds were the shouting of German guards and the crackling of buildings being engulfed by flames.

Those who had managed to escape from the boxcars didn't get far. The German escort and military police from the local garrison rushed back from their shelters as the sirens sounded the all clear, shouting and gesturing to the Americans to return to their boxcars. The prisoners, dazed, confused, and in some cases wounded by debris, milled about, uncertain what to do. The Germans, terrified that they were witnessing some kind of prisoner revolt, leveled their weapons at the Americans menacingly and advanced toward them.

"Get back on the train," bellowed the sergeant in charge. "*Schnell!*"

To emphasize his seriousness, he pointed his MP40 machine pistol into the air and fired off a couple of short bursts.[8] The automatic fire prompted the confused prisoners to cower down and retreat toward the train, while those still on board pressed themselves to any cracks or gaps to try and see what was going on.

"*Raus, raus!*" bellowed enraged German soldiers.

Another German sergeant was particularly crazed—he pulled out his Luger pistol and fired off the entire magazine in his frustration, this time toward the train. A bullet went through the thin wooden side of one of the boxcars, killing an American soldier.[9]

Once all the prisoners who were still alive had been rounded up and the doors to their fetid boxes once more firmly locked, the remains of the two burned wagons, still full of unrecognizable bodies destroyed by the bomb and the fire, were unhitched from the train. But if the prisoners thought they were leaving bomb-ravaged Diez they were mistaken—the track ahead of the train had been destroyed by a direct hit. It would take maintenance crews many hours of hard labor to put it right. The entire yard resembled a moonscape of craters, broken machinery, and torn-up tracks. The RAF's Mosquitos had done their job well.

*

Following the German tradition of giving presents on Christmas Eve, rather than on Christmas Day, guards started to roll back the boxcar doors on the evening of December 24. The POW train was still stuck in the station while repair crews worked on the tracks. Elderly Germans brought buckets of cold water to each car, two per sixty-plus prisoners. The dehydrated prisoners soon consumed these, which tasted better than the finest champagne. Some candles were lit and the prisoners tried to raise their morale by singing carols. The few padres with them gave prayers.

"It was just as if God hadn't forgotten us," recalled Pfc. Theodore Rosenberg.[10]

Later, the German guards unlocked the boxcars once again, and tubs of horrible ersatz coffee were provided, followed by some meager rations. Some cars were issued captured American tinned meat and loaves of black bread, one tin and a single loaf per six men. Other cars received black bread, margarine, and a little marmalade piled into American helmet shells.[11]

"Scanty though it was, there wasn't a man there who didn't appreciate it more than any Christmas present he had ever received before," wrote Rosenberg. "It was life over death—and we were near the balancing point of the two."[12]

With a little food and water in their stomachs, morale went up, and the low sound of carols being sung by exhausted but thankful men drifted across the rail yard, where buildings still smoldered from the raid and the track repair crews paused in their work to listen to the voices singing familiar songs in a language they didn't understand.

Just before midnight, church bells started to ring across Diez and Limburg, calling the faithful to Christmas Mass. They sounded shrill and clear on the cold night air,[13] but they were infinitely preferable to the bone-chilling terror of air-raid sirens and howling aircraft engines.

*

"We're moving," announced Hans Kasten to his boxcar.

The car shuddered and then gave a lurch, the locomotive

far down the line of cars giving a blast on its steam whistle. It was just before noon on Christmas Day. A wave of relief went through the Americans, who were thankful to be finally leaving the rail yard, a major Allied bombing target. They had spent their enforced idleness worrying that the British might return and bomb them again. Perhaps their long journey was finally nearing its end.

Soon the train was puffing once more through the white countryside. It had grown colder overnight, with an inch of frost on the iron bolts *inside* the cars.[14] The men shivered, their teeth chattering as they tried to stay warm, hungry again from lack of food.

An hour later the train stopped briefly in a small station. The men pressed against the tiny car windows and tried unsuccessfully to barter what personal effects the Germans had left them with passing civilians for food, but they had no luck.[15] The civilians stared back with sullen and hostile expressions on their faces, or waved a hand dismissively.

After a while, Kasten and the other observant prisoners noticed that the train had passed off the main track onto a branch line. Then, around 1400 hours, the train started to slow down again before slipping into a pretty little station in mountainous country.

Kasten peered through one of the little openings in his car and saw a sign.[16]

"It says 'Bad Orb,'" he relayed to the prisoners.

"What does it mean?" asked one.

"'Bad' means 'bath' in German," replied Kasten. "It means we've arrived in a spa town."

"Great!" quipped one of the others in a sarcastic tone. "Maybe I can finally get a wash."

A few of the others raised a tired chuckle. They all stank to high heaven.

"I wouldn't count on that just yet, soldier," replied Kasten, before guttural German shouting and the barking of dogs drowned him out.

*

Almost before the train had fully stopped, German guards in greatcoats and helmets were unlocking the boxcar doors and pulling them back on their runners.

"*Aus dem Wagen!*" they screamed, ordering the prisoners out of the cars. "*Ausgehen! Schnell!*"

Impatiently they pulled the prisoners nearest the doors out onto the platform, while the rest started to jump down, their limbs and joints protesting madly after so many days cramped into tiny spaces without exercise.[17]

Some Germans held straining Alsatians that were going crazy at the sight of the American prisoners. The din was tremendous and confusing, the cold intense and sharp.

"*Ausrichten!*" bellowed a German sergeant major in a crusher cap, who was strutting up and down the platform like an enraged bull. "Line up!" he screamed, this time in English.

Slowly, with the aid of much shouting, pushing, and hitting from the guards, the prisoners were mustered into groups of a hundred men and stood to attention for the agony of counting.

*

"*Marsch!*" bellowed the sergeant major, and with this command the bedraggled groups of prisoners started to shuffle out of the station and through the east side of town.[18]

"You've gotta be kidding," Kasten exclaimed as he turned a corner out of the station heading into Bad Orb. Emblazoned on the side of a building was a large and faded advertisement for Coca-Cola.

The experience of marching through Bad Orb was surreal. Many of the pretty stone houses and shops were bedecked with cheerful Christmas decorations. The war had thus far hardly affected this little German town nestled in the Spessart Mountains, thirty-one miles from the city of Frankfurt am Main. It was an affluent place, a prewar health resort and sanatorium town where the well-heeled had descended to drink its curative mineral waters and bathe in its warm thermal pools. But for the Americans, now trudging through the town toward a heavily forested hill called the Wegscheideküppel, the welcome was quite different.

Kasten and the others passed down a main street until the guards started yelling "*Halt*!" The enforced stop was not to allow the exhausted prisoners to rest; rather, it was so a German Army cameraman could record the event on film. They were surrounded by angry-looking groups of locals, who stood and stared at the prisoners with barely concealed loathing.[19] Kasten and the prisoners stood stone-faced or else stared at the ground while the cameraman flitted about the long column shooting his film for Dr. Goebbels.

"*Marsch*!" bellowed the sergeant major again once enough shots had been taken, and the weary column started again on its journey uphill. But they were soon halted once more, this time for the amusement of the local population. Soon, young Hitler Youths were pelting them with snowballs and stones while the older people booed and hissed.[20] The Americans had to stand there and take it—any display of resistance was brutally dealt with by their guards.

The march resumed, and the column moved out of town onto a steep road that was under four inches of snow. The Americans stumbled along for miles as the incline grew steeper, and they entered a forest road lined with great, ice-blown fir trees. The guards pushed and shoved any of the prisoners who fell down or were too slow, beating them with rifle butts, boots, and siccing the ever-present Alsatians on them. Then, a pair of wooden and barbed wire gates emerged out of the snow and mist. Set atop the gate was a large wooden Nazi eagle, its talons entwined around a wreathed swastika. Below the eagle, a white board painted in tall black Gothic script announced: MANNSCHAFTS-STAMMLAGER IX B.

"*Halt!*" bellowed the Germans. The column stopped before the gates, which were at least twelve feet tall and topped with more barbed wire.

Several Germans opened the gates and there was an exchange of salutes between the prisoner escort and the gate sentries, before a chit of paper was handed over. The German officer commanding the gate party examined the chit, nodded, and then beckoned the sergeant major to lead the prisoners in.

"Say, buddy, you speak German," a voice behind Kasten said. "What's that signboard say?"

Kasten glanced around. There were several men waiting for an answer as they all shuffled forward toward the towering portal.

"It says that this is Stalag Nine-B," replied Kasten. "It's a prison camp."

The Germans herded the column along a black cinder path through another gate, and then another, until they entered the main camp.

"*Russkiy! Russkiy!*"

Kasten glanced around with the other new arrivals at the strange shouting and saw faces pressed against the windows of huts in a fenced-off compound close by. They were drawn and pinched faces, the faces of men long used to hunger and privation.

"I think they're Russians," a corporal said close by.

The Soviet prisoners of war were cheering and waving and shouting out the word "*Russkiy*" over and over, trying to tell the new arrivals that they were Allies. Kasten and the others could manage only a few halfhearted waves in return, so tired were they after their exhausting journey.[21]

"Negroes!" exclaimed a man in the column behind Kasten, and everyone turned to look.

"They ours?" asked another, for plenty of African American troops had been captured in the Ardennes.

The US Army was segregated, with black soldiers manning transport companies, artillery batteries, and many other units during the recent fighting.

"Nah, look at their uniforms."

About a dozen black soldiers were emerging from a hut and staring at the Americans. They wore British battle dress uniforms, and their leader had the three large chevrons of a sergeant on one arm. He raised one hand in greeting.

"Where are you from?" shouted out Kasten.

"South Africa," yelled the sergeant, before a guard intervened and shooed the black soldiers away from the fence.

The new arrivals were marched farther into the camp until they were halted next to an earthen reservoir that stood ten feet tall. Close by, a tall, white-painted, wooden clock tower rose twenty feet into the air. It had a clock face on each side and space below the clock for a single guard, who was leaning on the edge looking down with a bored expression at the long line of prisoners. Kasten glanced about some more. He'd noticed that the three sets of fences they had passed through were substantial barriers, each consisting of two twelve-foot-tall wire fences set about eight feet apart, the space in between filled with yet more coils of barbed wire. Guard towers were spaced out every few hundred yards along the perimeter, some mounting MG34 machine guns. Several rows of dilapidated-looking, single-story, wooden huts stretched out on each side of the main path. The camp was huge, and Kasten couldn't see all of it from where he stood, but he sensed its dimensions. The camp was positioned atop the hill three miles outside Bad Orb, and the forest that surrounded it effectively hid the place from prying eyes.[22]

The prisoners were herded toward a large central square of mud and trampled snow, where they formed up once more into groups of one hundred to be counted again. Away to one side stood a group of German officers, who were watching the proceedings carefully and smoking cigarettes. The two oldest men caught Kasten's attention. One was slim, of medium height, and middle-aged. He wore a long greatcoat and a brown pistol belt, a visor cap, black jackboots, and gray gloves. His expression was severe. His shoulder epaulettes were of a full colonel. The man standing beside him was slightly taller, but of a similar age, and instead of a visor cap he wore an M43 field cap at a slightly jaunty angle. His rank badges indicated a lieutenant colonel. Kasten correctly guessed that the senior man was the camp commandant, and the other German must be his deputy.

"*Achtung*!" screamed a German sergeant, calling the parade to attention once the counting was complete.

The colonel strode over to a wooden dais placed in the mud, returned the sergeant's punctilious military salute, and then addressed the prisoners in loud and heavily accented English.

"I am Oberst Sieber, commandant of this camp. In a little while you will be processed and issued with your identity tags. You will provide us with your name, rank, serial number, and home address so we can inform the Red Cross that you are now prisoners of the Reich. Anyone who refuses will be punished. You are undoubtedly tired from your long journey. Therefore, once you have been processed and assigned to barracks you will be fed."

The commandant paused, then continued. "You will obey the camp rules, which will be told to you. Anyone who breaks these rules *will* be punished."

Sieber quickly ran through the major points, pulling no punches when it came to discussing the consequences for disobeying these regulations.[23] Then he pointed with one gloved hand toward the camp fence, which had a single strand of wire about eighteen inches high twenty inches in front of it.

"You see the single line of wire there," shouted Sieber menacingly, and hundreds of filthy, bearded, and lean faces turned to look. "That is the 'line of death.' Escape from this camp, gentlemen, is forbidden. If you cross this line, you *will* be shot." Sieber paused, his hard eyes scanning the crowd, a ghost of a smile creasing his lips.

"Welcome to Stalag Nine-B," Sieber finished. He was about to leave when he turned once more to the assembled prisoners.

"Oh, I almost forgot," he said, pausing melodramatically. "Merry Christmas."

CHAPTER 9

Abandon Hope

An aura of self-confidence surrounded Kasten. His blue eyes had the sharp, searching look of an eagle.

Pfc. Joe Littell

"You are currently classified by us, *and* the American authorities, as 'missing in action,'" stated the middle-aged German officer who was interrogating batches of prisoners as they were being processed into Stalag IX-B.

Hans Kasten sat on a hard wooden chair inside a drafty hut, as a long line of prisoners patiently waited outside in the snow and wind. On the table in front of the officer was a sheaf of papers inside a buff manila folder. Kasten shifted in his chair and waited, hunger gnawing at his stomach.

"Whether you are finally classified as 'killed in action' or 'prisoner of war' is *my* decision."[1]

The German was trying to sound intimidating, but he'd already been through this charade more than a hundred times that day, and his fatigue was starting to show.

"Cigarette?" asked the German, producing a packet of American Luckies.

Kasten took one and savored his first smoke in days. Then the German poured him coffee into a battered tin mug, placing it before him. If the German was trying to win Kasten over he failed, as Kasten detested coffee.[2]

"So, we begin," the German said, opening the folder, his English very good. "Name?"

"Kasten, Johann," replied the American.

"You have a German name," the interrogator said in a mock surprised tone. "Were you born in Germany?"

"No, I'm an American," replied Kasten coolly.

He knew the drill—name, rank, and number only; anything else you didn't have to answer. Kasten realized early on that the Germans were trying to trick prisoners into revealing some useful intelligence, but due to the massive volume of Americans that the camp staff was processing that day, they could do no more at this stage than perform a rather perfunctory interrogation.

"So, Kasten, you are from the Twenty-Eighth Infantry Division, *ja*?" asked the German.

"Right," muttered Kasten. He was wearing the division's "bloody bucket" keystone patch on his grubby uniform's shoulders, so there was no use in denying the obvious.

"So, let me see…" continued the German, rifling through several pages of tightly typed names, running his index finger down one page.

"Kasten, Kasten, ah yes," the German said, reading off Kasten's army number, regiment, and company. Kasten nodded—none of this was classified information.

"So, now we know who you are," the German said, evidently satisfied that the man on his list had been identified in person. He placed a tick next to Kasten's name.

"Do you speak German?" the interrogator asked suddenly.

"A little," replied Kasten calmly, keen not to announce his fluency to the authorities.

The interrogator switched to German and probed Kasten, but gave up and switched back to English when Kasten gave only vague one-word answers.

"So, Kasten, where were you born?" asked the German calmly.

Kasten replied with name, rank, and number. The German didn't seem fazed.

"You know, Kasten, I once lived in Detroit," the German said, smiling. "A fine city. Do you know it?"

Kasten smiled and once more gave his name, rank, and number.

"What is your religion?" the German said, changing the subject.

Kasten was surprised to be asked this and did not reply.

"I ask this so that if you die here, we will know what kind of service to give you."

"That's a cheery thought," replied Kasten. "Actually, I'm an atheist."

"An atheist!" exclaimed the interrogator, before making a note. "What did you do before the war?"

"Kasten, Johann, Private First Class..."

And so it went on, the German trying to get Kasten to reveal something personal about himself, or to discuss his capture or details about his unit. After a while the German, who didn't appear in the least bit angry at Kasten's refusal to answer his questions, admitted defeat and asked him to move to the identification station in an adjacent room.[3]

Once inside this room, Kasten was confronted by another desk, this time manned by an elderly corporal, who assigned Kasten his prisoner of war number.

"Stand by the wall," ordered the corporal, and Kasten was forced to hold up a chalkboard containing his number to be photographed; the old-fashioned flash temporarily blinded him. This mug shot was later developed and stapled to his file. Unlike many of the other prisoners who had their photograph taken that day, Kasten stared straight and proudly into the lens, no scowl of defeat on his face, his hard blue eyes seemingly searching for something. He stood with his shoulders back, and it was easy to see why so many of the men had gravitated toward this extraordinary personality, with his unique Vandyke beard and spare frame.

Another German took a large rectangular metal dog tag that was perforated down the middle so it could be broken into two parts and quickly hammered Kasten's POW number into it.[4]

"Do not lose this!" the corporal ordered curtly as he handed Kasten his tag, then pointed to another door.

Kasten passed through and formally entered Stalag IX-B as *Kriegsgefangener* No. 23400. The Germans worked overtime that Christmas Day, processing more than one thousand new arrivals. Over the coming days thousands more Americans would be added to the total, arriving at Bad Orb aboard several more cattle wagon trains from Gerolstein.[5]

*

"*Schweinhund!*" a German officer barked over to the processing hut.

A group of about two dozen American prisoners had completely refused to cooperate with their interrogators and had been taken out of the line and placed in a huddle. The duty officer was summoned and he started to shout at the prisoners in German, which none of them could understand. Tiring of this, he summoned two of his guards. In front of the hundreds of men still waiting to be processed into the camp, the two guards reversed their rifles and set about the Americans, beating them mercilessly with their rifle butts until they were screaming on the snowy ground, moaning and crying from their injuries. With a Luger pistol in his right hand, the German officer gestured for the men to stand up, while telling the waiting prisoners to continue to move forward into the interrogation hut. Those two dozen recalcitrant prisoners had learned a short, sharp lesson: In Commandant Sieber's camp, the inmates obeyed the rules that he had outlined to them, and obeyed without question. To ensure that they understood, they were forced to stand in the snow for four hours, suffering the agonies of frostbite and the onset of hypothermia.[6] The message that this example sent to the other prisoners was obvious—rock the boat and you could expect real trouble.

*

Next came assignment to a barrack block. Stalag IX-B had once been a holiday camp for children, but though the situation of the camp atop the forested mountain overlooking Bad Orb offered magnificent views, the camp buildings had deteriorated badly.

The camp consisted of about fifty buildings, mostly single-story wooden huts, but with a few large brick barracks and a large house outside the perimeter that served as the German camp headquarters, or *Kommandantur*. It was organized into various compounds for the different nationalities of prisoners.[7]

Like the camp itself, with its dilapidated buildings and old amenities, the men detailed to guard the prisoners had themselves seen better days. The guards were drawn from L Company, Landesschütz Battalion 633, originally raised in Fulda in June 1940. *Landesschützen* battalions were composed of a mixture of men who were not fit for frontline duty because of their age, or men whose battlefield injuries left them unable to fight. These reserve formations released younger, fitter soldiers to the front, while providing guards for POW camps and other rear echelon tasks. Most of the guards at Bad Orb were in their forties and fifties, and many wore medal ribbons and wound badges from World War I. Some of the younger men were missing arms or legs, yet were still forced to serve.[8] Most were unfit and looking for a quiet life, longing to return to their families. A few were harsh or cruel, but many were also easy to bribe for small luxuries, for by this stage of the war the German home front was in a parlous state, with drastic shortages of virtually everything.

Commanding this run-down and ever expanding camp was the commandant, Colonel Karl Sieber, a forty-nine-year-old infantryman and World War I veteran. He had been reactivated from the reserves in August 1939 and quickly routed into POW administration. He was awarded World War II bars to his Great War Iron Cross 1st and 2nd Class, and in April 1943 rewarded for his service in POW camps with the War Merit Cross 2nd Class with Swords, a pat on the head from Berlin for doing a good job.[9]

Stalag IX-B was typical of many late war camps—overcrowded beyond its authorized capacity by the influx of American prisoners from the Ardennes and evacuated Allied POWs from the east, whose camps were emptied ahead of the Red Army. Once the Americans were included, the camp's population grew to around nine thousand prisoners. Poorly resourced, Sieber was just about managing with the staff and supplies assigned to him, but he had had to make some grim decisions concerning rations, reducing prisoners to only about 1,800 calories a day in order to string out what he had.[10] This was somewhat below the recommended calorific intake for young men at the time. Red Cross parcels had made up this shortfall in the past, but due to Allied bombing of the rail network, these didn't arrive regularly and couldn't be relied upon as they once had.

Sieber maintained control over this huge, overcrowded, malnourished enterprise with a rod of iron. An old-school officer, he enforced harsh discipline against those who transgressed the camp rules and turned a blind eye to casual violence by his guards against the prisoners. In controlling the camp, he was ably assisted by his deputy, Oberstleutnant Albert Wodarg, a fifty-two-year-old lieutenant colonel from the Army Riding and Driving School Branch. Wodarg, like his boss, had a row of medal ribbons above his left breast pocket detailing plenty of World War I service, and he had also been awarded the War Merit Cross 2nd Class for his recent military service in the camps.[11] His job was the day-to-day running of the stalag. There were another dozen or so officers, including an army doctor, plus several hundred guards.

*

Once the prisoners had been processed, batches were marched under guard to their accommodation. Sieber had cleared Soviet prisoners out of fifteen barrack blocks to make room for the Americans, but it still meant horrendous overcrowding. The new American compound was at the top of the hill, where there were some large masonry barrack blocks as well as wooden huts in rows. A muddy road ran from the main gate through the Soviet compound, then through the US section of the camp and out through another well-guarded gate.[12]

When Kasten entered his assigned hut, his heart sank. It was, to use a word, primitive, and though better than the horse dung–festooned boxcars, it wasn't that much of an improvement. Kasten was among 160 prisoners who were to be housed in each wooden barrack; the accommodation was split into two huge communal dormitories that held eighty men each.[13]

He wandered over to a bunk and sat down, a group of men following him. He had already gathered about him quite a following of young GIs who looked to this older man as their leader. They had all witnessed his behavior during the march or on the train, and had been impressed. Needing leadership more than ever now, but separated from their officers and noncoms

by the Germans—the officers were housed in a special hut—
men like Kasten filled a void in the chain of command. Among
those who had fallen in with Kasten was Joe Littell. Kasten had
already noted Littell's excellent German, even though he was
not of German extraction.

The bunks were triple tiered with burlap sacking for mattresses. The hut was massive, measuring about one hundred feet
long by forty feet wide. But it was cold, as the wind howled
through spaces between the boards or through windows with
missing panes of glass.[14] It was clear that the Germans were not
wasting resources on maintaining the fabric of the camp.

The bunks were arranged along each side of the room, in
groups of four or five along the walls with a narrow aisle between the groups. In the middle of the room was a long pine
board table and a couple of benches. Two brick ovens were used
to heat the building, but they were not very efficient. Inside the
hut it was dark and dreary.[15] Kasten lay back on his bunk and
closed his eyes. It was fantastic to be able to finally stretch out
and rest. Many of the other guys were doing the same, while the
last of the cigarettes was being shared among groups of friends.
After the last few days, the atmosphere inside the hut was almost
convivial. The relief at being able to rest was only offset by the
hunger every man was feeling in the pit of his stomach. The
commandant had promised to feed them, but it looked as though
that was coming later.

*

After a little while, the door to the hut was thrown open,
and in strode a German sergeant in his midfifties. Speaking in
German, he demanded to know if anyone present spoke the
language. Kasten, whose eyes had shot open at the sound of
the door being opened, raised himself up on his elbows. No

one replied, but Kasten knew full well that several of the 160 men spoke some German, just like him. He noticed many of the prisoners were looking at him, deferring naturally to the man who had already provided leadership during the appalling journey to Bad Orb. He sighed, swung his long legs out, and stood up painfully.

"*Ich spreche Deutsch*," Kasten said, and the German sergeant immediately beckoned him over to act as his translator.

"He says he is the block leader, and is in charge of this barrack," Kasten said in a loud voice, translating the sergeant's words after he had introduced himself.

The German then proceeded to explain the rules and regulations of the camp.

"He says you cannot use the toilet during the day or when the barrack is unlocked," Kasten said.[16]

Many of the prisoners had already visited the "toilet" and been shocked by what they had discovered. Washing facilities for 160 men consisted of one single cold-water tap in a small, concrete-floored "bathroom" along with a latrine that consisted of a hole in the floor about ten inches in diameter, dropping through to a cesspool with an outside opening for cleaning.

"He says you must use the separate latrine building during the day," repeated Kasten, explaining that outside Barrack 43A there was a large pit with several poles that prisoners could sit on.[17]

There were a few humorous comments, and a ripple of laughter moved through the hut. The German sergeant smiled also. He appeared to be a decent sort, and he wore a couple of World War I ribbons above his left pocket. The prisoners would discover that most of these barrack noncoms had been called up from civilian life as the war situation for Germany deteriorated and more manpower was needed. They missed their families back home, and many had sons serving in the army at the front.

"You are not permitted to lay on the bunks with your shoes on," Kasten translated.[18]

Many of the men laughed at this, until Kasten explained—ironically, considering their surroundings—that the Germans were very clean people.

"You are to salute *all* German officers," translated Kasten.[19]

This was a military courtesy. The enlisted prisoners were not required to salute German enlisted personnel.

"Twice a day you will form up in the parade square for counting, what they call *Appell*," translated Kasten.[20]

After speaking for a few more moments, the sergeant smiled, nodded, and left. The prisoners relaxed and discussed their new situation among themselves. Kasten set about sorting out some issues in the barrack and helping to explain further how the Germans ran the camp. It was obvious that if they wanted to fend off illness, they would have to try and keep their accommodation as clean as possible. Kasten also asked for any medics to identify themselves.

*

"*Achtung!*" the German sergeant shouted when he reappeared sometime later, breaking up Kasten's meeting. "*Appell…Appell…raus, raus!*"

Kasten quickly translated and shouted out to the men that it was a counting parade—everybody outside for inspection. The sergeant hammered his orders home with several blasts on a whistle that he wore around his neck like a football coach.

The weary prisoners tugged on their battered boots and, still footsore and exhausted, they shuffled outside into the wind and formed up in ranks on the large parade ground. The parade took some time, as the German guards moved down the ranks carefully counting before reporting to Hauptmann Horn, the

German captain in charge of the American compound, that all prisoners were present and accounted for.

Next, a barrack at a time, the men were taken to a door where some grizzled-looking Soviet prisoners handed each man a receptacle to carry food in. The very lucky ones received old German or American mess tins, some got cooking pots, and some used their own steel helmets, while many had to make do with rusty and battered former Red Cross tins.[21] One particularly unlucky fellow received a flowerpot.

The prisoners were salivating by now, as they lined up for their first proper meal since capture, the smell of unidentified food wafting from the kitchen hut. There was an air of excitement as Kasten and the rest of the men from his barrack shuffled expectantly toward where some more Soviet cooks were ladling food out of large cauldrons that steamed in the freezing air.

"What the—!" Kasten exclaimed when a sour-faced Soviet prisoner ladled his portion into the battered tin he had been issued.

The meal was not as expected. Each man received three thimble-sized potatoes that swam in a thin soup of unidentified greens and a few turnip tops, as well as a slice of German black bread.[22] But for the prisoners, who were ordered to take this bounty back to their barracks to consume, it was as good as the best steak they'd ever had, and they hungrily wolfed it down. Unfortunately, it was discovered by about half the men that Soviet-prepared camp food was an excellent laxative, and they suffered from diarrhea for days afterward, overwhelming the primitive latrines.[23]

Kasten made a mental note that having Soviet prisoners in charge of cooking for the Americans was unacceptable. In fact, the Soviets seemed to be running large sections of the camp as the Germans used them to fetch, carry, cook, clean, and repair, and they were obviously operating a system to their own benefit. But the question was, who could change this system?

*

"You will elect a prisoner who will be your *Vertrauensmann*," translated Kasten.[24]

The block sergeant had returned the next day with the requirement that the prisoners organize their own council. He explained all this to Kasten in rapid German.

"What's a '*Vertrau*...' I mean, what he said," piped up one of the GIs.

"It means 'Man of Confidence,'" explained Kasten. "It's a prisoner that can speak German and interprets their instructions to his fellow prisoners while at the same time working on the prisoners' behalf."

"Sounds like a sweet number," another GI said sarcastically.

"No," replied Kasten firmly. "The *Vertrauensmann* receives no additional food or special favors."

The German sergeant grew impatient at all this chatter and interrupted, telling Kasten that the prisoners in the barrack must elect a leader, now.

"I think Kasten should do it," a prisoner said, and many other voices grunted in agreement.

"Now hold on, fellas," Kasten said. "Why pick on me? I don't want it."[25]

"You speak the language just like a real Heinie!" another said. "And we saw what you did on the march and at Gerolstein station."

"And on the train!" shouted another from the back of the room.

More voices chimed in, demanding or encouraging, all wanting Kasten to take the post.

"There's plenty of men who can speak some German," retorted

Kasten, alarmed and angry to be singled out, but his protests were quickly drowned out by the crowd.

"Wadya say, fellas?" shouted out a tough-looking GI in the front row. "All in favor of Kasten here as our Man of Confidence, raise your hands."

Before Kasten could protest further, most of the hands in the room went up, and Kasten was duly elected prisoner leader of the barrack.

"Just like city hall, ain't it?" joked the tough-faced GI to Kasten. "So wadya say, you our guy or what?"

Hans Kasten looked at the sea of raised arms and the expectant expressions on the rows of bearded dogfaces, and he finally nodded in defeat. A small cheer went through the room, and several of the prisoners clapped him on the back and shoulder. They probably thought that Kasten could solve all their problems, but he knew deep down that this new job was going to be a trial from the start. At that moment, Kasten thought himself to be the unluckiest SOB in this man's army.[26]

CHAPTER 10

Chief Man of Confidence

I as a Pfc assumed the position of a general or at least a full colonel.

Pfc. Hans Kasten

All those in favor of Pfc. Kasten as Chief Man of Confidence, raise your hands," ordered 1st Sgt. Gabriel Johnson, one of the newly elected barracks leaders.[1]

Most of the other fifteen men in the room raised their arms. At least half wore the chevrons of senior noncoms on their upper sleeves.

"Well, that's decided then," Johnson said, turning to Kasten. "Do you accept the appointment?"

Kasten was momentarily stunned—he looked around the room at the other men, many of them eminently more qualified, so he thought, to the position than he. Kasten had only been elected his barrack's Man of Confidence a few hours earlier. Now, at a meeting of all barrack leaders, the Germans had demanded that one of the sixteen be elected overall leader of the American camp. Kasten was chosen.

He couldn't figure out why. Eight of his fellow barrack leaders were master sergeants, first sergeants, or staff sergeants, men used to being in charge of other soldiers, many of them undoubtedly long-service veterans. But they wanted Kasten, a lowly Pfc, to take the post. He swallowed hard and croaked a response.

"Okay, Top, I accept."

"Good man," said M.Sgt. Wissinger, the head of Barrack 39.

Kasten suspected, due to the relieved looks on their faces, that more than a few of the men in the room thought that they had dodged a bullet by avoiding this particular post, a job that would involve day-to-day liaison with the enemy. After all, it was the Germans that had demanded that one of the sixteen men present be elected Chief Man of Confidence. This man would represent *all* of the American prisoners in the camp and have constant contact with the German commandant and his subordinates. Such a man would be expected to sort out the many problems the prisoners faced at Bad Orb, and to pass on often-unpopular German orders. A lot would be riding on his shoulders. And, perhaps most important to his fellow leaders, he would be expected to be responsible for the actions of every other prisoner in the American compound should there be a problem—the Germans took the line that the buck most definitely stopped with the Chief Man of Confidence, making this a potentially dangerous post.

Kasten was shocked by how fast things had changed since he had been taken prisoner. Now a twenty-seven-year-old whom the army had deemed not worthy of promotion beyond private first class had been put in command of what would eventually total four thousand US prisoners of war. The other prisoners captured in the Ardennes had been sent to several other camps.

"I as a Pfc assumed the position of a general or at least a full colonel," Kasten would write in stunned awe later.[2]

It was a terrible responsibility for anyone to assume, let alone someone who, though he might have demonstrated leadership potential over the past few days, had never officially commanded a single soldier. But it was a free vote, and the other men, particularly the highly experienced noncoms, perhaps saw something in Kasten that he couldn't see, something that others around him were waking up to: that Kasten was a natural-born leader of men and had the kind of dynamic and forceful personality that such a job required.

Another prisoner was quickly elected to Kasten's vacant position in his barrack block, leaving the council numbering sixteen Men of Confidence with Kasten as their overall leader.

*

"How'd you feel about helping me run things around here?" asked Kasten.

The two other Pfcs that he had called to his room were surprised by the request. Joe Littell and Ernesto Sinner glanced at each other and then back at Kasten, who, as Chief Man of Confidence, had been assigned a room in Barrack 24, what the Germans had decided would be the American compound headquarters.

"I need two assistants with an excellent grasp of German," continued Kasten, "and you two certainly have that. This camp is in a mess, and I've been handed the job of trying to sort things out. It's not going to be easy, but with your help I think some positive changes can be made. So what do you say?"

Sitting next to Kasten was his newly appointed deputy, Pvt. Edmund "Eddie" Pfannenstiel, another fluent German speaker.[3] Pfannenstiel had been a truck driver near Hays, Kansas, before enlisting and had been captured with the 130th Field Artillery in Kasten's Twenty-Eighth Infantry Division. He was a reliable man with a good sense of humor whose German was native, as both his parents were German immigrants and the language was spoken constantly in his community.

Ernesto Sinner spoke first. He was a short, dark-haired, half-Jewish soldier from New York City. He was born in Germany, and his family had emigrated to the United States when he was a young child, though his parents had continued to speak German at home and Sinner was completely fluent. Before he enlisted he'd been a waiter at the famous Elizabeth Flynn's Restaurant by Fulton Fish Market in the Bronx.[4]

"Sure, Hans, count me in," replied Sinner without any reservations, a wry smile on his face.

"Me too, Hans," Joe Littell said. He had come to respect Kasten in the few days that he had known him.

"Okay, thank you. I'm having you transferred here. You can bunk with us."

The Germans had assigned Kasten a cadre room on the right of the barracks. Inside the room were two triple-tier bunks, a battered table, and a couple of warped wooden chairs. It wasn't much, but from here Kasten would command the American compound.

Barrack 24 was well placed, standing opposite the American compound's kitchen block near the tall clock tower. Next to the kitchen was the firewood yard, where prisoners stockpiled wood gathered from the forest to fuel their inadequate little room stoves. The American compound hospital stood behind Barrack 24 to the northeast.[5]

"Your duties in the main will be to keep communications flowing between myself and the rest of the prisoners," Kasten said. "You will liaise with the other Men of Confidence and they'll inform their prisoners."[6]

Littell and Sinner nodded. They were, in effect, Kasten's personal staff—his military aides, assisting Kasten and Pfannenstiel in representing the US interest.

"Okay," sighed Kasten. "Your first task is to inform the other

Men of Confidence to convene here tonight after the second roll call for a meeting. It's time a few changes were made around here."

Sinner and Littell looked at Kasten, sitting behind the battered desk. He already looked businesslike and in command. As the two men took their leave, Kasten picked up a stub of pencil and started writing on the back of an old envelope, already lost in thought, one hand brushing his Vandyke beard as he worked.

*

"*Appell, Appell!*" was the familiar yell from the German barracks guards each morning at dawn, as they flung open the doors to the huts and screamed at the prisoners to get up and outside for counting. Within a few minutes the grumbling, exhausted, and hungry prisoners had formed up in ranks on the great parade square in the center of the American compound. Kasten stood by himself out in front of the thousands of Americans, commanding them. Behind him were his deputy, Pfannenstiel, and his two assistants, Littell and Sinner. Each of the fifteen Men of Confidence stood in front of their assembled barrack inmates while the whole operation was watched over by the guards in their towers, leaning on machine guns. Meanwhile, German sentries started the slow process of counting the prisoners. They strode along the ranks, many with sticks or clubs in their hands, ready to beat any American that refused to cooperate, while others stood away to the side with Alsatian dogs. Commanding this parade was the German officer assigned to the American Camp, Hauptmann Horn, trying to stifle a yawn as the parade and the counting dragged on for hour after stultifying hour.

Eventually, the Germans would be satisfied that the number of prisoners on parade matched the number of prisoners in the compound, and Horn would stride over to face Kasten.

"You may dismiss the parade, Herr Hauptvertrauensmann," Horn ordered curtly in German.

Kasten saluted and Horn returned his salute. Then Kasten smartly about-faced and addressed his men.

"Parade...dismiss!" he bellowed at the top of his lungs.

He saluted as the men drew themselves to attention and fell out. This hell was to be repeated again a few hours later, day in and day out, come rain or shine. It was the ritual of camp life.

*

"What I want from each of you is a list of your men," Kasten said to the assembled Men of Confidence. "Names, ranks, serial numbers, and POW numbers. We will create a central registry so we can keep track of the men. I'm told we should expect a lot more before the winter's out."

The Germans were still shipping in American captives from the Ardennes to camps, primarily to Bad Orb.

"Then I want a list of your requirements—what each of your barracks needs," Kasten continued in a businesslike tone.

"Well, we could sure do with some decent grub," piped up Pfc. Morton Goldstein of Barrack 32. A ripple of agreement went through the meeting.

"I hear you," Kasten replied, conscious of the rampant diarrhea the food was causing to the newly arrived American prisoners. "Leaving the Russians in charge of our kitchen is unacceptable. I'm going to talk to the Germans about having our own cooks replace them."

This was a sensible idea, for among the thousands of prisoners were plenty of decent army cooks. It would be better for everyone concerned to break the Soviet monopoly on food in the camp, and better in particular for the health of the prisoners.

When the prisoners had been processed into the camp, they

had all been asked their religion. Many, like Kasten, had been wary of saying anything, believing that under the Geneva Conventions they had to divulge only their name, rank, and service number. But many had been persuaded by the seemingly reasonable argument put forward by the Germans regarding religious services in the event of death. And many of those prisoners who were Jewish had answered this question honestly, some out of ignorance of the consequences, and some out of pride in their faith and identity. They didn't think there was anything to fear, as they were American soldiers, and therefore prisoners of war. Others had thrown away their dog tags at the point of capture. Many realized that admitting to being Jewish was not a wise move, and concealed their religion or simply lied.

Commandant Sieber had followed regulations that clearly stipulated that Jewish POWs were to be separated from other POWs in stalags, and he had placed any prisoner who had identified himself as Jewish in Barrack 32. An American officer had visited each of the barracks and told the men that this was German policy. He had even asked that all Jewish American prisoners identify themselves to prevent reprisals from the German authorities if they subsequently discovered Jews hiding among the other prisoners.

"If some of you guys are Jewish and they find out about it, dire things could happen," the officer had warned.[7]

Many of the Jewish American prisoners were forced to wrestle with their consciences, and more than one felt resentment against the American officer for backing up the Germans in this manner.

Colonel Sieber's rationale for this segregation was that the US Army segregated blacks from whites.[8] The Germans thought that the United States had double standards, criticizing their policy of excluding Jews from society when there was segregation in the US Army and in the Deep South.

Compared with the other barracks, where the prisoners usually numbered close to 150 men, Barrack 32 contained only seventy-eight.[9] It was already being routinely termed the "Jewish Barrack" among the general prisoner population. The Germans even placed a fence around the building and restricted the comings and goings of the occupants, but they knew full well that there were many more Jews who remained unidentified in the camp, and this infuriated Sieber and his officers.

The men in 32 had elected one of the camp's biggest characters as their Man of Confidence. Twenty-three-year-old Pfc. Morton Goldstein of the 590th Field Artillery, 106th Infantry Division, was easy to recognize in his reversible white army-issue parka, and as the person who ran the camp's craps games. From Egg Harbor Township, New Jersey, Goldstein operated almost as a kind of croupier, and his happy-go-lucky personality and quick wit had attracted quite a following. He was, to all intents and purposes, the "leader" of all the Jews at Bad Orb, a position that would expose him to severe danger in the future.

"So, as I said, get those lists of requirements to Sinner or Littell here as soon as you can," Hans Kasten said to the barrack leaders, gesturing to his two assistants, who were leaning against the wall by the window. "Now, up to now German guards have been leading work details."

Since the day the prisoners arrived, the Germans had been forming them into working parties that were given a variety of jobs throughout the camp, from collecting firewood in the surrounding forest to emptying out the communal latrine pits.

"They don't speak English and most of our guys don't speak German," Kasten said. "I've decided to approach the commandant with the idea of setting up our own military police unit. These men will actually lead each work detail in the American compound. They can also help to maintain discipline in our camp, as I'm sure you've noticed the problems at the main gate."

Kasten was referring to American POWs who regularly tried to barter with Germans at the gate. The commandant had threatened to shoot any prisoner seen near the gate. Kasten wanted to put some MPs on the gate alongside the Germans to forestall any further confrontations or shootings.

"I think about a dozen or so MPs will be appropriate," Kasten said. "Have a look at your own prisoners—I'd like tall men who have their own greatcoats and steel helmets."[10]

"Jeez, Hans, ain't that doing the Krauts' job for them?" Pvt. Thomas Reader of Barrack 24 said.

Several of the other Men of Confidence balked at the idea of American MPs, and said so in plain terms.

"Nonsense," replied Kasten, his blue eyes flashing with anger. "We *have* to control our own men. They've nothing to do all day, and we'll have major problems if we don't institute proper discipline. Better that we do it ourselves than leave it to the Germans. We all know what they are like."

It was a fair point. German justice was often brutal and occasionally terminal. No one wanted mob rule, jungle justice, or the creation of gangs inside the camp.

"Okay, gentlemen, I suggest we reconvene at the same time tomorrow. And remember, your job is simple—look after the men in your barrack. I'll deal with the Germans, but just make sure you back me up. Agreed?"

The Men of Confidence all muttered their agreements before filing out, chatting among themselves. Once Kasten was alone again with just Pfannenstiel, Sinner, and Littell he visibly relaxed a little. He had passed an unspoken test—he had the respect of the other leaders. They would do his bidding, even if they didn't yet fully agree with him on some of his ideas.

*

Incredibly, though no one really believed that Kasten would succeed, he soon managed to achieve a few small concessions from
Colonel Sieber. The commandant agreed to replace the Soviet
cooks with American ones. But this victory was short-lived, since
the Germans didn't increase the quality or quantity of rations.
The men continued to eke out an existence on about 1,800
calories a day,[11] while intestinal problems remained endemic.

The military police proved to be a greater success—the
commandant, undoubtedly happy that the prisoners would help
to guard themselves, even provided some white paint so that M1
helmets could be marked with the letters "MP" in proper US
Army fashion.[12] The German sentries relaxed a little as Kasten's
corps of MPs defused some of the tensions, and discipline among
the prisoners was somewhat restored.

*

On January 10, 1945, all American officer prisoners at Stalag IX-B
were sent elsewhere. The enlisted men and noncoms watched
as their military leaders from the Twenty-Eighth and 106th
Infantry Divisions were assembled on the parade square before
being marched out of the camp to the station in Bad Orb. They
were bound for an officers' camp, Oflag XIII-B at Hammelburg
in western Germany.[13] But not every officer was removed. The
Germans left just five behind, whose professional services as
doctors, chaplains, and dentists were desperately needed. And
though they were commissioned officers, Hans Kasten, as Chief
Man of Confidence, theoretically outranked them all—he now
commanded the prisoners, and the officers, two doctors, two
chaplains, and a dentist[14]—so they merely performed ancillary
roles to Kasten and his prisoners' council.

Soon afterward, the two chaplains, 1st Lt. Sam Neel of 422nd Infantry Regiment and 1st Lt. Father E. J. Hurley, visited Kasten with a problem.

They told Kasten that one of the prisoners was in a bad way—he had told the chaplains that he had been forsaken by God and wanted to die.[15] Kasten raised one eyebrow as the priests talked.

"Surely this is the Church's problem, not mine?" Kasten said when the priests had finished explaining. "I'm an atheist, and I know nothing of such matters."

"I know, my son," said Father Hurley, the young Catholic chaplain, "but we would like you to see this man, to talk to him."

"But I can't see what I could possibly do," replied Kasten, spreading his palms.

"Just come with us and talk to the man," said the Reverend Neel, the Protestant chaplain. "We think it would help."

Rather reluctantly, Kasten accompanied the two chaplains to the man's hut, where they found the young private bundled up beneath a couple of thin blankets on a lower bunk, his face ashen and drawn. Kasten sat down beside the man, the chaplains hovering in the background, wringing their hands with concern. Kasten tried to talk to the man, but his response was familiar.

"I've been forsaken by God," he croaked weakly. "I want to die."

Kasten found the man's wallet and extracted a small black-and-white photograph of the private's family. He held it up to the young soldier's face.

"Your family is expecting you back," Kasten said in a harsh tone, "and if you don't have the guts to live for yourself, you *have* to live for them." But Kasten's strong words seemingly had no effect on the man, who continued to mutter and to say that he must die.

Eventually Kasten sighed, stood, and shook his head.

"Well, I've tried," he said with a defeated expression on his face. "I think this man is beyond my help."

"We'll pray for him, Kasten," replied Neel solemnly.

"And we'll pray for you, too," added Father Hurley, placing a hand on Kasten's arm.

Kasten stared back at the two chaplains without saying anything. He knew they were good men, but what good was prayer to men like the sorry creature lying in the bunk? The man needed proper food, medical care, and a purpose. It was an increasingly common problem in the camp as the full horror of captivity was starting to bite, and bite hard. Two days later the man died, one of three such cases that week. Neither Kasten nor the chaplains could do anything to stop it. Once a man had given up on life, the body soon followed. Kasten remained convinced of the futility of religion and spoke bluntly to the chaplains.

"If that's all the strength your religion gives these men," he said in a weary and exasperated voice, "I'm glad I am an atheist."

*

"Look!" someone cried out, pointing to the horizon. Hundreds of prisoners were milling around the parade square or beside their huts after morning roll call with little to do, smoking whatever cigarettes they had or simply chatting. An ominous roaring was coming toward the camp and the men stopped what they were doing, staring into the far distance as two dots rapidly resolved themselves into aircraft.

A German Messerschmitt Bf 109 fighter was thundering toward the camp, weaving and moving rapidly from side to side as it came on. A few hundred yards behind the German was an American P-51 Mustang, a weak sun glinting off its silver wings and fuselage.

"He's right on the Kraut's tail!" someone shouted.

The Mustang fired, tracer rounds spewing forth from the machine guns, and the big rounds dropped short before suddenly finding their mark and pummeling the Messerschmitt. The prisoners threw themselves to the ground in panic as some of the Mustang's bullets passed close by overhead, whacking into the forested mountaintop. Then the burning German fighter tore past, no more than two hundred feet above the huts, its engine screaming while thick black smoke trailed behind the stricken machine. The Mustang howled overhead, still firing, and hundreds of spent cartridge cases clattered on the roofs of the prisoners' huts or landed in the parade square, where they lay steaming in the mud. Seconds later there was a heavy explosion close by the camp, and a tall column of smoke began to climb into the winter sky as the victorious Mustang peeled away and climbed up toward the heavens, the weak sun glinting off its silver wings as it disappeared in the haze.

The prisoners slowly clambered back to their feet, brushing mud and snow from their uniforms, a quiet cheer rippling through their ranks as they stood and watched the smoke rising higher and higher. There were no overt displays of victory— the prisoners were fearful that the guards might punish them for any gloating just a very quiet cheer that was soon extinguished by angry Germans, who bellowed at the prisoners to return to their huts, their faces like thunder after witnessing the Messerschmitt's demise.

The prisoners had been on edge and fearing retribution since one of their number had daubed a message for the Germans in white paint on the wall of their staff building. In three-foot-high letters it read:

"One, two! Eins, zwei!
Soon you'll all eat pig shit pie!"[16]

The war couldn't last much longer, many of the prisoners said, if American fighters were so bold in taking on the Luftwaffe deep inside Germany. For this day, at least, a visible illustration of Germany's imminent military defeat raised the morale of the prisoners. The terrible food, itching body lice, mud, and squalid latrines were temporarily forgotten thanks to the flashing silver and roaring engine of a "Cadillac of the Skies." And for the Germans who'd witnessed the fight, the graffito on the side of their staff building perhaps had more than a whiff of prophecy about it.

*

Since shortly after his election, Hans Kasten had been asking the camp authorities to delouse the prisoners. The camp was filthy with vermin. Among the worst culprits were body lice that lived in the seams of uniforms and armpits, causing the prisoners to constantly scratch themselves. The chances of a major epidemic outbreak, such as typhus, was growing more likely each day as the Germans ignored the body lice problem, until, quite out of the blue, Kasten was informed that all prisoners would be deloused on January 24, 1945.

When the day came, the thousands of Americans were formed up after morning *Appell* into long queues and processed through the delousing routine. German guards under the supervision of the camp doctor, Oberst Jaitner, stood ready to deal with each batch of prisoners. Jaitner and his orderlies, wearing surgical masks and gloves, ordered the prisoners to strip completely naked. Kasten, Littell, and Sinner were among the first group to receive this treatment. Once naked and shivering in the frigid air, the prisoners were herded into washrooms, which were normally not used, and permitted for the first time in weeks to take a shower. The lukewarm water that fell from the shower heads was an immense relief to the filthy prisoners, who were each permitted a minute or two to quickly soap themselves all over. The wastewater, brown with dirt, ran off the men and into the drains.

The German guards kept the human conveyer belt running, and each batch of freshly showered prisoners was quickly dusted with antilice powder by overzealous Germans, leaving them looking as though they had been pelted with flour as they emerged from the sheds coughing like miners. In the meantime, their lousy uniforms had been fumigated. For five minutes, the prisoners experienced pure joy as the dreaded bugs finally left their bodies and they were free of the constant itching and scratching.[17]

But if Kasten believed it was because of his complaints and demands that the Germans had granted this unexpected largesse, he was mistaken. The real reason soon became apparent when buckets of precious coal suddenly appeared beside the stoves in all the barracks.

"Do *not* touch this," warned the German guards, pointing sternly at coal buckets. The prisoners would continue to use wood to heat their drafty lodgings. Anyone who touched the coal would be severely punished, added the guards menacingly. At the same time, working parties of prisoners were set to work repairing windows and patching holes in the huts and generally tidying up the camp.

Something was definitely afoot.

CHAPTER 11

Herr Buchmuller Recommends

In my opinion, the present accommodation is untenable.
Werner Buchmuller, Swiss Legation, Berlin

Kasten," Colonel Sieber said, almost spitting the word out. "I have to inform you that a visit by the Protecting Power will occur at this camp tomorrow."

The commandant was sitting behind his desk in his office. Hans Kasten had been summoned and stood to attention in front of Sieber, the American compound officer Hauptmann Horn at his side. Behind Sieber a large portrait of Adolf Hitler glared down at Kasten, the Führer's pale gray eyes boring into his. Unlike everyone else at Stalag IX-B, including the illustrious commandant, Kasten was the only man to have met Hitler in the flesh—as a young man in Germany just before the war—and looked into those allegedly mesmerizing eyes for real. He hadn't been impressed then, and he sure wasn't impressed now.

"Now, Kasten, listen to me very carefully," Sieber said with a snarl. The commandant proceeded to outline exactly what Kasten could say to the visitors and what he could not.[1] These instructions were completely in violation of the Man of Confidence principle and the Geneva Conventions, but Sieber clearly couldn't have cared less.

"You understand, Kasten?" Sieber said, tapping an index finger on his desk blotter, clearly extremely uneasy at the thought of the Swiss poking their noses into his business.

Kasten said nothing, simply nodded curtly.

"You are dismissed," Sieber said.

Kasten was escorted back to the American compound. He was excited. Regardless of Sieber's illegal warning, Kasten knew that he had a golden opportunity to help his fellow prisoners.

*

"I've found out what's going on," Kasten said to a meeting of the Men of Confidence.

They all hushed. The sudden German willingness to clean up the inmates and sort out some of the major issues with the infrastructure of the camp had mystified everyone. It was a volte-face on the part of Colonel Sieber, whose attitude thus far had been to leave the prisoners to stew in their own filth while enforcing draconian measures against anyone who resisted such degrading treatment.

"It seems, gentlemen," Kasten said, leaning on the edge of his desk with his arms folded, a slight smile of satisfaction ghosting his lips, "that the Red Cross is coming."

*

A small convoy of cars pulled up outside the American camp's main gate on the morning of January 24, 1945. Led by a German Kübelwagen field car, a black saloon car was trailed in turn by the camp commandant's camouflaged vehicle. The whole party had driven up from the *Kommandantur*. To the watching prisoners there seemed to be a commotion of saluting guards, and German officers shaking hands with civilians as the VIPs made their way on foot into the camp and toward the American compound.

Colonel Sieber walked along dressed in his usual greatcoat, brown pistol belt, and visor cap. Beside him was a taller, middle-aged man in a black homburg hat and a long civilian coat, flanked by a German major whom none of the prisoners recognized. Bringing up the rear was Deputy Commandant Wodarg, Hauptmann Horn, and one more civilian. The prisoners watched as the party came to a halt on the parade square. Sieber talked briefly to the civilians, saluted, and departed, leaving just Horn and the Wehrmacht major to accompany the civilians around the camp. In their hands, the civilians held clipboards and pencils.

Hans Kasten and his assistants were drawn up in a line waiting for the civilians outside their barrack.

"Herr Buchmuller," Captain Horn said in German, "may I present Private Kasten, the American *Hauptvertrauensmann*."

"A pleasure, Herr Kasten," Werner Buchmuller said in excellent English. He was from the Swiss Legation in Berlin, and he offered his hand before introducing the other civilian, his assistant.

Kasten saluted, then shook the Swiss official's hand, introducing Pfannenstiel, Littell, and Sinner, who all saluted.

"And this is my liaison from the German high command, Major Siegmann," Buchmuller said, referring to the mysterious army major, who nodded curtly, his hard eyes like a wolf's under the brim of his visor cap as the Americans saluted.[2]

"Perhaps we might speak later, Herr Kasten, in private?" enquired Buchmuller.

"That will be fine, sir," replied Kasten, smiling. He was looking forward to telling the Red Cross all about the conditions at Bad Orb.

"Herr Buchmuller," interrupted Siegmann, glancing at his wristwatch nervously, "you *must* begin the inspection."

"Yes, yes, Major," replied Buchmuller, slightly irritated. "Well, Herr Kasten, I will visit you later."

With that, the Red Cross party began its tour of the camp, peering into barracks, talking to prisoners, and inspecting everything from latrines to kitchens to stoves to the hospital. Regardless of Commandant Sieber's attempts at window dressing in the days preceding the inspection, the stern looks on the faces of the inspectors and their furious note scribbling soon told Captain Horn all he needed to know about what the Red Cross thought of the camp.

*

A few hours later, it was Kasten's turn to be interviewed in his office. This time no Germans were present, just Buchmuller and his assistant. Kasten seated himself behind his desk while the two Swiss perched uncomfortably on hard wooden chairs opposite him.

"So, as the Chief Man of Confidence," began Buchmuller, "we would like to hear what you have to say about this camp."

"Before I begin," Kasten said, "will what I have to say be entirely in confidence?"

"Of course," guffawed Buchmuller in a surprised tone. "Absolutely."[3]

For the next two and a half hours Kasten laid it all out for the Red Cross. Everything: the abuses and denial of food and water on the march to Gerolstein, the appalling cattle wagon journey to Bad Orb, the deprived conditions in the camp, the lack of food, hygiene, hope. It poured out of him in a furious diatribe, one voice that represented everyone's grievances, everyone's disgust and anger at being treated in this manner. Buchmuller and his assistant wrote everything down in notebooks, their pencils flying across the pages as they listened to Kasten's condemnation of Stalag IX-B and the German military that had inflicted such indignities upon them.

And then, at the conclusion of this confidential meeting, Buchmuller and his assistant stood and intimated that Kasten must accompany them to the commandant's office for a meeting. The first stirrings of nervous misgivings began at this request, but assured that what he had said had been taken in confidence, Kasten assumed that his presence at the final meeting with Colonel Sieber and his staff was merely a formality because of his position of responsibility in the camp.

He was right to be nervous.

*

When Kasten followed Buchmuller and his assistant into the large meeting room inside the German *Kommandantur* building outside the main gate, he was the only prisoner present. He took a seat beside the Swiss delegates and scanned the faces around the room.

Colonel Sieber sat opposite Kasten. The Germans had all removed their caps, and Sieber looked relaxed as he smoked a cigarette. Beside him was Lieutenant-Colonel Wodarg, a not entirely convincing affable smile on his face. Then Colonel Jaitner, the camp medical officer, an elderly and harmless doctor in uniform. Captain Horn, the American camp officer, was also present and looking nervous, his eyes flicking about the room, along with Major Siegmann from headquarters, who looked bored by the entire proceedings and lounged in his chair.

"So, Herr Oberst," began Buchmuller, addressing the commandant, "the strength of the American camp is listed as two medical officers, one officer dentist, two officer chaplains, 1,263 non-commissioned officers, and 2,807 privates."[4]

Sieber glanced to his left at Horn.

"Yes, sir, that is correct," Horn said, referring to a typed sheet of paper in front of him.

"Turning to accommodations," Buchmuller said, referring to his notes. "Herr Oberst, many of the prisoners have not been issued German blankets, and those that have been issued are worn out and threadbare. Up to a few days ago, Herr Kasten here informs me that there were still thirty men without blankets at all."

At the mention of Kasten's name, the German officers' heads snapped up. Kasten was shocked—what he had told the Red Cross was in the strictest confidence, but Buchmuller appeared to be ignoring this.

"My inspection has revealed that many of the stoves used to heat the barracks are in bad repair and, in any case, are far too small to heat rooms of this size. The fuel position is exceedingly bad. Herr Kasten informs me that no coal is given out and all that is obtainable from the German authorities is a quantity of wood sufficient to provide heating for a few hours a day."[5]

Sieber's eyes met Kasten's for a moment—the look was contemplative and not pleasant.

"Because of the poor heating the ceilings of some barracks are always damp, is that not so, Herr Kasten?"

At this point, Kasten rather wished that the floor would open up and swallow him. All the German officers were staring at the American Chief Man of Confidence like a gaggle of snakes staring at a mouse.

"That's right," Kasten croaked miserably.

"The damp is aggravated by the fact that so many windows are broken and replaced by only cardboard or wood," continued Buchmuller confidently. "Herr Kommandant, the lighting in the barracks is unsatisfactory; each of the big rooms is fitted with a weak bulb which is not strong enough to permit reading after dark. Also, in very few of the barracks that I visited was there adequate furniture, such as chairs and tables. In my opinion—and in Herr Kasten's, I might add—the present accommodation is untenable."[6]

Buchmuller paused to allow Sieber to respond. The commandant shifted uncomfortably in his chair, slowly stubbed out his cigarette, and linked his fingers together on the table in front of him.

"This is *only* a transit camp, Herr Buchmuller," Sieber said calmly. "The prisoners will be transferred elsewhere at the earliest possible opportunity."

"I think, Herr Kommandant, in light of the present situation in Germany, an early transfer is unlikely," countered Buchmuller. "Therefore, I must insist that improvements in the accommodation should be made at once."[7]

"Herr Buchmuller, if I may," interjected Captain Horn, the American camp's German officer. "The noncommissioned officers that you referred to earlier are to be transferred elsewhere tomorrow. The overcrowding in the barracks will be greatly lessened and beds for all prisoners made available."

Sieber and Wodarg nodded seriously in agreement.

"These NCOs will be leaving their blankets behind when they leave the camp, so there will now be a sufficient amount for all of the prisoners remaining."[8]

"As for the stoves, I shall have them all repaired immediately," added Sieber, smiling. "And I shall put in a request for more stoves, as well."

"Good. In the meantime, will you permit more men to collect firewood than at present?" asked Buchmuller.

"Of course," replied Sieber generously. "But I can do nothing about the lighting owing to the very strict saving measures now applied all over Germany."[9]

"Herr Kasten informs me that the prisoners have only been permitted one hot bath and deloused once since entering the camp," Buchmuller said, changing tack.

Sieber's and the other Germans' eyes flashed once more at Kasten. "From the looks on the faces of the Germans I could foretell my fate," Kasten would write later.[10]

"Fortnightly baths will be available for *every* man," Sieber said curtly.

"In my opinion, the current washing facilities in the barracks are completely inadequate," continued Buchmuller. "I ask you to do all in your power to make some improvements at the first opportunity."[11]

"Of course," Sieber replied through gritted teeth.

"Also, the latrine facilities are similarly inadequate. Herr Kasten informs me that no toilet paper has been issued . . . *except* today."

Sieber shifted again uncomfortably in his seat, furious that one of his little window-dressing props had been found out. He glanced again at Kasten, his eyes narrowed.

"This *too* will be remedied," Sieber muttered through his teeth.

"Now, let us turn to food and cooking," Buchmuller said in a businesslike voice. "I have found that the kitchens are adequately equipped, but no ration scale has been posted up in the kitchen."

"That will be corrected," interjected Sieber.

"Thank you. Now, as far as I can ascertain, the German rations are correct but the prisoners have told me that they are suffering from the change in diet, having had much more and better food previous to their capture. In addition, Herr Kommandant, there is no stock of Red Cross food whatsoever, and the German rations are scarcely sufficient. The lack of Red Cross food is most deeply felt and is, as Herr Kasten informs me, having an adverse effect on the morale of the prisoners."[12]

Sieber sighed and shot Kasten another look.

"The French prisoners have a stock of Red Cross food," Sieber said, referring to a section of the camp full of Frenchmen captured in 1940. "I can perhaps ask them to make a loan of some food to the American compound. But we are not in a position to issue bigger German rations to the prisoners. We are currently waiting for a consignment of Red Cross parcels."[13]

The grilling that Sieber and his officers were receiving from Herr Buchmuller was not over yet. Buchmuller ranged over several other issues, from the health of the prisoners to clothing to religious activities to recreation, or lack thereof. Much to Kasten's chagrin, Buchmuller kept referring to him throughout. Undoubtedly the Swiss believed that he was acting in the best interests of the prisoners, but by the end of a far-reaching interview, Kasten was sure that Sieber would seek some kind of payback for his humiliation. Kasten might have been Chief Man of Confidence, but he was still just another prisoner of war in the middle of Germany.

*

True to his word, on the morning of January 25, all the American noncoms were gathered together after roll call and marched out to the railroad station. Numbering 1,263 men, they were to be shipped to Stalag IX-A at Ziegenhain.[14] Apart from five officers, all the American prisoners at Bad Orb were now either privates or Pfcs. But if Kasten and the other prisoners believed that this was the last transfer, they were wrong. Colonel Sieber and his officers had not forgotten nor forgiven Kasten's damning testimony to the Swiss representatives. Sieber wanted to be rid of his troublesome Chief Man of Confidence, and an opportunity to do just that had suddenly presented itself. Sieber seized it with both hands—and he owed this opportunity to his own cousin.

*

On another muddy parade square 125 miles from Bad Orb, Colonel Sieber's younger cousin had stood watching the latest batch of prisoners formed up in ranks for counting. It was early January 1945 and he was a man in a very bad mood. This was, unlike Stalag IX-B, no prisoner of war camp. The innocuous wooden sign above the main gate read: ARBEITSLAGER 650.

Willi Hack, Sieber's cousin, was a slim, good-looking thirty-two-year old with dark brown hair. But on this day, his face was far from pleasant. His lips curled in disgust as he watched his guards form the prisoners up for inspection.

"My God," Hack said, turning to a colleague, "look at this garbage."

He was referring to the prisoners, emaciated and sickly looking, with gray skin and sunken cheeks and eyes, who stood shivering in thin blue-and-white-striped uniforms, their heads shaved and their feet inside wooden clogs or battered old boots.

"What am I supposed to accomplish with this?" Hack asked, casting one immaculately gloved hand in the prisoners' general direction. "Do those fools at Buchenwald not realize the importance of my work?"

It was a rhetorical question, and the two other officers standing with Hack said nothing.

"Well, let us begin," Hack sighed, smoothing out his uniform before striding toward the prisoners.

They all stiffened and visibly blanched at Hack's approach—he looked like the very angel of death descending upon them. He wore an expensively tailored field-gray leather greatcoat open at the collar to reveal his service tunic collar beneath. On Hack's right collar tab was a silver death's-head skull and crossbones set on a black background, the symbol of the Third

141

SS Totenkopf Division. These were worn in place of the usual SS sig runes. On his left collar tab he wore the three diagonal rank pips and one silver bar of an *Obersturmführer*, or first lieutenant. His arm of service color, black for construction engineers, underlined his silver shoulder straps. He wore a black belt around his waist, with a round silver buckle adorned with a Nazi eagle and swastika, a motto beneath reading *"Meine Ehre heisst Treue"* (My Honor Is Loyalty). A Luger pistol sat in a black leather holster. His field-gray visor cap, displaying another death's head beneath an SS eagle, was worn at a slight angle, giving Hack an arrogant, devil-may-care appearance. He knew full well the effect he had on prisoners; he had been in charge of slave labor on several previous projects for the Reich.

Hack moved slowly down the first rank of prisoners, whose eyes were downcast at the ground, many shivering uncontrollably from the biting cold and fear. Hack's other officers followed close behind. Five hundred fresh slave laborers had arrived from Buchenwald concentration camp to join the several hundred others already hard at work on Operation Schwalbe, Hack's top secret project near the town of Berga on the White Elster River. These new arrivals were to replace "natural wastage," as Hack euphemistically termed death from overwork, exhaustion, disease, beatings, or execution. The fresh draft had been left under no illusions that SS-Obersturmführer Hack and his cronies ran things at Berga no differently from any other concentration camp in Germany: On a rudimentary scaffold beside the main gate the corpses of two prisoners swung suspended by their broken necks, recently hanged on Hack's express order for some minor infraction of camp rules.

"What I need are strong backs for the important work to be done here," Hack said irritably as he stalked along the line of living skeletons. He stopped and seemed to think for a moment.

"I shall have to look elsewhere for what I need," Hack said. He turned, closely followed by his officers, and walked rapidly back toward his office, past the run-down wooden huts and barbed wire fences that made up his kingdom, past the dangling bodies of his victims, his mind alive with a fresh and, he thought, brilliant new way to solve his labor problem. He would ask his older cousin for help.

CHAPTER 12

The Reprisal

No one, under any circumstances, is to admit to being Jewish.
Pfc. Hans Kasten

S it, Kasten," Colonel Sieber ordered, gesturing to a chair before the large wooden table around which seven German officers sat.

Hans Kasten had climbed the stairs to this second-floor office inside the camp's *Kommandantur* on the morning of January 26, 1945, perplexed as to what it could be about. Kasten looked pale and thin, his olive drab uniform grubby and showing signs of hasty repairs. He'd been a prisoner at Stalag IX-B for a little more than three weeks since his capture in the Ardennes, and it had taken a toll on him and all of the other inmates. There were dark smudges of exhaustion beneath his eyes, but those eyes still sparkled with the defiance and assurance that had gotten him elected the American compound's Chief Man of Confidence.

Colonel Sieber glared at Kasten like a headmaster interviewing a particularly troublesome child. He was still furious about the visit of the Swiss representatives and Kasten's secret machinations with Werner Buchmuller that had led to such a damning report on the camp and his command. Kasten's appearance also infuriated Sieber, particularly the way Kasten wore a moustache and chin beard, the ends of his moustache waxed up German style. Hans Kasten, the American with the German name, German parents, fluent language ability, and even German-style facial adornments. Was such a man *really* an American?

Sieber and many other German officers had asked themselves this question when confronted by Kasten and so many other American prisoners whose ancestry was from the Fatherland. Was Kasten instead a German in an American uniform? Were he and his kind traitors to the Fatherland? Even among the non-Germanic POWs, reservations had been expressed at having a German American Chief Man of Confidence. Pvt. Pete House, for instance, was never fully convinced that Kasten was who he was presented to be, regardless of his demonstrable defense of prisoners' rights.

"I often felt that he might be a German plant," House wrote.[1] But if there were any doubt as to where Hans Kasten's loyalties lay, what was about to occur would settle this question once and for all.

*

Colonel Sieber cleared his throat loudly, a signal that the little meeting was opened. In front of Hans Kasten's chair, placed prominently upon the table, was a large object draped in a cloth. Kasten sat cautiously, his eyes passing around the long table, staring at the German officers, whose own hard eyes glanced back at him without pity or sympathy. Sieber shifted impatiently in his chair while deputy commandant Lieutenant Colonel Wodarg slowly smoked a cigarette, his blue eyes boring into Kasten's as smoke rose to the ceiling in lazy blue curls.

The room, unlike everywhere else in the camp, was pleasantly warm, logs in a large, open fireplace at one end crackling and popping. The contrast to the prisoners' frigid huts was stark, and for the first time in weeks Kasten actually felt warm. But though the room might have been warm, the attitude of the Germans present was decidedly chilly.

The American compound's German officer, Captain Horn, stood, his chair scraping on the wooden floor, walked over to where Kasten was seated, and unwrapped the object on the table in front of him with a flourish. It was a large loaf of German rye bread.[2] Horn said nothing and resumed his seat. The bread transfixed Kasten's eyes. The rations in the camp were pitiful and really fit only for hogs, consisting of small ladles of oat, rotten potato, and rotten carrot or pea soup, with a little canned meat and thin slices of black bread. Five American prisoners had already died of illness exacerbated by the low-calorie diet.

"Kasten," Colonel Sieber said, speaking in German in an almost conversational, mock-friendly tone, "we want you to supply us with the names of all those of the Jewish faith in the American sector of the camp."[3]

Kasten didn't move or speak. The silence around the table was palpable. He glanced at the bread, then at the hard faces of the Germans who stared at him awaiting an answer, then back at the bread. He was hungry—hungrier than he had ever been in his life before. The Germans still kept camp rations to a minimum, claiming logistical problems for the ongoing food shortages that the Swiss had highlighted, but many of the prisoners believed that it was deliberate—the Germans were starving the hated Americans to punish them for all the ills that had befallen Germany since D-Day.

Kasten thought immediately of Pfc. Morton Goldstein, the happy-go-lucky leader of Barrack 32. Sieber had segregated him and seventy-seven other Jews who had unwisely given their religion during processing into the camp in December 1944. Kasten, like Sieber, knew that many more of the prisoners in the general population at Bad Orb were Jews or half Jews, including one of his own assistants, Ernesto Sinner, whose mother had been a German Jew.

The Jewish GIs had answered their nation's call the same as every other young man in America, but their capture had posed serious problems. Many were the sons or grandsons of Jews who had escaped poverty and persecution in prewar Europe for the political and religious freedoms of America, only to find themselves once more beneath the yoke of a cruel and intolerant master. But the fact remained that regardless of their religion, Jewish American POWs were afforded the same rights and protections under the Geneva Conventions as prisoners of any other faith held by the Germans. Up to this moment in the office at Stalag IX-B, the Germans had appeared to grudgingly respect that rule, even though they had tried to have *all* the Jewish prisoners herded into one barrack. Sieber was well within the regulations of the German Army in doing so, for the most recent version of regulations for the treatment of Jewish prisoners of war had been promulgated by Berlin on March 11, 1942. Part one of these regulations stated:

> The bringing together of Jewish prisoners of war in separate camps is not intended; on the other hand, all Jewish prisoners of war are to be kept separated from the other prisoners of war in Stalags and officers' camps.[4]

What Sieber was asking was for Kasten to *willingly* betray his fellow soldiers for some uncertain and as yet unexplained reason, which was, judging by the thunderous expression on Sieber's face, undoubtedly sinister, in return for a loaf of black bread. Nowhere in American regulations did it state that prisoners of war must identify themselves to the Germans as Jews—in fact, the Geneva Conventions stated that a prisoner was not under any obligation to give his captor his religious faith.

Disgusted and appalled, Hans Kasten took a deep breath. He knew what he had to say. With great, almost theatrical, deliberation, he raised his right hand and pushed the loaf into the center of the table. Then he leaned back in his chair and locked eyes with Colonel Sieber.

"We are *all* Americans," he said.

The Germans shifted in their seats angrily. Kasten spoke again.

"*We* don't differentiate between religions."[5]

Sieber's eyes grew wide and then narrowed with fury. He turned and nodded at two junior officers who jumped to their feet. Their jackboots rang as they strode around the table and reached for Kasten, hauling him up from his chair by his uniform lapels.

"*Amerikanische Schweinehund!*" bellowed the older of the two officers, before he curtly backhanded Kasten across the face, the slap echoing around the room. Kasten grunted out in pain, before both of the Germans hit him again several times about the head and body. Sieber did nothing to stop this illegal abuse.

"You will give us the names of the Jewish vermin in the American camp," screamed the older German into Kasten's bloodied face.

Bang, another blow on the cheek. Kasten's head was swimming. Then, without hesitation, the Germans started to drag Kasten across the floor to the top of the staircase. Kasten closed his eyes, tasting the blood in his mouth from his busted nose. He opened one rapidly swelling eye and saw that he was at the top of the long flight of hard wooden steps. The Germans gripped him under both armpits and prepared to heave him out into space.

*

Kasten lay at the bottom of the flight of stairs half-conscious. The German officers had gone—there was just one middle-aged private with a Mauser rifle slung over his right shoulder who was supposed to escort Kasten back to his compound. Kasten groaned and, gripping the wall, pulled himself painfully to his feet. He staggered a couple of steps through the doorway before collapsing in the dirt outside. The German sentry did nothing to help; he simply stared at the Chief Man of Confidence as he lay on the ground. Kasten began to run his hands over his body, checking for breaks.[6] There were none, but his face was swollen and bloody from the beating, and his chest and legs hurt from the tumble down the hard stairs. Regardless of his injuries, Kasten knew that he had to get back to the American compound as fast as possible to warn his comrades of Sieber's diabolical plan.

Kasten pulled himself to his feet, wincing from his many wounds, his head still woozy, and started to stagger back toward the camp. The sentry walked slowly alongside him with a concerned look on his face. Limping, Kasten was helped by several other American prisoners the moment he was through the gates of his compound. They half carried him to his quarters, where Joe Littell and Ernesto Sinner came out to greet him with shock etched into their faces.

"Call a meeting," croaked Kasten painfully. "Have all barracks leaders gather here immediately."

"Shouldn't we fetch a medical officer?" asked Sinner in a concerned voice.

"Later," snapped Kasten breathlessly. "I'm all right. Fetch them here, *now*!"

Littell and Sinner left immediately to track down the sixteen barracks leaders while Kasten lay down on his bunk. A couple of prisoners used damp cloths to wipe away the blood on his face.

*

Since the noncoms had been shipped out of Stalag IX-B, new men had been hastily elected to fill eight vacant Men of Confidence positions. They and the eight originals rushed over to Barrack 24, Kasten's headquarters. They were all shocked by the state they discovered their leader in.

Kasten slowly raised himself up to a sitting position and started to speak. He explained what had happened during the Red Cross visit, how angry Commandant Sieber had been, and the outrageous demand to name Jewish American prisoners.[7] Morton Goldstein started when Kasten croaked out this part of his story, blanching visibly.

"Now listen, all of you," Kasten said in a fierce whisper, one hand holding his ribs and the other gripping the side of the bunk. "Go back to your barracks and tell your men everything that I have just said. Give them the whole story."

He paused to catch his breath. "Tell them that in all probability there will soon be repercussions. And tell them to get this absolutely straight: No one, under any circumstances, is to admit to being Jewish."

The Men of Confidence all voiced their agreement, virtually as one, and darted away toward their huts and their men. But Goldstein staggered out of the meeting with a look of knowing horror etched across his young face—he and his men were already clearly identified as Jews. Whatever was coming, it would be coming for them first.

*

One of the camp's two prisoner doctors was called to treat Kasten. Capt. O. C. Buxton was from Kasten's own Twenty-Eighth Infantry Division.[8] He knelt beside Kasten's bunk and checked him over.

"Nothing broken, soldier," Buxton said after examining Kasten, who lay still on his mattress, one eye puffed shut. "But they banged you up pretty good."

"Is he going to be okay, Doc?" asked Joe Littell, who was hovering nearby with Sinner.

"Some contusions and nasty bruises. He'll feel pretty sore for a couple of days, but with rest he'll soon recover," Buxton said. "Here, give him some of these. It'll help with the pain." He passed Littell a small bottle of aspirin from his precious medical supplies.

"Thanks, Doc," croaked Kasten.

*

"*Appell*!" screamed German soldiers, as they went from hut to hut in the early afternoon, smashing open the doors and yelling in guttural German at the prisoners. The German guards seemed more agitated than normal, and as the prisoners hastily poured from their barracks and formed up for the usual counting ritual they began to notice that something was different this time.

Hans Kasten hobbled painfully over to take his place at the front of the parade, with his assistants falling in behind him and the sixteen Men of Confidence in front of each of their paraded barracks. The German guard presence was much heavier than usual. Wearing steel helmets and greatcoats, the guards were formed up to cover the parade. Once more snarling Alsatians were being held on the sidelines by yet more sentries. This time, the Germans didn't start counting; rather, a strange hush descended on the parade. They were clearly waiting for something or someone.

"*Achtung*!" yelled a German sergeant major. A group of German officers was approaching the parade square, led by Colonel Sieber. The German guards all jumped to attention.

"Parade...ten hut!" shouted Kasten, wincing a little from his bruised ribs, and the Americans did likewise.

Sieber, Wodarg, and the officers halted on the sidelines and stood watching as Captain Horn, the American compound commander, strode over to where two German soldiers had placed a small wooden dais. He quickly mounted the platform and stood, his eyes scanning the thousands of American faces. There was a pause, and then Horn spoke.

"All Jews, one step forward!"[9]

Every man on the parade heard Horn's loud voice that afternoon. Kasten had been right—the Germans, frustrated by Kasten's refusal to sell out the Jewish American prisoners, were now resorting to a more direct approach.

As per Kasten's instructions, not one man moved. Horn stood on the dais, his face a mask, his eyes darting around the various barrack groups. There was no talking—just silence, a cold wind blowing snow across the square mixed with smoke from the camp kitchens. How long Horn stood waiting, no one was quite sure, but it was probably less than half a minute.

He repeated his order, "All Jews, one pace forward!"

Again, Horn's order was met by a stony silence from the 2,800 watching Americans. He glanced once at Colonel Sieber, who nodded curtly. Horn suddenly sprung into action. He jumped down from the dais and strode over to the nearest sentry, snatching a Mauser 98K rifle from his hands.

Kasten watched in horror as Horn advanced toward him, the rifle in his hands. Kasten was convinced that the German officer was going to shoot him dead on the spot. But when Horn was a few paces from Kasten, he reversed the rifle as he walked, holding it by the barrel with the wooden butt facing upward. Horn didn't say a word, but he swung that rifle like Babe Ruth, and the butt connected painfully with Kasten's chest. Kasten flew back several feet, landing in the dirty snow and mud, badly winded and with terrible pain spreading across his chest. He

Pfc. Johann "Hans" Kasten. The son of German immigrants, Kasten would be captured in the Ardennes and elected Chief Man of Confidence at Stalag IX-B, representing thousands of his fellow GIs. *(Courtesy of IndianaMilitary.org)*

The twisting series of hairpin bends leading into Clervaux, in Luxembourg, where Hans Kasten and a desperate group of GIs, tasked with defending the town's medieval castle, watched Sherman tanks try to stop advancing German Panzers. *(Photo by Mark Felton)*

Clervaux Castle, Luxembourg, where Hans Kasten and a group of surrounded GIs made a gallant last stand during the Battle of the Bulge. *(Photo by Mark Felton)*

Pfc. Joseph Littell *(right)* would become Kasten's trusted assistant during their imprisonment and ultimately escape alongside him. *(Courtesy of Julia Littell)*

Stalag IX-B POW camp at Bad Orb, in Germany, was widely regarded as the worst prison camp to have held American prisoners. *(Courtesy of IndianaMilitary.org)*

Stalag IX-B Commandant Colonel Karl Sieber *(left)*, photographed just after the liberation of the camp. Sieber was forced to remove the standard Nazi eagle from the crown of his cap. *(Courtesy of IndianaMilitary.org)*

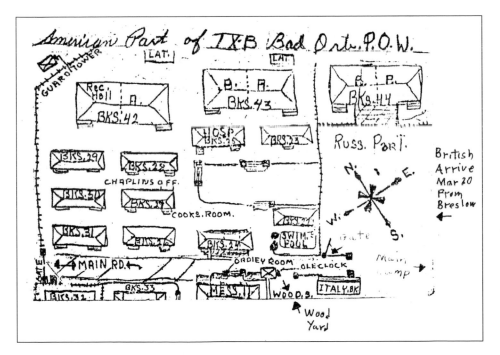

Hand-drawn diagram of Stalag IX-B made secretly by Pfc. Raymond Brown in 1945. *(Courtesy of IndianaMilitary.org)*

Stalag IX-B photographed after liberation, June 9, 1945.
(Courtesy of IndianaMilitary.org)

US prisoners at Stalag IX-B carrying a soup barrel.
(Courtesy of IndianaMilitary.org)

Hans Kasten as Chief Man of Confidence at Stalag IX-B, wearing a Soviet fur hat that enraged Commandant Karl Sieber.
(Courtesy of IndianaMilitary.org)

Pfc. Peter Iosso, photographed before being sent to Europe. *(Courtesy of IndianaMilitary.org)*

Pfc. Eddie Pfannenstiel, pictured before shipping out to Europe. He was Kasten's deputy at Stalag IX-B and took over as Chief Man of Confidence after Kasten was sent to Berga Concentration Camp. *(Courtesy of IndianaMilitary.org)*

1st Lt. Edward J. Hurley, one of two chaplains at Stalag IX-B, distributing food to liberated American POWS. *(Courtesy of Indiana Military.org)*

An example of the overcrowded prisoner accommodation at Stalag IX-B; these US prisoners are shown just after liberation. *(Courtesy of IndianaMilitary.org)*

The hutted enclosure at Berga concentration camp that housed US POWs brought to slave on the secret Nazi project Operation Swallow. *(Courtesy of IndianaMilitary.org)*

The working area below the Operation Swallow tunnels at Berga an der Elster concentration camp in 1945. Here US prisoners unloaded railway cars full of rubble under constant physical abuse by German guards. *(Courtesy of IndianaMilitary.org)*

The entrance to one of the unfinished Operation Swallow tunnels at Berga in 1945. US POWs worked inside these tunnels without protective clothing or breathing masks, with terrible consequences for their health. Many died as a result of these conditions and abuse by their German guards. *(Courtesy of IndianaMilitary.org)*

Allied war crimes investigators exhume the bodies of American prisoners who died at Berga concentration camp. *(Courtesy of the United States Holocaust Memorial Museum)*

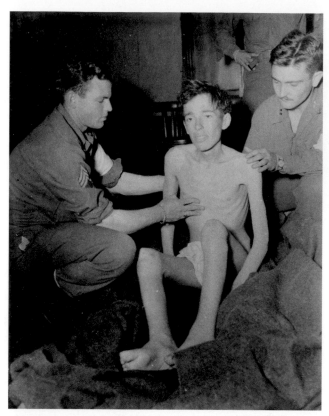

An emaciated GI who survived slave labor at Berga concentration camp and the later death march organized by SS Commandant Hack at the end of the war. *(Courtesy of the United States Holocaust Memorial Museum)*

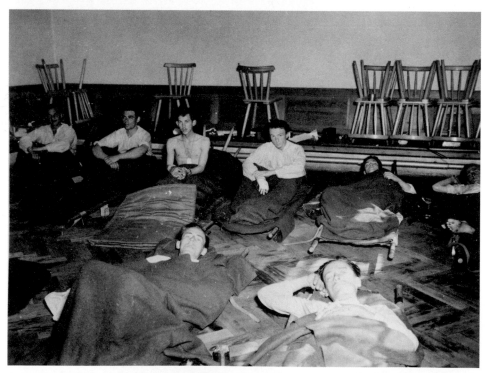

American POWs rescued from the Berga death march receiving medical attention following their horrific ordeal. *(Courtesy of the United States Holocaust Memorial Museum)*

couldn't move and was struggling to breathe. He thought that he was done for.[10]

Horn bellowed orders and, as Kasten lay in agony staring up at the gray sky, the German sentries started to move into the square. Within seconds they were wrenching out men that they either knew to be Jews or suspected of being Jewish. Morton Goldstein and his seventy-seven Jewish American GIs were immediately pulled from the parade, the guards using rifle butts to herd their victims to one side. They were swiftly joined by anyone who looked Jewish. This included Italian Americans, Hispanics, and quite a few Jewish Americans who had tried to disguise their religious faith when they first entered Stalag IX-B. But this was not enough—soon other men were being jerked from the lines, anyone who had come to the attention of the camp authorities, the troublemakers, or just men in the wrong place at the wrong time.

After thirty minutes of pushing, shoving, and yelling, the Germans had managed to assemble 347 Americans. These men were now all labeled as Jews and had their POW numbers entered on a final list for transfer out of the camp. Captain Horn's final act was to march back over to where Kasten still lay prostrate on the ground, struggling for breath.

He looked down at Kasten's face, twisted with pain, and smiled. "Kasten, you and your two assistants also."[11]

Commandant Sieber was now to be finally rid of the troublesome Chief Man of Confidence and his helpers. "This was my payment for the Red Cross affair and my morning refusal regarding our Jewish troops," Kasten would later write.[12]

As Littell and Sinner helped Kasten to his feet, he glanced up and watched as Colonel Sieber, a large grin plastered to his face, turned and strode out of the American compound with Horn and his other officers. They were laughing.

CHAPTER 13

Blue Sunday

The Germans said we would have to stand there until the guilty ones were found.

Pfc. John Reinfenrath, 106th Infantry Division

Two shadows stole across the open ground between huts, flitting like wraiths, unseen and unheard. In the early hours of Sunday, January 28, 1945, Stalag IX-B was quiet, the men inside their barracks sleeping or shivering beneath their thin blankets. The sounds of bombing drifted over the camp from many miles away, like rumbling summer thunder, but hardly anyone took any notice anymore.[1] The RAF was hammering German cities every night, its Lancasters often droning over the camp. By day, it was the turn of the high-flying B-17 Flying Fortresses of the US Army Air Forces.

The only lights in the camp were the dim glow of bulbs illuminating the twelve-foot-high perimeter fences and the occasional sweep of a searchlight from one of the guard towers. German sentries stood at the gates, stamping their feet and blowing on their hands as they tried to stay warm on the bitterly cold night, while others walked lonely beats along the outside of the fences, rifles slung over their shoulders, their boots crunching in the fresh snow.

The two unseen figures quietly pried open a small window and clambered gingerly into the kitchen block. The two American prisoners were on the hunt for food, launching a secret raid on the stores in the hope of illicitly filling their empty stomachs.[2] The raid was not known to the other prisoners in the American compound and would not have been authorized, for these men were intent on stealing rations destined for the entire prison population. It was an act of selfish desperation driven entirely by hunger. An act that if discovered by Hans Kasten or the other barracks leaders would have resulted in the prisoners themselves punishing these men.

Whispering to each other, the two thieves soon located the main food store and started to fill the pockets of their tatty great-coats with potatoes, carrots, and tinned meat. Then suddenly they froze. A sound from the far end of the block sent a shiver of fear up their spines. Someone was coming. The two prisoners ducked down, one behind some crates of vegetables and the other under a table, and waited, trying to control their breathing. A door was unlocked, the key rattling in the lock, and then came the sound of hobnailed boots ringing on the building's concrete floor. Suddenly, the beam of a flashlight played about the room where the two thieves crouched. Taking a quick peek, one of the prisoners spotted the figure of the German mess sergeant making his rounds. He was dressed in a greatcoat and forage cap, a pistol on his belt. He was working his way closer and closer to where the two men crouched, and they knew that if he discovered them, they would be severely punished. One of the men looked around his hiding place, spotting a meat cleaver used by the cooks. He leaned over, his hand curling around its cold wooden handle.

"*Halt!*" shouted the German sergeant. He had seen two feet underneath the table in the gloom and immediately turned his flashlight on to the pair of dirty American combat boots. "*Aus!*"

he ordered, quickly unbuckling his black holster and pulling out a Walther P .38 service pistol.[3] But he never saw the other American, who left his hiding place and crept up behind the German, hitting him over and over in the head and shoulders with the cleaver. The German crumpled unconscious to the floor, blood pouring from his horrible wounds. The American dropped the bloody cleaver and instinctively wiped his hands on his clothes, the blood warm and sticky.

"Come on," he said in a fierce but shaky whisper to his friend, "let's get outta here." Within seconds the German's assailants had vanished into the night, leaving the sergeant where he fell, his breathing shallow and irregular.

*

Something was very wrong at Stalag IX-B that Sunday morning. The prisoners were used to hearing the guards rousing the cooks to start preparing coffee and the noon soup about 0600, but on this day nothing happened. The prisoners were further mystified when the barrack guards did not unlock the hut doors at 0900.[4] Then the prisoners heard an ominous sound: the rattle and thump of Germans in full combat order filing past the huts. The prisoners crowded against the frosted-up windows, quickly scraping holes to peer through. German soldiers in steel helmets, carrying rifles and MP40 machine pistols, were marching down the camp's main street. Ominously, some of them had stick grenades tucked into their belts. They were not camp guards, but much younger, fit-looking soldiers.[5]

"Maybe the war's over," piped up one optimistic private in one of the barracks.[6] But they didn't have long to wait for an answer. At 1000 precisely the usual guards and the heavily armed soldiers began to descend on the huts, flinging open the doors and yelling at the tops of their voices.

156

"*Raus*! *Raus*!" was the familiar cry, only this time the Germans were in large groups and very aggressive, as they bundled the prisoners out into the four inches of snow that lay on the parade square.

"Grab all your kit!" yelled Pfc. Pete House from his hut, warning the prisoners to take plenty of clothing with them.[7]

It was a wise warning, for the Germans would be keeping the Americans outside for most of the day. The Germans lined the prisoners up in the snow. They looked furious and pointed their weapons menacingly at them. They looked ready and willing to open fire. All they needed was an excuse.

Hans Kasten was bundled outside with his assistants and the other occupants of his hut. The Protestant chaplain, 1st Lt. Sam Neel, joined him.[8]

"What in the hell's going on, sir?" demanded Kasten.

"There was an incident last night in the kitchens," Neel said, shivering. "Some of our men broke in, the Germans think two or three, and assaulted the mess sergeant with an ax."

"What?" exclaimed Kasten in shock. "Is he dead?"

"I'm not sure," Neel said. "The Germans told me that the sergeant was struck many times from behind and is badly injured."

Kasten was extremely dismayed. This was a major breakdown of discipline for which they would all suffer. Someone had fouled up big-time.

*

The Germans herded the prisoners toward the air-raid trenches behind the huts and formed them up in ranks. Then Colonel Sieber appeared, his face even more thunderous than usual, and strode out to address the camp.

"In the early hours of this morning," shouted Sieber angrily, "a member of the German staff was assaulted by two or more American prisoners. The men who committed this crime *will* be found and punished. I will now give you a choice." Sieber paused for effect, the camp inmates standing miserably in the wind and snow waiting, still surrounded by armed Germans who seemed to be itching to start shooting.

"Either the guilty men give themselves up," yelled Sieber, "or there will be no food, no coffee, and no firewood until they do."[9]

Sieber's threat hung in the air. The commandant was not fooling—he meant every word of his threat. He had decided that the prisoners themselves could find the assailants or be punished for the sins of the tiniest minority. It placed the Americans in an invidious position—they would have to rat out their own to save themselves from Sieber's wrath.

"Think about what I have said," finished Sieber, his eyes scanning the twenty-six hundred American faces.

Kasten was given permission to bring his barrack leaders together and talk. They stood in a huddle in the snow and tried to decide what was best.[10] Though Kasten was one of the 350 men who'd been selected for transport out of the camp, he was still the Chief Man of Confidence, and he had a responsibility to all of the Americans at Stalag IX-B until he departed.

"What those men did is not only in violation of the camp rules," stated Kasten to the others, "but a violation of US Army regulations." The other Men of Confidence all nodded.

"So, what do we do?" demanded Pfc. Anthony Urban of Barrack 23.

"Talk to your men," replied Kasten. "Somebody must have seen something. They would have tried to wash the blood out of their clothes afterward. Talk to your men and make them see the light. The guilty *have* to be found and handed over. Their actions have endangered every man in this camp, and we can't condone that."

Some of the other leaders were shocked at handing over Americans to the Germans for punishment, but Kasten was insistent, and was strongly supported by many of the others.

"That son of a bitch means what he says, believe me," Kasten said, casting a glance over at Colonel Sieber, who stood talking to several other German officers. Kasten was still in pain from the two beatings that he had suffered on Sieber's orders. "We are in a bad spot. Our sick won't last long without food, and we'll all freeze without heating. The hospital is already full, and we've already lost five of our guys to sickness since we arrived in this dump."

Kasten and his council discussed the problem for a little while longer before a consensus was reached: The barrack leaders would return to the parade and explain the situation to their men, impressing upon them the seriousness of the problem and what they must do to help.[11] The two chaplains would join them in pleading with the men.

*

While the prisoners stood freezing in the wind and snow they could hear the Germans moving from one hut to another, tearing them apart in their hunt for bloodstained clothing. Hunger was now gnawing maddeningly at every man, and several fainted away or became delirious. For hours, the Germans investigated, until suddenly around 1600 hours the word started to travel around the huge parade that the guilty had been found. Smoke was seen rising from the kitchen chimney, and the prisoners were told that as soon as the kitchen was cleaned of blood, a meal would be prepared.

A bloody field jacket had been found stuffed behind a bunk in Barrack 42.[12] Then a pair of bloody boots was discovered. Men from this barrack identified the two assailants to Kasten, who had them brought to his office.

The two attempted murderers were a pair of scared kids, two buck privates who now looked as though they wouldn't say boo to a goose as they stood to attention before Kasten's desk. A couple of Kasten's MPs shadowed the two miscreants, Privates Parks and William Lewandowsky, while the rest of Kasten's staff sat around the room. Kasten had Parks taken out into the corridor, questioning Lewandowsky alone.

"So, whose bright idea was it to break into the kitchens?" asked Kasten, a piece of paper in front of him on which to record Lewandowsky's statement.

The young private fidgeted uncomfortably on his chair. "Mine, it was my idea," he replied sullenly.[13]

"Tell me what happened," Kasten said, picking up his pencil.

"We, that is me and Parks, we went to the kitchen after the evening count. We pried open a window. Once we was inside we kinda stood by the stove, warming ourselves, then we took some bread and butter."

"What happened when the German duty sergeant arrived?" asked Kasten.

"I jumped under the table...when he came up he checked the window. Then he saw me, and told me to come out. I started out and then I saw him lying on the floor. Parks kept hitting him with the ax. I didn't touch him, wrestle with him or nothin'."

Kasten sighed, pausing his pencil, and looked up. "What did you do after?" he asked.

"We, we went back to the barrack. Lewandowsky had a lot of blood on him, so we washed in the snow at our barrack, then finished with a basin of water at the washroom."[14]

Kasten had Parks in next for questioning. Unlike Lewandowsky, Private Parks was more evasive in his answers, initially unwilling to take the blame for hitting the guard. He said that he was the man under the table, not Lewandowsky.

"Then how do you account for the fact that Lewandowsky had no blood on his uniform?" asked Kasten, raising one eyebrow quizzically, his piercing eyes glaring at Parks.[15]

"I wanna wait until I see the results of the fingerprinting," replied Parks moodily, referring to the fact that the German military police would take prints off the ax. "I didn't hit him the first time, I was under the table. It was Lewandowsky that hit the Kraut, not me."[16]

Kasten questioned Parks some more, and eventually he admitted that most of what Lewandowsky had said was correct, but he still refused to admit to repeatedly striking the German sergeant with the ax.[17]

Kasten finished taking notes and had Parks taken out by an MP. He called in his staff and the two chaplains.

"Seems that Private Parks was the one who assaulted the German," Kasten said. "Private Lewandowsky was an accomplice. But it was Lewandowsky's idea to break into the kitchen."

"So what happens now?" asked Chaplain Neel, his face a mask of concern.

"I have to hand them over to Sieber," replied Kasten matter-of-factly. "The issue is out of my hands. I'll write up a report for the commandant explaining what happened, but the Germans will want to try these men under their own military code."

Neel and the other men in the room knew that there was nothing they could do for Parks and Lewandowsky. They had sealed their fate the moment the ax had connected with the German guard's head.

Privates Parks and Lewandowsky were last seen being marched out of the compound toward a waiting truck, their wrists shackled with iron handcuffs. When Kasten tried to find out what would happen to them, he was curtly informed that they "were to be tried."[18] What actually became of these men, nobody knew, but most could guess. Incredibly, the German mess sergeant survived the horrific assault.

By now, few of the prisoners cared much about the details of the incident, they were simply happy to finally have a bowl of hot oatmeal soup and a thin slice of bread and margarine to fill their aching stomachs.[19] As for their two comrades hauled off to God knew where—the general consensus was those men had brought it upon themselves through their selfish actions.

*

The telephone rang in Hauptmann Ludwig Merz's office at Greiz, in the German state of Thuringia. He picked up the receiver. It was his commanding officer, Major Heinrich Otto, based at Gera, thirty-four miles south of Leipzig.[20]

"Merz, you are to provide a detachment of two dozen guards at Labor Camp 650 at Berga an der Elster," ordered Otto, who commanded Landesschütz Battalion 621.[21] Merz was a fifty-six-year-old reserve captain who commanded the battalion's First Company. Unusual among army officers, this former elementary school teacher had been a Nazi Party member since May 1, 1933, shortly after Hitler had assumed power.[22] He was, nonetheless, surprised at Major Otto's request. Berga was eight miles southeast of Gera.

"Surely this is an SS affair, Herr Major," he replied, the term *labor camp* uppermost in his mind.

"Not on this occasion, Merz," replied Otto. "A detachment of Allied prisoners of war is to be transferred to Berga for a special project."

"Prisoners of war?" queried Merz.

"*Ja*, Americans from Stalag Nine-B."

"Americans?" Merz said in a surprised tone. "But, sir, Allied prisoners of war fall under army jurisdiction, not that of the SS."

"I know that, Merz," replied Major Otto impatiently, "but these are *not* ordinary prisoners. They are American Jews."

Merz was even more surprised. He knew POW regulations as well as any man involved in providing guards for the camps, and they explicitly stated that Jewish prisoners of war could not be sent to labor camps.

"This is an SS special project, Merz, and they have jurisdiction in these matters. It is out of my hands," Otto said. "A special camp is being constructed for them at Berga. You are to send a detachment under a sergeant to provide the guard detail at once. Report to SS-Obersturmführer Hack. He commands operations there."

"When will the Americans arrive at Berga, Herr Major?" asked Merz, noting Hack's name on a pad of paper in front of him.

"Mid-February," growled the colonel.

"*Zu Befehl*, Herr Major," replied Merz formally, replacing the receiver in its cradle.

He sat back in his chair for a moment, thinking. The SS was not to be argued with. Since the July 1944 Bomb Plot against Hitler, the SS had been consolidating its power in the Reich and had carte blanche authority to obtain labor for its nefarious projects from wherever it chose, including, it appeared, from prisoner of war camps. Merz sighed and called in his secretary.

"Find Feldwebel Kunz," he ordered, "and have him report to me at once."

*

As Kasten, Littell, Sinner, and the other men selected for removal from Stalag IX-B waited each day to be shipped out—for "farm work," according to the Germans—a minor miracle occurred. On Wednesday, January 31, a line of German Army trucks unexpectedly arrived at the camp gates. A detail of prisoners was immediately escorted down to unload the vehicles. When the tailgates were opened and the awnings pulled back, an audible gasp of surprise ran through the assembled prisoners. Neatly stacked in the backs of the lorries were wooden crates, on the sides of which had been stenciled in black letters "International Red Cross" along with the organization's symbol in red. Each crate was full of cardboard boxes containing care packages, seven hundred in total.[23] An almost delirious atmosphere descended upon the camp, and for the first time in weeks the prisoners could be seen smiling and laughing as they awaited the distribution of the packages with bated breath.

That evening, each barrack was finally issued its packages, one cardboard box to four men. The contents were literally lifesaving for men eking out a precarious existence on rotten potatoes and carrots, oatmeal soup, and sawdust-adulterated "bread." The men ate canned Spam, powdered milk, cheese, chocolate, and salmon, and they bartered quality cigarettes among themselves for high prices. Many became ill from overindulgence, but they were all happy for perhaps the first time since capture—it was as if Christmas had finally been celebrated.[24] Such was the festive atmosphere that the Germans relaxed the usual regulations, allowing the Americans to stay up to one in the morning before they were finally locked inside their barracks and the lights extinguished.[25]

*

The air raid siren went off just after the noon soup had been served on February 6. Some prisoners were still making their way back to their barracks with their precious food while others were already eating inside. Allied aircraft were an increasingly common daytime sight for the prisoners, usually high-altitude B-17 Flying Fortresses.[26] They left long vapor trails across the sky on clear days as they droned overhead in vast armadas on their way to flatten yet another German city. But today was different. Many prisoners looked up as a louder sound cut in over the wail of the siren—the screaming of high-powered aircraft engines. Men pointed and gawked as a German Messerschmitt Bf. 109 fighter dived toward the camp, hotly pursued by a pair of American P-47 Thunderbolts.[27]

The German was trailing smoke, and then the P-47s let rip with their big .50-caliber machine guns. American prisoners hit the dirt, or flung themselves into hut doorways, their soup spilling onto the dirt as machine-gun bullets tore across the entire camp. The American pilots sprayed death at the weaving German plane, which was at almost treetop height. The tracer bullets stitched across several huts and spurted across the parade square before the planes passed by. German guards and prisoners were soon running around in confusion as cries for help mingled with the screams of wounded men.

Barracks 22, 23, and 24 had been raked, the heavy slugs blowing gaping holes in the roofs and peppering the interiors, while the open space between Barracks 26 and 27 had also been strafed.[28] Three American prisoners had been killed, while at least six were wounded.[29] About fifteen Soviet, fifteen French, and some Serbian prisoners had also been killed,[30] with many more wounded, as the strafing had thundered through their compounds as well. Soon, stretcher bearers from the hospital were carrying their sad cargoes from the huts, the prisoner doctors and medics doing what they could to stem bleeding. It was an accident, but it wasn't the first time that the camp had been accidentally strafed by American planes, and there was some feeling on the matter among the put-upon prisoners.

Getting killed by your own side was truly the most wretched and awful thing to occur. But such was the continuing tragedy of imprisonment at Stalag IX-B.

*

"We will be leaving on the eighth," Hans Kasten said.

He had been visiting the different huts to inform those who had been selected for transfer what was happening. Each hut contained several men who'd had their names placed on the evacuation list, but as he stood inside Barrack 32, the Jewish Barrack, he knew that every man there had been chosen.

"I've been informed that the rest of the camp will be following eventually," Kasten said,[31] scanning the expectant faces of the seventy-eight Jewish American GIs who sat on bunks or stood in the aisles listening carefully.

"You believe that?" asked Morton Goldstein, the barrack leader.

"I don't know what to think," replied Kasten levelly. "All I know is we had better all be ready for transfer on the eighth."

"Where are they taking us?" asked Goldstein.

"I don't know," Kasten said, shrugging his shoulders, "but I was told that there will be an ample supply of Red Cross packages at this new camp, and that the conditions will be much better than here."[32]

Several of the men present laughed at this. No one believed the Germans anymore. The way the men had been selected for the transfer was obviously sinister—demanding that Jews identify themselves, and then the assault on Kasten in plain view of everyone.

"Well," replied Goldstein jovially, "it won't take a heck of a lot to beat this dump, am I right?"[33] But the expression on his face, shared by many of the men in the room, was about as far removed from good humor as it was possible to go.

CHAPTER 14

Berga

I know all about you, Kasten.

SS Obersturmführer Willi Hack

It was so horribly familiar to the 350 men, led by Hans Kasten, who were to be transferred out of Stalag IX-B. It was simply a reversal of their experience of arriving at Bad Orb on Christmas 1944. Formed up into a long column that was guarded by German sentries with dogs, the men marched out of the camp's main gate and down the hill toward the quiet town, and thence on to the railroad station.[1]

"Not again!" Pfc. John Reinfenrath exclaimed when he rounded the corner onto the long station platform and was confronted by the familiar sight of a long line of wooden boxcars, their doors standing open to reveal straw scattered about inside.[2]

Hans Kasten was not surprised, and neither were a great many of the men, but a widespread panic and fear gripped many at the thought of another claustrophobic journey locked inside the cars, sitting in their own filth and squalor.

"Line up!" shouted the German guards. They pushed and shoved the American prisoners into long queues to collect rations for the journey. Unlike the journey to Bad Orb, which had been marked by near starvation, this time the Germans provided some rations. Each pair of men was issued with one small Red Cross package to last them for the duration of the journey.[3] But, frustratingly, the Germans refused to say how long that journey would be. Kasten and some of the others guessed at three or four days, judging by the quantity of food that was issued, and warned the men to eke out their rations carefully.[4]

Then, once the process of handing out food was completed, the men were herded into the wagons like sheep, encouraged here and there with a rifle butt or fist. The Germans packed forty men into each car.

John Reinfenrath and his comrades were surprised that the cars were much cleaner this time, free of animal dung and urine, the straw relatively fresh.[5] But it was still a squeeze for everyone, and even as Kasten and the other leaders tried to organize the men, it was evident that no one was going to be able to rest properly on the journey. Once again, the Germans failed to provide even a bucket in each car for the calls of nature, and reacted angrily to demands for such articles. Fortunately, many of the men still had their M1 steel helmets.

Joe Littell tried several times to get water issued to the men, talking to the Germans in their own language, pleading with them, but the guards told him to be quiet or simply ignored him. Though they had some food this time, it looked as though they would be suffering badly from dehydration.[6]

*

"How many of the men are actually Jewish?" asked Ernesto Sinner once the train had been underway for a few hours.

Kasten grimaced.

"I estimate no more than eighty," he replied. Sinner and Littell had stuck close to their leader in the first wagon behind the coal car and locomotive. "Sieber had a quota to fill," continued Kasten, "and he emptied his camp of every man who ever was in trouble or raised his voice about the conditions."[7]

"Including us," Littell said morosely.

"I'm sorry," Kasten said, leaning back against the cold wooden wall as the wagon lurched and swayed on the tracks.

"Don't be a dope," Sinner said in his tough Bronx accent. "You asked us to be your assistants, and we accepted—we're all in this together."

"That's right," Littell added, a grim smile on his lips.

"I appreciate it," Kasten replied, his defiant eyes flashing in the wagon's half light, the yellowed bruises around one socket and across one cheek still visible from the beating he had taken inside the German *Kommandantur* when he had refused to name the Jews.

"So where do you think we're going?" asked Sinner, scratching his stubbly chin. It was a question being asked in every wagon along the whole length of the train.

"That SOB Sieber was adamant that we are being sent to an Americans-only camp," Kasten replied, almost spitting out the hated commandant's name. "He said that Bad Orb was only a holding camp for many nationalities."[8]

"Makes sense," Littell said.

"Maybe," Kasten answered, "but I don't buy it. For one thing, why the interest in Jewish prisoners?"

The car gave a lurch and brakes squealed up ahead.

"God damn!" exclaimed another soldier farther down the car who had his face pressed against one of the small, barbed wire–latticed, open windows at one end. "We're stopping again!"

A groan went through the huddled mass of prisoners.

"Did you see any signs?" shouted back Kasten.

"Nah," the soldier replied. "Just some houses, and plenty of snow. Anyhow, it's getting dark."

Since setting out from Bad Orb on February 8, the journey had been extremely slow, with frequent long stops in sidings where the Germans stored unused locomotives and freight cars. Kasten presumed that Allied bombing was becoming more intense and disruptive to the German railroad system. They all feared being trapped for long periods of time inside the cars; everyone remembered what happened when British Mosquitos had bombed the first train they had been aboard while traveling from Gerolstein to Bad Orb. The constant knot of tension never left their stomachs, as their ears were almost preternaturally attuned to any strange background noises above the groaning, puffing, and squeaking of the locomotive that might herald an aerial attack.

"Well," sighed Kasten, as the train came to a complete stop in another siding outside some unidentified small German town, "I know one thing. Wherever we're headed, the Germans are not in any hurry to get us there."

*

It took the train five slow and tortuous days to reach its destination, traveling via the cities of Fulda, Gotha, Erfurt, and Weimar, a journey of only 124 miles. If anyone needed a lesson in how bad the war situation was becoming inside Germany, then one needed look no further than the chaos and delays on the national railway system as Allied planes destroyed rail yards, switching and signaling equipment, and rolling stock. The Luftwaffe was now almost powerless to stop them, with many of its aircraft grounded by lack of fuel and a shortage of trained pilots. Nazi Germany was entering terminal military decline by the second month of 1945, and was snatching at anything that might stave off defeat. The Ardennes Offensive had failed; the Germans suffered heavy casualties and the loss of much precious armor, which severely affected their ability to defend the Siegfried Line against fresh Anglo-American offensives. In the east, a massive Red Army winter offensive had swept all before it, the Soviets rapidly approaching the Reich's eastern frontiers in East Prussia. The overstretched German forces were doing everything they could to stabilize the Eastern Front, but were unequal to the task. Hitler had returned from the Adlerhorst, his Western Front headquarters, to Berlin aboard his special armored train and disappeared into his bunker beneath the bomb-shattered Reich Chancellery. From there he would direct the final battles, increasingly out of touch with military reality. But Himmler's massive SS state continued to function, and it was now at the forefront of a series of desperate, last-ditch secret projects to somehow turn around the fortunes of the Reich before the Soviets reached the gates of Berlin and the Western Allies jumped the Rhine. One such secret program was now to involve the 350 American prisoners of war who huddled dejectedly inside their freezing-cold boxcars.

The Germans refused to allow the Americans off the train to relieve themselves, but on two occasions they did provide large tubs of ersatz coffee in lieu of fresh water. Allied aircraft did not attack, which was a massive relief to the men trapped inside the wooden boxcars.[9]

*

On the morning of February 13, 1945, the call went through the boxcars once more: "We're slowing down again!"

Those that could pressed their faces against the small end windows and tried to see where they were. The locomotive was definitely slowing. They were gliding into another station.

"Berga!" shouted a voice in Kasten's wagon. "I see signs that read 'Berga.' B-E-R-G-A!"

Was this just another temporary stop or the end of their journey? No one knew for certain. After five days crammed inside the wagons, the prisoners were desperate for some space and somewhere to lie down properly. The hard triple-tiered bunks that they had left behind at Stalag IX-B seemed almost like the Waldorf in comparison.

The locomotive gave several loud blasts on its steam whistle as it coasted into the station and slowed to a walking pace.

"Lots of Heinies…and dogs!" reported one of the watchers. Kasten stood and climbed up to a window and peered outside. The long platform was lined with German soldiers in steel helmets, some with Alsatians. It was quite some welcoming committee.

"Looks like we've arrived, boys," announced Kasten to the car.

The train lurched a few more times then shuddered to a standstill, steam blowing off with a loud hiss. The German soldiers immediately started unlocking the wagon doors and hauling them back on their runners.

"*Aus, aus!*" they yelled and screamed, bodily dragging off those Americans closest to the doors. The prisoners had been through this all before, but these guards seemed more aggressive.

"*Schnell!*" screamed a purple-faced German corporal into Kasten's face as he climbed down from the wagon. "Get in line!"

Kasten was pushed roughly toward the long file of prisoners that was forming up on the platform. The noise was incredible—shouting and hollering Germans, whistles, and the incessant, loud barking of the guard dogs. The prisoners were dazed and confused after five days of quiet inside their boxcars.

Kasten took his place at the head of the line, and Littell and Sinner fell in behind him. Two German officers were chatting at the end of the platform. Kasten could see that the one facing him was a middle-aged army captain, probably the guard commander.

He had noticed that the Germans doing the unloading were *Landeschützen*, just like the guards at Stalag IX-B. The German officer with his back to Kasten now turned, flicked his cigarette onto the tracks, and started toward the Americans. With stunned horror, Kasten took in his uniform cap and collar tabs.

"What the heck?" exclaimed Kasten. "That guy's SS!"

Littell and Sinner shared his disbelief, nervous tension lancing through their stomachs at this unexpected turn of events.

The SS officer halted in front of Kasten. The American was slightly taller, but the young SS officer looked fit and strong in comparison to the emaciated Kasten.

"I am Obersturmführer Hack," the SS officer announced in clipped German. "And you are Chief Man of Confidence Kasten." It wasn't a question. Hack smiled slightly. "I know *all* about you, Kasten," he said, almost cheerfully.[10]

Kasten said nothing, just looked into Hack's hard eyes and thought, *Once again I'm nailed in advance.*[11]

Kasten's second intimation that all was not well at Berga was the sight that greeted him just outside the town's railroad station. It was a sight that was to remain with every American who witnessed it, and it was deeply disturbing, particularly following the unexpected appearance of the SS officer on the platform a few minutes before.

A long line of skeletal figures dressed in striped pajama-like clothes and caps stood watching silently from behind a tall barbed wire fence as the Americans were formed up into a long column outside Berga railway station. The Americans stared at the listless and dead-eyed faces of the prisoners behind the wire and shuddered. Kasten asked a guard who the emaciated prisoners were.

"Jews" was the guard's dismissive reply.

The Americans had only a brief glimpse of Berga I, the small labor camp that had been established in the town itself, before their guards moved the column off.

Thirty minutes later, and after a climb up a hilly road, the Americans discovered their destination: A wooden gate with a guard tower gave access to a large rectangular space upon which stood four large wooden barracks. A painted wooden sign was fixed atop the main gate—it read "Arbeitsdienstlager 625." They had arrived at Berga II American concentration camp.[12] The prisoners filed onto the main parade square. A count was taken, and Kasten and his assistants noticed SS Lieutenant Hack standing with a couple of NCOs and watching the proceedings with a bored expression on his face. Kasten and the Americans were relieved to discover that Wehrmacht rather than SS troops guarded the US camp.

Herded into the brand-new wooden huts, the Americans' spirits rose. Conditions were better than at Bad Orb. Each barrack still smelled of freshly cut wood, with two large rooms and a common entryway. The rooms were dominated by wooden bunks stacked three high. There was electricity, one bulb for each room, which was left on at night, and an outside latrine. The compound was well lit, and guards patrolled the perimeter wire or stood watch in wooden towers.[13] They would also discover that, at least initially, the food was better than at Bad Orb. Some of the Americans believed that their lot had improved.

Once again, the prisoners elected Men of Confidence to represent them, and Kasten was appointed Chief Man of Confidence. The Jewish POWs from Bad Orb moved into one barrack, while the rest of the men whom the Germans had mistakenly thought were Jews or had labeled as troublemakers occupied the other three. The Germans also organized the barracks into work shifts. The nature of that "work" remained a mystery to the Americans, but SS-Obersturmführer Hack would soon ensure that the mystery would be solved.

CHAPTER 15

The Devil's Mountain

Geilenberg used as many as 350,000 men for the repair, rebuilding, and dispersal of the bombed [oil] plants and for new underground construction.

Army Air Forces in World War II, USAAF,
May 12, 1944

Obersturmführer Hack leaned over the large table and carefully examined architectural blueprints. Beside him was the project architect, Wilhelm Fricke, as well as another SS officer. The plans showed a series of seventeen tunnels driving into the mountain on the opposite side of the Elster River from the town of Berga.

"Progress thus far has been less than satisfactory," Hack announced.

Fricke nodded solemnly.

"I'm hoping that with the addition of the American labor, we can speed construction up," Hack continued. Fricke agreed wholeheartedly.

The two men had a good working relationship, and Fricke knew that Hack was under considerable pressure. At the top of the blueprint was the name of the project in bold— **Schwalbe V.** *Schwalbe*, the German word for the swallow bird, was part of a top secret fuel-generation scheme headed by SS-Obergruppenführer Hans Kammler, who also ran the V-2

175

ballistic missile program for Himmler. There were seven Swallow projects, all under Kammler's supervision. The intention was simple—Germany needed fuel to keep its armed forces fighting, due to the loss of oil fields to enemy forces and the massive bombing campaign by the Allied air forces.

On May 30, 1944, a mineral oil emergency decentralization operation codenamed "the Geilenberg Program" was initiated under its namesake, Nazi official Edmund Geilenberg. The Germans were wise to plan ahead. Air raids during July 1944 caused 98 percent of surface aviation fuel production to fail as the plants were destroyed or badly damaged. One day after the raids, the oil-saving plan was approved by Berlin. Hitler personally commanded Geilenberg to relocate German synthetic fuel production underground. But this was easier said than done.

The biggest headache the Germans faced was finding suitable tunnels to house the vast amount of machinery required to produce fuel. Mining companies began examining underground rooms and mines, with no success. Most of the mines were too small or lacked necessary infrastructure. Project Swallow needed access to a lot of water. The high-pressure hydrogenation chambers produced massive amounts of heat. So each of the Swallow plants would be constructed with a large number of gallery mouths or entrances into long tunnels. These would then be linked together underground to form a vast working space. The hydrogenation furnaces required rooms at least fifty yards high, but the rock was able to withstand high temperatures.

All of the Swallow plants were built in new tunnels, near a river and a railroad. Vast quantities of water were essential for the hydrogenation process. Geologically stable mountains were also required, and the SS required that the roofs of the hydrogenation rooms must consist of at least forty yards of uncracked rock to make them bombproof. The best places were limestone or sandstone quarries where rapid tunneling could be achieved.[1]

Construction of Swallow V at Berga began in October 1944. German mining engineers had first arrived in Berga in September 1944 to investigate shifting an already operational hydrogenation plant to the area. The Swallow program's chief engineer, Dr. Nerge, chose Berga personally. On October 1, the site manager, SS-Obersturmführer Hack, arrived and immediately commandeered the local town hall for his headquarters. Hack told the mayor that he was responsible for the entire project. He was soon laboring under enormous pressure to get the project completed as swiftly as possible. Hack reported directly to Kammler, who in turn reported directly to Reichsführer-SS Himmler himself. That was how important this program was to the SS at this time. Hack had a stellar reputation in SS circles from his previous work on underground facilities, and much was expected of him. Hack controlled a budget for the Berga project of 20 million *Reichsmarks* (the equivalent today of $114 million).

Although at thirty-two years old Wilhelm Hack held the comparatively junior rank of first lieutenant, he was nonetheless a long-serving member of the SS. His background was in engineering, having studied at a technical school in Stuttgart near his hometown of Reutlingen, before joining the SS in March 1934. He had seen the sharp end of war as a sergeant in the Third Panzer Pioneer Battalion, part of the Third SS Panzer Totenkopf Division, on the Eastern Front before being commissioned as an *Untersturmführer* in February 1942 and transferred to Amtsgruppe C (Buildings and Works) of the SS-Wirtschafts-Verwaltungshauptamt, the Main Economic and Administrative Office, responsible for the grandiose and top secret construction projects so beloved of Himmler's dreaded organization.

Hack had been on the staff at the infamous Mittelbau-Dora concentration camp, where he directed construction of the subcamp at Niedersachswerfen, overseeing slave labor in the construction of a massive underground engine factory for V-2 missiles. He had gotten the job done, to his superiors' satisfaction, though over the dead bodies of hundreds of prisoners. After being promoted to *Obersturmführer* in November 1944, Hack had been assigned the present construction task at Berga an der Elster, with every expectation that he would complete the project within the required time frame. Hack did not have any intention of disappointing his superiors and tarnishing his impeccable record. Success at Berga would bring promotion and even more high-level projects.[2]

He had been married since 1935, and had one young son. His marriage had been a cause of some friction for him, as it was necessary to obtain a marriage permit from the SS Race and Resettlement Office to ensure that his spouse was of pure Aryan stock. In 1935, Hack's marriage had not been approved, but he had gone ahead anyway, demonstrating his impatient nature, and applied again for a permit in 1937. The blood cleanliness issue had hovered like a specter over his marriage and career, never having fully satisfied the SS that his family was free of non-Aryan blood. He had certainly made up for any doubts by his brutal treatment of slave laborers on the secret engineering projects that he had become involved with since returning from the Eastern Front. He was a man with something to prove to the organization he had devoted eleven years of his life to serving faithfully.

Castle Dryfels, an imposing medieval fortress overlooking Berga, was also confiscated by the SS and became the construction management office for the civil engineering company that would actually build the facility.[3]

What the Germans had decided to do at Berga was a major undertaking. Across the White Elster River from the town was a small, heavily wooded mountain. Here, Hack's workforce, consisting in the beginning of professional miners, began to excavate seventeen parallel tunnels into the mountainside. At the same time, other workers cut down a huge volume of timber and began to build four bridges across the river, three massive barracks for offices and SS accommodation beside the Elster, plus twelve more barracks for the workers and for shoring up the tunnel entrances. Seven miles of narrow gauge railway track was laid, leading out of each tunnel to a main line, where small railcars were used to haul away the rock blasted out of the tunnels with dynamite charges and dumped close by. The entire production area was massive, encompassing many acres of mountainside and riverbank.[4]

Hack turned to the other man attending the meeting in his office. SS-Hauptsturmführer Richard Rohr was the highly brutal *Lagerführer*, or commandant, of the small concentration camp that the SS had established in Berga town to house slave laborers supplied by the main camp at Buchenwald. Soon after Hack had arrived on-site, he had applied to the SS Main Office in Berlin for additional help, and begun to receive regular shipments of prisoners from Buchenwald.

"Have the Americans settled in?" Hack asked, turning to the issue of his latest batch of "helpers," as though he was discussing the arrival of dear friends.

"Yes, I'm keeping them separate from my prisoners, both in their accommodations and at the work site," Rohr replied. The concentration camp slaves and the Americans would be kept as separate from each other as was feasible. It was window dressing.

Rohr briefly described the Americans' new camp. "They are

guarded by an army detachment, and not by my men, as per POW regulations," he said, his voice full of annoyance at this bureaucratic sham. In Rohr's opinion, *all* the prisoners at Berga should have fallen under SS jurisdiction.

"Excellent," Hack responded, happy that the illusion of correct POW treatment was being observed. "I want them put to work as *soon* as possible. We can't afford any delays, and the natural wastage of prisoners from your camp means we are shorthanded, particularly for the heavier labor inside the tunnels."

Rohr nodded grimly. He would pass on the instructions to Hauptmann Merz, the army officer who commanded the *Landesschütz* unit providing guards for the Americans, who in turn would instruct the guard commander, Feldwebel Kunz.

Hack could issue such instructions to Rohr, who was a captain and a rank higher, because of his unique position as project manager for the Swallow V construction. Hack's word was law, regardless of rank badges or military protocol.

Detached from the main Buchenwald camp himself, Rohr presided over his own little version of hell on earth. Thousands of concentration camp prisoners had been sent in drafts to Berga, but due to malnutrition, disease, overwork, and brutal treatment, they were dying in large numbers, necessitating constant requests for replacements. The 350 Americans were nothing short of a godsend to Hack and his cronies—fresh, strong backs to speed up the construction of the tunnels. But the Americans were not the "strong backs" that Hack thought— they were run-down, underweight, and suffering from various medical complaints.

"So, Fricke," Hack said, turning to the project architect to discuss another important aspect of Swallow V, "are we still on track?"

Fricke grimaced and turned to a sheaf of papers on another

table, daily reports and lists of facts and figures pertaining to how much rock had been moved, the current length and height of each tunnel, the workforce's daily numbers, et cetera, et cetera. Reams of facts and figures, all annotated and analyzed with a clinical and dispassionate eye by Fricke and his staff, who ignored the hundreds of slave laborers that were, with German efficiency, worked to death then shipped back to Buchenwald as corpses where they were carefully recorded, tallied, and then disposed of. The project administrators ignored the prisoners maimed by explosions, and those beaten half to death by SS guards and civilian foremen. They pretended not to see the starved, shambling wrecks of human beings clad in the striped suits of the slave labor system being marched daily past their offices, where these neat and tidy bureaucrats studied their blueprints and their production graphs and time management studies. Fricke looked glum—not because of the suffering and death that he and his staff were an intimate cause of, but because the work was not progressing fast enough to satisfy either Hack or SS headquarters.

"I'm sorry, Herr Obersturmführer," Fricke said. "Our initial deadline was *too* optimistic." Hack nodded in polite agreement, but his eyes sparkled with a furious glimmer.

"We cannot expect completion before March 1946, at the earliest," Fricke stated, before outlining the reasons for this new date. At the time the Americans arrived, the tunnels had only progressed between seven and sixteen yards into the mountain.

"Have faith, Fricke," Hack grunted. "I shall extract the maximum possible effort from our new American prisoners. They will help us to complete the project much faster than you think." A distinctly vulpine leer crossed Hack's face when he spoke of the Americans. And he was the kind of man to make good on his promises.

*

Feldwebel Kunz divided the American prisoners into two units of approximately eighty men each. There were two shifts each day, with about half the men in each American work unit taken out each time for hours of unremitting slave labor.[5] The daily third shift at the site was always performed by concentration camp prisoners, meaning the Americans had a little respite from the backbreaking labor. The remaining men were either resting, sick, or doing other work duties at the site or in their prison camp.

The first shift formed up on the *Appellplatz*, or parade square, on the afternoon of February 14, 1945. They were the men from the Jewish Barrack, led by Pfc. Morton Goldstein. There was a heavy guard detail, all with steel helmets and fixed bayonets on their rifles, as if they expected resistance. The prisoners would be working from 1400 until 2230 hours, with a new shift beginning at 0600 the following day.

"*Marsch!*" bellowed Kunz. He kept a clipboard containing the names and POW numbers of the men constituting the first shift tucked under his right arm as he led the prisoners to work. The Americans tramped along, out through the little camp's main gate and across a bridge over the White Elster River and into the work site. As the Americans approached the site they could see the tunnel entrances above the river, dozens of slave laborers in their striped uniforms busily at work under the command of civilian overseers armed with staves. The miniature railroad line was busy with carts being manhandled by exhausted workers, thick dust billowing as they dumped their loads of rock at assigned places along the riverbank.

"Jesus!" exclaimed several of the Americans, ducking involuntarily as an explosion went off in one of the tunnels. A choking cloud of impenetrable dust and smoke emerged from the tunnel mouth as the dynamite's booming report echoed off the surrounding hills.

As the column of Americans approached the entrance to the first tunnel, Kunz halted and quickly called off ten names from his list. Hard-looking German foremen in flat caps and dusty work clothes stood ready to take charge of each batch of prisoners. At each tunnel mouth a detachment of ten men was assigned. The prisoners noticed that once they had been handed over to the civilian overseers, their army guards disappeared. For the next twelve hours, they were under the control of a group of sadistic and intolerant foremen who were quicker to anger and beat their workers than the German camp guards. These civilians were under Obersturmführer Hack's command, and they were pushing the project on as fast as possible to please their capricious SS master—and if that meant over the dead bodies of their workers, then so be it.

*

It was no coincidence that the first shift consisted of those Americans who had been positively identified as Jewish. The pathetic remains of men laboring all around the site in concentration camp garb was deeply shocking to the Jewish American prisoners. Pfc. Gerald Daub walked with his little work group to one of the shaft entrances. Daub watched as a German foreman mercilessly beat a concentration camp prisoner who had fallen in the dirt and dust as he loaded rocks into one of the small mine railcars. The man soon stopped moving as the foreman rained down blows with a stick and his boots. Eventually tiring of the effort, the foreman stopped and turned, spotting Daub and his nine comrades waiting to begin work.

The foreman strode over to where the Americans stood, horrified and frightened by what they had just witnessed. He walked slowly down the line, looking at each man in turn. Though they were malnourished and exhausted, in comparison to the walking dead concentration camp slaves, the Americans looked in the full bloom of youth.

"*Amerikaners*," the foreman stated angrily as he walked along, shaking his head at these unpopular arrivals. Many of the Germans working at Berga had lost relatives during the Allied bombing campaign, and they would later turn increasingly bitter and aggressive toward American POWs.

The foreman stopped in front of Daub, one of the smallest men in the line. He glared down at Daub. The foreman was a large, well-built, and well-fed man in comparison to the short, skinny American.

"You, come with me," ordered the foreman in German. Daub didn't quite understand, but someone quickly translated. He followed the German past the body of the unconscious prisoner still lying facedown in the dirt at the mouth of the tunnel, the other concentration camp slaves averting their haunted eyes and speeding up their work as he passed.

The tunnels were fairly large; the Jewish labor from Buchenwald had been terrorized sufficiently that they had managed to burrow between fifty and seventy feet into the bluff above the river, each tunnel standing twenty feet high and fifteen feet wide.[6] But the cost in human life had been great, and the Americans had been drafted in specifically to help Hack speed up the construction.

Inside the tunnel, the air was dusty and cloying. The foreman picked up a long drill and showed Daub how he wanted it used. Daub then felt the heft of the contraption, which was six feet long and very heavy. His job was to bore small holes two inches in diameter and six feet in depth for the placing of dynamite charges for blasting.[7] When the drill was started the noise was tremendous, but the worst was the vibration, which made Daub's thin little body tremble and his arms and back ache.[8]

Heavy dust filled the tunnel constantly as the drillers worked under close supervision from the overseers.[9] Soon the rest of Daub's group was put to work clearing dislodged rock from inside the tunnel, filling the railroad cars and pushing them down the track for about one hundred feet before being emptied beside the river.

When a dynamite charge was lit, the German foremen quickly hurried from the tunnel, taking cover, but the warnings issued to the American POWs were insufficient, and several were caught close to the blasts, suffering lacerations from flying rock shards. These would soon fester without medical care. The Americans were not issued gloves, face masks, or hard hats, and they were herded straight back into the smoke- and dust-filled tunnels, where visibility was no more than three feet,[10] to begin loading up the loose rock, breathing in dangerous levels of dust that had them all coughing and spitting. The Germans issued no water during the shift. The Americans' hands were soon raw and split from handling the sharp rocks. Any goldbricking or refusal to work was met with blows from the foremen's rubber hoses, truncheons, or clubs. The fortunate few still had their M1 helmets, but it was labor the likes of which no one had ever experienced before.

*

By the time Daub and the other prisoners from the Jewish Barrack arrived back in camp, it was just after 2230. The Jewish American group came through the gates looking disheveled and filthy, their uniforms torn, faces and hair dusty, and many nursing injuries. They dragged themselves into their barrack and drank whatever water they could find, completely exhausted.

Hans Kasten went straight to meet them, to talk to Morton Goldstein and some of his men.

"Don't let any more of our men go down there," Goldstein said, nodding his head in disbelief. "It's murder, Kasten, sheer goddam murder."

Goldstein and a handful of his men carefully outlined what the shift had entailed, and the treatment they had received from the civilian foremen. Kasten was horrified by what he heard, and promised to do what he could to stop the work. What the Germans were doing was in complete violation of the Geneva Conventions' ruling that prisoners of war could not be used as labor. It was expressly forbidden to force POWs to work on military projects of any description. It was time to confront Obersturmführer Hack.

CHAPTER 16

Mutiny

*The prisoners have been brought here to work, and that's
what they will do.*

SS-Obersturmführer Willi Hack

T he next morning, Kasten could not prevent the next shift
from being assembled and marched out of camp at 0600
hours. But he immediately approached Sergeant Kunz, demanding, as the prisoners' Chief Man of Confidence, an interview
with Obersturmführer Hack, who had relocated the main SS office to Schloss Dryfels, the small but imposing medieval castle
located atop a wooded hill on the other side of Berga from the
American camp, where the construction firms and architects all
had their offices as well.[1]

"You two had better come with me," Kasten told Joe Littell
and Ernesto Sinner. He knew that this interview was not going
to be easy. After what happened to him on the two occasions he
tried to resist German camp authorities at Stalag IX-B, Kasten
was probably keen to have witnesses along with him this time.

*

Kasten, Sinner, and Littell sat on a wooden bench inside
Obersturmführer Hack's outer office. A bored-looking German
Landesschütz guard stood close by, a Mauser rifle slung over

his shoulder. He had escorted the three from the camp to the castle. Outside the door was a desk with a black typewriter and telephone upon it, and a filing cabinet against the wall. Hack's secretary, Gerda Teichert, sat behind the desk. She glanced up disapprovingly several times from her paperwork, glaring at Kasten and his companions with barely concealed loathing.

The Americans were now under SS jurisdiction in all but name. Despite German attempts to make it appear as though the Americans were still being housed and guarded as prisoners of war belonging to the Wehrmacht, Kasten was wise enough to know where the real power at Berga lay, and that was with Obersturmführer Hack, the project manager.

The room was deathly quiet except for the scratching of Teichert's fountain pen on paper and the muffled detonations from the excavation site as the new shift continued blasting and clearing operations in the tunnels. Kasten and the others looked around. Compared to where they had been living for the past few weeks, the room was elegant and pleasant: a large rug on the floor, paintings on the white walls, and a fire burning in the grate. The telephone rang suddenly, and the Americans all jumped. Teichert snatched up the receiver, listened, and then replaced it in its cradle. Without speaking, she gestured at the three Americans with her pen and pointed toward Hack's office door. They stood and entered.

Hack sat behind his desk, hatless, writing something, when Kasten's party entered. His office was also pleasantly furnished and comfortable. He glanced up at his visitors, his expression annoyed.

"What do you want?" he growled impatiently.

"We've come to ask that you not put the prisoners to work," Kasten said confidently, noting how Hack's expression looked even more thunderous. "They are far too weak," he added.

"They will not survive. I respectfully request that you comply with the provisions of the Geneva Convention that pertain to the treatment of prisoners of war."[2]

Hack leaned back in his creaking leather chair, his cold eyes fixing Kasten's impassively.

"The prisoners have been brought here to work, and that's what they will do," the SS officer replied slowly, unused to having his methods questioned by mere slaves.

"Herr Obersturmführer," Kasten said, more forcefully this time, "I'm sure you are aware that forcing prisoners of war to perform hard labor is a direct violation of the Geneva Convention. I'm sure you also know that anyone who issues such an order will one day be held to account for his actions."[3]

Hack's fingers drummed impatiently on his desktop. Then, the faint ghost of a twisted smile formed on his lips.

"Show me your identity disks," he ordered.[4] This request wrong-footed Kasten for a second or two but, sighing, he reached under his shirt and pulled out his US Army tags. Hack rose from his chair and advanced around the table, taking hold of the tags. He held them beneath his nose and read slowly, in a sarcastic tone: "Johann Carl Friedrich Kasten."

His eyes swiveled back to Kasten's face. "You are a German who has come over here to destroy the Third Reich. You are a traitor to your country."[5]

Kasten opened his mouth to reply, but Hack held up a hand to silence him.

"You know, Kasten, there is only one thing in the world that is more despicable than a Jew. Do you know what that is? It's a German who betrays his country. I should have *you* working in those tunnels—not just like everyone else, but working a double shift." Hack paused, letting the threat hang in the air for a moment or two.

"But I won't do that," Hack said. "You see, *Kasten*, I have something more interesting in mind for you. Something *much* more interesting."[6] His index finger gently tapped Kasten on the chest as he spoke.

Hack lowered his arm and walked over to the window, gazing out on his empire with a proprietorial eye. Then he turned and suddenly pointed at Joe Littell, who was standing with Sinner beside Kasten.

"Are you Jewish?" Hack shouted. Littell was temporarily taken aback by the direct question, not to mention Hack's sudden change of subject.

"I'm a Christian," Littell replied, "a follower of Jesus Christ. And Jesus was a Jew," he added, his confidence coming back.[7]

"Don't talk to me about Jesus," Hack shouted, his face twisted with disgust. "I asked you only if you're Jewish." Hack's eyes swiveled around and he glared at Sinner.

"Are you Jewish?" Hack demanded. Sinner struggled to maintain his composure, for he *was* half-Jewish on his mother's side.

"No," he said confidently, his eyes locking with Hack's.[8] The SS officer gazed at Sinner for a few seconds, as if trying to decide whether to pursue this line of questioning further, before he abruptly strode back to his desk and sat down.

"It's time to end this meeting," Hack announced in a reasonable voice. "I am very busy. You are dismissed."[9]

Kasten, Littell, and Sinner came to attention and saluted, then filed out to be escorted back to the camp. One thing had become abundantly clear to all three of them now that they had properly met Obersturmführer Hack for the first time. He was quite possibly unbalanced, and he had taken a very personal dislike to Kasten from the moment he had laid eyes on him at Berga station. The way he had threatened Kasten in front of his assistants, and his strange questioning about their religious faith, had left a distinctly unpleasant impression. If Kasten thought his job as Chief Man of Confidence at Stalag IX-B had been trying, then it appeared that performing his duty to his men at Arbeitsdienstlager 625 was going to be much tougher, perhaps even impossible.

*

Shortly before 1400 hours a commotion began in the American camp. The new shift was supposed to have mustered on the *Appellplatz* so that Sergeant Kunz could check off the names of the eighty or so prisoners, and the parade fallen in and marched down to the excavations. But no matter how many times German guards yelled and blew their whistles, not one American soldier emerged from the barrack.[10] Kunz turned purple with rage and sent messages to both the concentration camp and to Hack's headquarters. The prisoners were refusing to muster—this was mutiny.

A Kübelwagen field car swung into the American compound followed by two Opel Blitz trucks. Hack climbed out of the back of the field car, accompanied by the commandant of the concentration camp, Hauptsturmführer Rohr. The two trucks quickly disgorged their contents—two dozen heavily armed SS troops. The riot squad, a special guard detail held back in case of rebellion or escape attempts, had been called out from the concentration camp. Rohr quickly directed his men, who were wearing steel helmets, greatcoats, and full battle order equipment, and carrying rifles, machine pistols, and even stick grenades. The SS men fanned out to strengthen the cordon of *Landesschütz* army guards in surrounding all of the American buildings. Two SS men also set up a fast-firing MG42 machine gun on a tripod facing the barrack that had refused to report for work, one man opening a can of ammunition and running a belt of bullets through the breech before the gunner cocked the weapon menacingly.

Hack stood watching the troops moving into position before he walked closer to the barrack and demanded to know why the Americans were refusing to muster.

"The work violates the Geneva Convention," a voice shouted from inside the barrack. "We are American prisoners of war, and you can't make us work. We know our rights."

Hack stood thinking for a moment. Then he shouted back.

"All prisoners will report to the *Appellplatz* immediately." There was no movement from any of the huts. Hack turned and pointed to a handful of growling Alsatian guard dogs held by their SS handlers by the main gate.

"You see these dogs," Hack shouted. "Either you report for counting, or I send the dogs into the barracks. You have one minute to decide."[11]

There were the sounds of heated discussions inside the four barracks buildings, as Hack theatrically looked at his wristwatch.

"Thirty seconds!" Hack yelled.

He turned and gave several orders in guttural German. The dog handlers moved several paces forward, the Alsatians straining at their leashes, growling and barking.

Suddenly there was the sound of a door opening, and Hans Kasten stepped out of one of the other barracks, holding up his hands.

"That won't be necessary, Herr Obersturmführer. We are coming out." As he spoke, the doors of the other three barracks swung in and American prisoners started to emerge timidly from within, many with their hands in the air as they saw the large array of armed and determined-looking SS and *Landesschützen* all pointing weapons at them.

Hack's head swiveled around and he gave a nod to Hauptsturmführer Rohr and Feldwebel Kunz, who immediately issued a stream of orders to their respective men. The Germans advanced at the double toward all the barracks, forcing their way inside with maximum violence. Soon the air was filled with the screams of orders being delivered in German, accompanied by pushing, shoving, beating, and the sounds of breaking glass and overturned furniture. The guards, particularly the SS, were very heavy-handed, and within a few minutes all the American prisoners had been mustered on the *Appellplatz*, many nursing bruised arms and faces, split lips, or bloody noses.

Hans Kasten took his place at the head of the parade, and he wondered for a moment if Hack wasn't about to set his dogs on him as an example to the rest. But instead of more violence, the guards carefully counted the prisoners, and then Kunz selected the men for the next shift. The rest of the parade was dismissed, while Kunz marched the new shift to work. So ended the brief mutiny.

It was now abundantly clear to Kasten that Hack was not to be trifled with, and although the Americans occupied their own camp, with regular army guards, this was just for show. In reality, Kasten and the 349 other men had no more rights or protection than those enjoyed by the emaciated, diseased, and cruelly abused Jewish prisoners at Rohr's concentration camp.

The Americans were now lost inside the parallel universe of the labor camp system.

*

Pfc. David Goldin was totally exhausted. His arms ached desperately as he held up the heavy drill on the morning shift on February 19, 1945, the vibration making his whole body shake. Thin, ill, and covered in rock dust, Goldin had been drilling in shifts for five days in one of the tunnels at Berga, under the supervision of a German foreman who was not slow to hit him if he showed signs of fatigue. Five days of hell, broken only by the march to and from the camp and a miserable sleep jammed up against another prisoner in the freezing barracks, assailed all night long by hunger pangs and lice.

Goldin was, at thirty-four, the oldest American prisoner at Berga. A proud Virginian in the Seventy-Ninth Infantry Division, he had been captured just after the Battle of the Bulge and sent to Bad Orb, where he had been selected along with the other 349 men for transfer to Berga.

He didn't think he could hold up the drill much longer without collapsing. The air inside the tunnel was dense with thick smoke from dynamiting, and Goldin coughed continuously as he breathed in rock fragments that made his lungs bleed, while his hands and face were covered in infected scratches and cuts—the Germans provided no gloves or head protection. The boom of detonations from neighboring tunnels and the deafening racket of the drill assaulted his ears. Other American prisoners scurried around in the gloom, loading the little railroad cars with rocks and debris, another German overseer armed with a length of rubber hose hastening them along.

Goldin was desperately thirsty, but the Germans provided no drinking water during the shift. His tongue felt too large for his mouth and his eyes were crusty with dust. Suddenly there was a cry from the German foreman standing near him. Goldin heard a loud noise before there was blackness. A large rock fell suddenly from the tunnel roof, striking him in the head. Goldin crumpled to the floor, blood gushing from a nasty scalp laceration. Several other American prisoners rushed to his aid. One fortunately still had some sulfur powder used to prevent wounds from becoming infected on the battlefield, and he carefully applied this and a rudimentary bandage from a piece of a torn-off shirt, before the yelling German overseer ordered them to pick up Goldin and carry him outside of the tunnel.[12] There he lay unconscious for four hours, unattended and ignored, as the Germans refused to allow a doctor to treat him. The overseers instead chased the other prisoners back to work. Later, at the end of their shift, a group of prisoners carried him back to the camp where they laid him on a bunk and did what they could for him.

The next day another man was nearly killed in one of the tunnels, but this time it was not a falling rock that caused his injuries; rather it was a shovel in the hands of a brutal German foreman. The enraged foreman attacked Pvt. David Young, from Kasten's Twenty-Eighth Infantry Division, striking him across the back with a shovel. The German felt that Young was not working hard enough. But he didn't stop with the first blow. As Young lay moaning in pain on the floor of the tunnel, the German beat him mercilessly, bringing the shovel down repeatedly on Young's prostrate body until the American didn't move anymore.[13] The prisoners also hauled Young's broken body back to the barracks, where he lay in a semicomatose state until his death in late March, denied medical attention.

Hack's regime of terror was starting to claim victims on a daily basis, as the Americans, weakened by starvation and disease, were felled by accidents, suffocated by rock dust, or beaten half to death by impatient German overseers. Kasten kept record, and it was clear to him by the time of the Young incident that something had to change or all of the Americans at Berga were doomed to be slowly killed off. Starvation was a big part of how run-down and sickly the Americans had become, opening them to illness and disease, and levels of fatigue that led to beatings. The Americans were still Allied prisoners of war, and he decided to try and find out why their camp was not receiving Red Cross parcels, the contents of which would go a massive way to alleviating the suffering that was by now endemic.

*

"Herr Obersturmführer," Kasten said, standing once more in Hack's office at the castle. "I'd like to know when our Red Cross parcels will arrive."

Hack looked up from his paperwork, a disinterested expression on his face. "Red Cross parcels?"

"Herr Obersturmführer, as prisoners of war we should be receiving our Red Cross parcels sent on from Stalag Nine-B."

"Should you?" Hack replied. "Well, unfortunately, due to other priorities, the parcels have been sent elsewhere."

"Elsewhere," Kasten exclaimed, shocked. "But, that's against—"

"They have been sent to the German field hospital at Breslau," Hack said, cutting Kasten off midsentence.[14]

"On whose authority?" Kasten demanded, his face thunderous.

"Mine," Hack replied, smiling.

"But my men are dying of starvation," Kasten shouted, his rage causing him to forget who he was speaking to.

"Nonsense," Hack snapped back. "The prisoners receive adequate rations."

Kasten could barely contain himself. But he knew that trying to convince Hack otherwise was futile—the SS officer had evidently sent the Red Cross parcels elsewhere on purpose, to add to the suffering of the Americans under his control. Kasten, his mind racing with furious thoughts, was abruptly dismissed and escorted back to the camp.

*

When Kasten explained to Littell and Sinner what Hack had done with the Red Cross parcels, they were also in an uproar. They felt rage and frustration at Hack, the camp, and the entire terrible situation that they had all been dumped into against their will.

"If only someone could get word to the Allied forces about the plight of the prisoners here," Littell said, frowning.

Sinner nodded vigorously. The three of them were standing outside of their barrack's main door. Littell looked at Kasten, who was staring at the twelve-foot-tall perimeter fence. His face had a preoccupied look on it, a look that Littell and Sinner hadn't seen before. Then, slowly and almost to himself, he spoke:

"If only someone could find a way to get out of Berga."

No one responded. It seemed an impossible proposition. And who should go on such a mission? And where were the Allies, anyway? It was killing Kasten that he wasn't able to actually influence events, to do something positive to try and sort this mess out. He might have been Chief Man of Confidence, but for all intents and purposes, he was as powerless as any man in the camp. Hack didn't want to listen to him or even care to entertain alleviating any of the Americans' suffering. He seemed to revel in it. With the disappearance of the Red Cross parcels it was now abundantly clear to Kasten and everyone else in the American camp that the umbilical link with the army stalag system had been broken. Though on the surface they remained separate from Hauptsturmführer Rohr's concentration camp, they were now but an offshoot, a subcamp of that hell. They were no more prisoners of war, under the terms of the Geneva Conventions or international law, than the poor fellows in the striped pajamas who labored alongside them in those infernal tunnels. But Kasten was right—the Allies needed to know what was happening at Berga.

The burning question was—how to get word to them?

CHAPTER 17

The Dogs of War

Conditions were so reprehensible that it was a question of whether you died obediently in the Berga work camp, or whether you might be shot and killed escaping.

Pfc. Joe Mark

Kasten," a voice shouted loudly. Kasten, who was standing outside one of the barracks on the morning of March 2, 1945, talking to some of the men, turned at the sound of his name being called. Obersturmführer Hack was striding toward him across the snowy parade square, accompanied by Hauptsturmführer Rohr, Sergeant Kunz, and a couple of SS noncoms.

"I have news!" declared Hack loudly as he approached Kasten, his voice having a mock enthusiastic tone.

He stopped a couple of paces in front of Kasten. He was grinning, and turned to his companions and winked. The other Germans all grinned back or laughed. Kasten said nothing—he just stood and stared at Hack, an undisguised expression of contempt on his face. The other Americans had all made themselves scarce at the sight of the SS.

"Well, Kasten," Hack said, turning back to the American. "The camp has just acquired two dogs. They are attack dogs, Kasten, trained to hunt people down."[1]

Hack paused, as if awaiting some reaction from Kasten. But the American just stood and stared back without a word.

"Listen, Kasten," Hack continued in a conspiratorial tone, "try to get a good night's sleep tonight because tomorrow we plan to turn you loose and see if the dogs can get you."[2]

For a moment Kasten thought that he had misheard Hack, but the leering, self-satisfied grin plastered to the SS officer's face meant that he hadn't. The color drained from Kasten's face and his stomach flipped in horror. Hack really meant to kill him. His mind raced with responses, but before he could utter a word Hack took a step closer.

"They're trained to kill, Kasten," Hack said quietly, "but such dogs should, by constant practice, be kept in top condition, don't you think?"[3]

Kasten scanned Hack's face for some sign that he was joking, but looking into the SS officer's dead eyes made it clear that he meant every word of what he had just said. For administrative purposes, the Germans could simply report that Kasten had died trying to escape. It was a monstrous plan—the scheme of a psychopath. But looking into Hack's eyes, it was now clear to Kasten that Hack was truly deranged, even by the twisted standards of Berga.

For a few seconds Hack glared triumphantly at Kasten. Then, without speaking, he turned on his heel and strode back toward the gate followed by the other Germans, his leather greatcoat skirts flapping in the freezing cold breeze, leaving Kasten alone with his disturbed thoughts. Kasten turned slowly and walked across the frozen mud and compacted, dirty snow toward his barrack, hardly noticing his surroundings. He was a man who'd just had a terrible shock. The question was, what was Kasten going to do about Hack's diabolical plan?

*

Joc Littell and Ernesto Sinner were almost openmouthed when Kasten explained what Hack had said.

"I'm not staying here," Kasten announced. The three of them had fallen into an uncomfortable silence following his revelations.

"What do you mean?" Littell demanded, concerned.

"I'm not staying here to be torn apart by dogs," Kasten replied fiercely.

"You mean escape?" Sinner asked.

"Yes," Kasten replied. His eyes had a faraway look. His mind had already begun to reduce the problem, as he had done with every other setback he had been presented with as Chief Man of Confidence. "I'm going to escape."

Before Littell and Sinner could reply, Kasten raised a hand to silence them.

"I need time to think," he said in a low, distracted voice.

Littell and Sinner glanced at each other. Kasten had just had a great shock.

"Sure, Hans," Littell replied, "we'll talk later. Whenever you're ready."

Littell and Sinner stood and went to the door. As he was leaving, Littell glanced back. Kasten was standing in the window, gazing out at the fence yonder, motionless like a statue.

*

At noon, Kasten sought out his friends. Littell knew the moment he saw him that he had something in mind—his face no longer wore a shocked, ruminative expression, but had a hard look, his eyes searching and bright.

"I'm making an escape try after dark tonight," Kasten stated.[4] Littell and Sinner both started in their chairs.

"Take me with you," Littell said, almost without thinking.

"Me too," Sinner said.[5] There was a silence in the room for a moment as Kasten seemed to contemplate what his two subordinates had said. Then he shook his head.

"Absolutely not," Kasten replied, slowly enunciating each word.

"Please!" Sinner exclaimed, excited. "We can help you to escape!"

Kasten's face remained set.

"And the three of us can all work together to get back to American lines," Littell pleaded.

"Look," Kasten said sharply, "you're both staying here. In the first place, that son of a bitch Hack has nothing against the two of you."

Littell and Sinner both started to speak, but Kasten raised his hand to silence them.

"In the second place, the chances of success are about one percent. The answer is no."[6]

But Littell and Sinner were having none of it. They pressed Kasten over and over, shooting down his arguments and objections until they eventually won him over. It would make more sense for the three of them to go than just one man. They could support each other. They all spoke fluent German and could hopefully blend in to the local population. The objective of the escape was twofold: to save Kasten's life, and to follow his original plan of getting word about what was happening at Berga to the Allies. Three men would have a greater chance of success than just one man on his own.

"We'll need supplies," Kasten said, once he had grudgingly accepted the offer of their company.

"I'll see what I can find," Sinner replied. He knew that pickings would be slim, as everyone was on virtual starvation rations.

A long discussion followed about where to go. The prisoners had only very scanty information about where the front line was located, and it appeared that Berga was still a long way from the action. In the west, the Anglo-American forces were busy clearing out the remaining German units west of the Rhine, before planning to leapfrog the river in a huge offensive in late March. Before this got underway, the Americans would score a notable success when they chanced upon and captured an intact bridge over the Rhine at Remagen on March 7. So, on March 2, when Kasten made his decision to escape, he and his companions were more than three hundred miles from the nearest American lines.

In the east, the Red Army had steamrolled through Poland and entered Pomerania, driving up to the east bank of the Oder River. Budapest had fallen and other Soviet forces were threatening Vienna and eastern Austria. The closest Soviet forces to Berga were about 250 miles away. Kasten took the decision to head roughly west toward the advancing American forces.

Even if everything went according to plan, the journey on foot would take weeks, and the three of them could not have been more ill prepared. Hack's sudden announcement had forestalled any proper escape planning—everything was to be ad hoc and spur of the moment. But there was no choice. If Kasten stayed put, Hack would undoubtedly carry out his threat on March 3.

After a few hours of scrounging around the camp, Kasten, Littell, and Sinner reassembled in their barrack with their meager supplies.

"I managed to get half a loaf of bread," Sinner said, placing one of the German's horrid black rye concoctions on the table. "And this," he continued, producing a small tin from his pocket that contained a little margarine.[7]

"We won't get far on that," Littell said, sighing. It was all the food they could manage to find in the camp, such was the dire state of the supplies the Germans issued.[8]

"I've got some *Reichsmarks*," Kasten said, pulling out a few crumpled banknotes from inside his jacket. Some of the more enterprising GIs had managed to hide some banknotes in the linings of jackets, avoiding German searches.

"How much?" Sinner asked.

"Sixty," Kasten replied. "It's enough to buy some food and perhaps the occasional roof over our heads."[9] Kasten also explained that he intended to mostly live off the land.

"The farmers stack sugar beets in the corners of their fields to feed their cattle during the winter. We can eat those."[10] It wasn't particularly appetizing, but better than starvation.

"Anything else?" Littell asked.

"Just these," Kasten said, placing a safety razor and two blades on the table. "We'll need to keep up our appearances. If we look like bums, we'll be arrested for sure."

"But what about our clothes, Hans?" Sinner asked, concerned. The three of them glanced at their own uniforms and those of their companions.

"I'm afraid there just isn't time to try and alter them much," Kasten said. Under normal circumstances, any escapee would try and obtain civilian clothes, or at least modify his uniform so that it looked less "Allied."

"I guess we could cut the buttons and epaulettes off your coats," Kasten said.[11] Over their regular uniforms, Littell and Sinner had retained their US Army olive drab greatcoats, which were fitted with brass buttons embossed with the American eagle. Kasten was better off—he still had an olive drab reversible to white smock-like combat jacket. It was agreed that they would alter their clothing once out of the camp, to avoid drawing any attention from the guards. Kasten also said that he would shave off his moustache and beard. He was too easily recognizable, and once the Germans discovered they had escaped at morning roll call on March 3, the search would begin, with their descriptions widely distributed. Better to not stand out.

Kasten glanced out of the window. Snow was falling steadily.

"We'll move around at night and try to use the snow to

disguise our uniforms." Relying on Nature's camouflage was a massive risk, but there was no choice.

"Finally, there are these," Kasten said, placing six sticks of dynamite and their blasting caps on the table. Littell and Sinner both looked at Kasten in alarm. He had had the sticks smuggled to him from shifts working in the tunnels.

"Just in case," Kasten said, a grim smile on his thin face.[12]

*

"Take me with you," Pfc. Morton Goldstein, the de facto leader of the eighty Jewish American prisoners at Berga, begged.[13]

"What?" a surprised Kasten responded. Seconds earlier, Goldstein had breezed into Kasten's barracks. Though exhausted by labor in the tunnels, Goldstein had lost none of his can-do spirit, even in the appallingly trying circumstances he and his fellow Jews found themselves in.

"Don't play coy with me, Kasten," Goldstein said. "I want in on your escape."

"No way," Kasten replied firmly.

"Come on, Kasten," Goldstein implored. "What's one more body? I got to get away from here. I have to."

"I told you, no," Kasten said flatly.

"Look," Goldstein said, his voice desperate. "How much?"

"Come again?" Kasten replied.

"How much for a place on the escape?"

"Forget it," Kasten said, increasingly annoyed by Goldstein's persistence.

"Twenty thousand dollars," Goldstein blurted out as Kasten started to walk away.

Kasten turned and stared at Goldstein.

"That's right, twenty thousand dollars in New York if you'll take me along," Goldstein said.[14]

Kasten shook his head slowly—he understood Goldstein's desperation, but so far as he knew Obersturmführer Hack had not threatened to kill him. Anyway, three young men traveling across Germany was suspicious enough, but four, well, that was bound to draw a lot of attention.

"I'm sorry, Goldstein," Kasten said. "I've made my decision." Then he stalked off to sort out some aspect of his escape, leaving Goldstein behind, alone with his disturbed thoughts.

*

"So, here's the plan," Kasten said, drawing a piece of paper from his pocket and flattening it out on the table.

Kasten had drawn a simple diagram of the American compound. The perimeter fence formed a large rectangle, with the main gate on the short western side. The rectangular barrack huts were arranged in a quadrant, with their doorways facing south. Kasten's hut occupied the northeast corner of the compound.

"First, we make a hole in the hut floor," Kasten said, pointing to the rough floorboards. "From here we can access the crawl space beneath."

In all German prisoner of war camps where the inmates lived in wooden barrack blocks, the huts were raised about eighteen inches off the ground on brick footings to prevent prisoners from digging tunnels directly from their accommodations.

"We then crawl over to here," Kasten said, using a pencil stub to indicate the long northern side of the barrack that faced the fence.

"What about the lights?" Littell asked.

The American camp was too small for guard towers mounting searchlights, but the Germans had erected four floodlights in each corner of the rectangle. These powerful beams illuminated the dead ground between the huts and the fence and created a complex pattern of shadows beside and below the huts themselves.

"There's nothing we can do about them," Kasten replied solemnly. "We will need to carefully time our move to the wire. We will move when the sentry turns at the end of his beat."

At night, Sergeant Kunz always detailed two armed sentries who patrolled clearly defined "beats" along the perimeter fence. They didn't patrol the entire fence line; rather, one was stationed in the southwest corner of the camp and the other patrolled the ground in the northeast of the camp, including outside Kasten's hut. Each sentry would walk part of the way along one of the short sides of the fenced rectangular camp, turn ninety degrees, and continue along the fence before he about-faced and traced his steps. The plan was for Kasten and his companions to wait until the sentry reached the limit of his beat, turned, and started back the way he had come. Once he had disappeared out of the line of sight, the trio would emerge from their hiding place and quickly cross the well-lit ground to the fence, which was on a slight incline.

"That's going to be tight," Sinner exclaimed. "Very tight." He was referring to the sentry. "How much time are we going to have before the Heinie reappears?"

"Well, we can't make a move until he's out of earshot," Kasten replied. "He may have his back to us as he marches away, but he could hear us crawling out from under the barracks, or see our footsteps in the snow. I think we should have about two minutes before he reappears, maybe less."

"Jeez!" Sinner said. "Is that going to be enough time?"

"And what about the other sentry, the one patrolling near the main gate?" Littell added.

The other sentry's beat extended to under the floodlight in

the northwest corner of the fence, before he about-faced and quickly disappeared out of the line of sight behind a hut.

"We will have to watch both sentries for a while from under the hut," Kasten replied. "Understand their patrol pattern. Then we make our move."

"Jeez, Hans, I don't like it," Sinner said, scratching his head. "It's going to be tight, very tight."

"I know," Kasten replied. "I *did* tell you this has about a one percent chance of success, remember?"

"Okay, so we manage to cross the ground to the fence without being seen," Littell interrupted. "Then what?"

"We make a hole in the fence," Kasten said, reaching into his pocket. "With these." He laid a pair of homemade wire cutters on the table. They were pretty rudimentary but would get the job done.

"Where'd you get those?" Sinner asked, intrigued.

"While you guys were trying to find us some rations for the trip, I spoke to a few people," Kasten replied, smiling. "They'll do."

"And then what?" Littell asked.

"Then, gentlemen, we head west. I calculate that we need to march at least twenty-five miles a day," Kasten said.

"For how long?" demanded Sinner.

"About twelve days should do it," Kasten said. "Twelve days of hard marching and we'll be home free in American lines."

"Twelve days marching in that," replied Sinner, pointing out the window at the snow that was falling steadily, blanketing the region. "On half a loaf of bread and some beets?"

Kasten picked up the diagram and walked over to a potbellied stove, where a low fire glowed inside. He opened the stove and pushed the paper inside, where it flared briefly before turning to ash. Then he turned to his friends.

"What's the first rule in the army?" he asked. "Never volunteer." Then he smiled broadly, his tired face lighting up with good humor that broke the tension.

Littell and Sinner, the two volunteers, grinned as well. Looking at Kasten, it was hard to believe that they wouldn't succeed—he still exuded confidence like a warm sun on a cold winter's day. They had chosen this path themselves. Now it was up to the three of them to make the escape a success.

"When do we leave?" asked Littell.

"An hour after the barracks are locked for the night," replied Kasten without any hesitation. It was almost impossible to believe that, all going well, the three of them would soon be free, free for the first time since capture in the Ardennes, and, most importantly, free of the hell of Berga.

*

A few hours later, Kasten, Littell, and Sinner lay on their bellies under the barrack. It was completely dark underneath the building. They listened as guards shuttered the barracks' windows and bolted the doors, closing the prisoners in for the night.

The three fugitives lay still, shivering violently from a combination of biting cold and fear. The floodlights had been switched on, and, peering ahead of them, they realized that an opportunity had presented itself. The two floodlights at the northern end of the camp, including the one beside Kasten's hut, had failed to come on. There was evidently some electrical fault.[15] Kasten could see that the two floodlights at the southern end of the camp backlit his hut, causing the building to throw a shadow across half the space he and his friends needed to cover to reach the fence. They had caught a lucky break.

Littell tugged at Kasten's sleeve. He turned. Littell pointed off to the side, where a pair of boots could be seen slowly tramping along in the snow past the barrack. Kasten nodded and smiled. The sentry had come on duty just like normal. He began to watch those boots carefully as they appeared and disappeared like clockwork. Kasten had no watch, so he counted silently beneath his breath, his teeth chattering. After a while he had the sentry's timings down pat. As the guard walked past once more, heading away from Kasten's hut, Kasten beckoned to Littell and Sinner to follow.

Crawling on their bellies, the three prisoners carefully approached the edge of the dark area beneath the hut. Beyond they could see the tall perimeter fence, glistening with ice and moisture. Then the sound of boots came again as the sentry returned. This time they could see him fully as he reached the corner, turned ninety degrees, and walked along between the hidden escapees and the fence before reaching the limit of his beat and returning. The German was evidently cold. He had the collar of his greatcoat turned up to his eyebrows, almost meeting the brim of his steel helmet.[16] A Mauser rifle was slung over his right shoulder, and his breath plumed in the frigid air like smoke.

Kasten watched the sentry walk back to the light at the corner and march out of sight. He quickly looked left to where the other sentry would occasionally appear, but the broken flood light made it impossible to see anything. He didn't hesitate.

"Now, come on!" he said in a fierce whisper, shaking Littell and Sinner out of their trancelike states. With their hearts beating in their mouths, the trio struggled free from beneath the hut and began to commando-crawl across the snow toward the fence, their thin bodies aching with cold and tension.

The crawl lasted only a few seconds, but for Kasten and friends it felt like an hour as they powered through the snow, out from under the shadow cast by the building, and into the strong glare thrown by the other floodlights. Kasten reached into his pocket and with shaking fingers managed to get the wire cutter's teeth to connect with the fence, as the other two held it steady to prevent any noise. Each time the cutters bit through another link, the snap sounded as loud as gunshots to the terrified prisoners.

Once an opening had been made, Kasten and Littell pulled the fence apart and Sinner squeezed through the gap. Then he pulled from the outside, while Kasten pulled inside and Littell flung himself through the gap. Finally, Sinner and Littell held the fence apart for Kasten. He was halfway through when the guard reappeared at the corner and began to advance along the path toward where the three Americans had frozen in place, lying as still as they could in the deep snow, trying to control their breathing and trembling.[17]

Littell closed his eyes. All he could hear was the sound of boots tramping down the snow, coming closer and closer...

CHAPTER 18

Breakout

If you want to see our papers, why don't you call the police?
Pfc. Hans Kasten

Kasten, Littell, and Sinner hardly dared to breathe as the sentry approached. It seemed inconceivable that he would not see the three bodies lying in the snow. Only Kasten had a modicum of camouflage, with his reversible white combat jacket. Though they lay in the long shadow cast by the building, they must be plainly visible.

The guard's boots crunched closer and then his footfalls abruptly stopped. Littell screwed his eyes closed and waited for the shot, trying not to think about the sticks of dynamite in Kasten's pockets—if the guard fired and hit one of them, the results could be catastrophic for everyone.[1]

After what felt like minutes, but were in fact the briefest of seconds, the guard about-faced and began to tramp back the way he had come. It was unbelievable, for the German had halted only a few paces from where the three Americans lay in the snow, but he hadn't seen them. Probably he was so bundled up against the biting cold, the collar of his greatcoat turned up to meet the bottom of his steel helmet, that he simply couldn't see much.[2]

The three escapees let out their breath, and then Kasten

resumed pulling his frame through the gap in the wire while Littell and Sinner grasped the fence to help him. They lay still for a moment considering their options. The ground beyond the fence was well lit and wide open, with the guards' wooden barracks close by. To cross this would involve completely exposing themselves to view.

Kasten looked about himself with the furtive expression of a hunted animal. He knew they couldn't stay put—the sentry would be back to make his rounds in a few minutes. It seemed doubtful that he would miss the three prostrate men again.

When to make the attempt to cross the open ground? One mistake at this stage, one mistimed step, and they were dead men. It looked clear. Kasten glanced at Littell and nodded. The three of them rose to their feet and were about to make the dash when a bloodcurdling banshee wailing pierced the night, a noise so loud that the three Americans threw themselves once more to the ground and froze. Thinking initially that they had set off some kind of alarm, they realized seconds later that it was an air raid alert. They had barely processed this when all of the camp lights were abruptly extinguished, plunging the fence and the open ground beyond into stygian darkness.[3]

Kasten didn't hesitate.

"Run! Run!" he whispered fiercely to his companions, and the three of them leaped to their feet and started to charge forward.[4]

But at that exact moment the door to the guardroom was suddenly flung open, and sentries started to tumble out of the building, hastily pulling on greatcoats or helmets, clutching rifles and machine pistols as they swore and cursed. There was no time for Kasten and the others to stop. Seconds later, the Americans tore right through the straggling line of guards and were away. By a great stroke of luck, the guards had dashed from a well-lit room into total darkness, and their eyes had not adjusted in time to see the three prisoners fly past and disappear into the snowy night.[5]

Kasten, Littell, and Sinner moved as fast as they could away from the camp. The wail of the air raid siren still deafening, the racket covered the sounds of their feet and legs hauling through the deep snow.

*

The trio pressed on through the night, trying to make as much distance as possible before dawn. But it was not easy. The weather greatly complicated matters. They were not only fighting the cold but also experiencing problems navigating. They had no compass, and the overcast, snowy weather meant that navigating by the stars was out of the question. Instead, they relied on Kasten's intuition and went resolutely on, avoiding any villages or farms as they hiked cross-country.[6] But it was slow going, and as the first tendrils of light began to appear on the horizon they slowed and started to look for somewhere to hide and rest up for a while. Kasten picked a stand of timber, and once they were hunkered down among the fir trees, they could rest their aching legs and feet.

"How far do you think we've come?" asked Littell, rubbing his sore, cold feet with his hands.

"I'd say no more than fifteen miles," replied Kasten. He extracted a razor blade from his pocket. "We'd better do what we can about our appearances," he continued, pointing to Littell and Sinner's US Army greatcoats.

For the next half an hour the trio tried to change how they looked. They cut off the shoulder straps on the two greatcoats and then sliced off the brass buttons embossed with an American eagle, tossing them away into the undergrowth. Then Kasten took the safety razor and painfully shaved off his moustache and beard, which was difficult without hot water and soap.[7] His two companions stared at him afterward—without his Vandyke, Kasten looked younger and more vulnerable somehow, all except his eyes, which still had the searching, piercing look of a bird of prey.

Kasten carefully distributed their meager supply of black bread and margarine among them, and they ate virgin snow to quench their thirsts, for though it was freezing cold, the pace of the night march had left all three of them thirsty. They were very out of shape after weeks of imprisonment, and Kasten told Littell and Sinner to get some shut-eye—he would remain on watch and swap with one of his companions later. Littell and Sinner gratefully lay down on some spruce boughs, trying to stay off the wet snow, and soon fell into a heavy, exhausted sleep after their thin breakfast.

Kasten remained on watch, sitting on a log, his eyes darting here and there among the trees, listening to the sounds of the forest coming to life as March 3, 1945, dawned overcast and dreary. His mind was not in this little patch of German woodland but miles away at the American camp at Berga. There, too, Americans were beginning to stir from a restless slumber. Kasten sighed, for he knew that within the hour the disappearance of three American prisoners would become known to the Germans—and hell would surely follow.

*

The prisoners assembled on the *Appellplatz* as usual on the morning of March 3, 1945. It was their morning torture before one group left to labor inside the hellish tunnels. Standing in the snow, the Americans were arranged in four groups, each group corresponding to the four huts and standing in ranks five deep to make counting easier and quicker. A German junior noncom moved down the ranks of each group, making his count aloud. As each barrack was counted, the noncom would march over to Sergeant Kunz, the American camp's guard commander, and salute.

"All prisoners present and correct, Herr Feldwebel," each of the noncoms would bellow, before Kunz would return his salute.

But this morning things were not all present and correct. The noncom counting Kasten's hut first thought that he had made a mistake. He began again. Still short three prisoners. By now, many of the American prisoners knew that something was amiss, though not all had been let into Kasten's escape plan. Those who were in the know could only stand and wait, hopeful that their friends had managed to place as much territory as possible between themselves and Berga during the hours of darkness.

His face distressed, the corporal in charge of the count strode over to Kunz to report.

"Three prisoners are missing, Herr Feldwebel," he said in a low and timid voice.

"What!" exclaimed Kunz angrily. "Are you sure?"

The little corporal nodded, adjusting his spectacles and frowning. Kunz, a clipboard under his right arm, strode over to the corporal's group and started to count them himself. The corporal was right; three men were not present. Quickly, he ordered a couple of sentries to search the barracks. No one was home. Kunz tugged at his collar, which was seemingly much tighter this morning. Three prisoners had escaped on his watch. He ordered a complete search of the camp by his available guards. This took some time, but again, the three missing men were not found.

Kunz kept Kasten's hut on parade while dismissing the other three to work or other duties. Then he was called to the perimeter wire. When he arrived two sentries were bent down examining the fence. Kunz could see immediately that the fence had been cut.[8] The snow around was still disturbed, though further snowfall had made it difficult to completely understand the scene. Kunz, his stomach now full of butterflies, had to admit the truth—three American prisoners had escaped during the night. Now he had to do three things: find out which ones had gone; telephone his commanding officer, Hauptmann Merz, to report what had happened; and worst of all, inform SS-Obersturmführer Hack.

*

"Which prisoners?" demanded Hack, seated behind his desk at Castle Dryfels, the telephone receiver clamped to his ear as he listened to Sergeant Kunz's report. "What are their names, you idiot?"

"Littell, Sinner, and Kasten, Herr Obersturmführer," Kunz replied, eager to please.

"Kasten!" yelled Hack, jumping up from his chair. "Did you say Kasten?"

"Yes, Herr Obersturmführer," replied Kunz, thoroughly demoralized.

"Kasten!" roared Hack, slamming down the receiver. He marched quickly to a coat stand beside the door, pulled on his greatcoat, pistol belt, and cap, and flung open the office door. A startled Frau Teichert looked up from her typewriter.

"There has been an escape at the American camp," growled Hack menacingly. "Inform local army command and all SS and police units in a fifty-mile radius from Berga. Tell them to look for three men. I will send over descriptions shortly. Have you got that?"

"Yes, Herr Obersturmführer," replied Teichert, lifting the receiver on her telephone as Hack strode from the office and outside to where his Kübelwagen field car stood in the courtyard.

His SS private driver came to attention and saluted when Hack appeared.

"Never mind all that," growled Hack impatiently, ignoring the salute, wrenching open a rear door. "To the American camp, quickly!"

Hack's order would place all German military and police units on full alert. Within minutes of receiving this information, troops were being packed aboard trucks and ordered to set up checkpoints on all major roads and bridges, and at railroad stations. The local Hitler Youth, Nazi Party, and Volkssturm, the German Home Guard, were also alerted to be on the lookout for the three escapees. Hack sat in the back of the Kübelwagen as it hurtled toward the American compound, feeling sure that on foot in the snowy, freezing weather, the half-starved Kasten and his two companions would not get far. And when Kasten was apprehended, Hack intended to make him pay for this embarrassment, and pay in full.

*

At the camp, Hack stared at the fence and the ragged cut where Kasten and his companions had squeezed through and escaped. Sergeant Kunz and some other guards were beside him, Kunz's face a rictus of concern and fear. Hack turned to the sergeant, his furious eyes blazing.

"You idiot, Kunz," hissed Hack. "How could this have happened?"

Kunz visibly cringed under Hack's penetrating glare. "I don't know, Herr Obersturmführer," he muttered, casting his eyes to the ground.

"This is incompetence, Kunz, rank incompetence," bellowed Hack. "This is what comes of putting old men and cripples in charge of security!"

He demanded to see the sentry who had been on duty in this sector of the camp during the night. The man, a middle-aged private, was plainly as terrified as Kunz. Hack bellowed at him as well, refusing to listen to the man's explanation.

"I will see that you are dismissed for this, Kunz," Hack said in a low, menacing voice.[9] Then he turned on his heel and stalked off through the snow. Heads were going to roll at Berga; there was no doubt about it. And Hack would be the one holding the ax.

*

Kasten and his companions could not afford to sleep for long. By late morning they were on the road again, heading roughly northwest. They were careful to avoid main roads, along which German patrols would be driving, looking for them. Instead they moved cross-country, what British POW escapees called "boy scouting": moving across snowy fields and through quiet woods, occasionally making use of deserted tracks and minor roads. It was very hard work, the differences in terrain exhausting for men who were permanently hungry.

They stopped occasionally to dig beets out of the piles stacked in the corners of fields where German farmers had placed the fodder for their livestock through the harsh winter. Kasten's party eagerly sliced the beets up with razors and chewed down the raw vegetables, slaking their thirst as always on mouthfuls of snow.[10] They shivered constantly, and their boots were soon soaked after wading through ankle-deep snow. Kasten was particularly impatient—they weren't making enough time, and by the end of their first full day of freedom he estimated that they had hiked about sixteen or seventeen miles. They needed to quicken their pace if they stood any chance of reaching the American lines far to the west. The pressure to get west would lead Kasten and his friends to take a risk, always a dangerous decision.

*

When the trio awoke on the morning of March 4 from a cold and uncomfortable night spent huddled together for warmth under fir boughs deep inside a stand of timber, it was a terrible effort to get up. Every fiber in their thin bodies ached from the previous day's exertions.[11] At this point, huddled for warmth in the snowy woods, the barracks at Berga looked almost palatial in comparison. But they reminded themselves that they were free, and they intended to remain so. After a hurried breakfast of raw sugar beet and snow, the three men started off.

Around 1400 hours, the sky grew more overcast and then it started to snow. Kasten stopped and looked up.

"We can use the snow for cover," he told the others.[12] He intended to make up more time by using main roads, regardless of the risk of running into Germans. The snow would coat their clothing, helping to disguise them. It seemed like a sensible decision. They hooked off the field they were crossing and soon found a good road pointed roughly west. They stuck to this for the rest of the day, the level surface making for much easier going. Every so often, they would pass a German civilian going the other way. They hardly paid the three Americans any attention, for everyone's clothing and hair was white with snow. The stranger would give a jaunty *"Heil Hitler!"* which Kasten and his friends soon became accustomed to returning with gusto.[13]

At 2100 the Americans approached the small town of Göschwitz.[14] They had made up plenty of time and had managed to march more than fifty miles from Berga in two days. But being outside in the winter elements was starting to take its toll on all three of them. They needed to get inside and warmed up before they developed hypothermia. But that would mean going into the town and interacting with local Germans. The language barrier was no problem for any of them, but their appearances might give the game away—three young men in strange clothes, particularly as the alert concerning their escape from Berga must have gone out. Fortunately, Göschwitz was just beyond the fifty-mile limit of the security cordon the Germans always erected once prisoners escaped from a POW camp. But, still, the Germans were not stupid—if they failed to apprehend them, they would simply extend the search area until they did. Kasten was in a quandary. Night had fallen, and the darkness and snow would provide excellent camouflage for them to enter the town.

"We'll try and get a room for the night," explained Kasten, who still had 60 *Reichsmarks* in his pocket. "We can get some hot food and have a proper rest."[15] Littell and Sinner agreed to the plan. Both trusted Kasten's judgment completely.

The first inn that they came to looked inviting, a warm glow emanating from the doorway when the innkeeper wrenched it open.

Kasten asked for a room, his German perfect. The innkeeper guffawed loudly.

"Are you crazy?" he asked. "Don't you know that since the bombings people have been sleeping in the hallways? Try the inn up the street."[16] Then he shut the door in their faces.

Kasten looked at his companions, who shrugged their shoulders. They walked farther into Göschwitz, quickly finding the inn. But the reaction of the innkeeper was the same as that of the first: There was no room. The evacuation of civilians from the nearby cities, which were being pounded at night by the RAF and by day by the USAAF, meant that Göschwitz had absorbed a huge number of refugees. This was good news for

Kasten's group—what were three more strange faces among hundreds?—but bad news on the accommodation front.

"What about there?" asked Sinner, pointing to the tavern attached to the inn. It was crowded.

"A bit public, don't you think?" Littell said, concerned.

"We can blend in with the crowd," replied Kasten. "We need to get indoors for a few hours, and get some hot chow inside us." It was decided. They would enter the tavern.[17]

Kasten led the way, opening the door. The three of them were immediately assailed by warmth, wood, and cigarette smoke, loud conversation, laughter, and the clink of glasses. They pushed into the large, dimly lit room and looked for a table. Kasten led them through the crowd, most of whom barely glanced at the newcomers, and they sat down at a corner table, where the light was poor. To sit on a chair after the few days they had had was heavenly. To feel the warmth from the big open fireplace seeping into their frozen bones was the best feeling in the world. And perhaps it was this sudden conviviality that made them forget for a moment who they were, and where they were.

A waiter came over and took their order for sausages and beer, before disappearing back into the crowd. Kasten sat back, resting his aching back against the chair. Sinner was expectant of the meal to come; Littell was equally happy. Littell glanced at the table next to his, which he hadn't really noticed when he had arrived. His stomach gave an immediate flip. Among the patrons was a German Air Force officer. The German looked up from the conversation he was having with his companions and caught Littell's eyes. He glanced only briefly, but a little bit longer than normal, before returning to his conversation. Littell felt nonetheless uncomfortable, as if the Luftwaffe officer had seen into his very soul. He tried to ignore the growing feeling inside of him that he and his two companions were sticking out like the proverbial sore thumbs. So when the waiter returned bearing a platter of steaming sausages and three steins of beer, Littell made a big play of being absolutely normal.

"I have a terrible thirst," he announced to the waiter in a loud voice, realizing a moment too late that in his enthusiasm he had actually made a grammatical error in his German.[18] The waiter seemed not to notice or to care but, hiding his panic badly, Littell glanced at the Luftwaffe officer at the next table, who was staring at him suspiciously. Kasten and Sinner seemed not to have noticed Littell's language error, but the German officer's inquisitive look convinced Littell that he had been discovered.

CHAPTER 19

Forgive Us Our Trespasses

You realize, of course, that you will be shot.

SS Guard at Torhaus Gera

The Luftwaffe officer kept glancing at Littell's table. He had obviously heard what Littell had said to the waiter, and perhaps he had picked up on his incorrect grammar. Either way, Littell beat himself up about it inside while he, Kasten, and Sinner nibbled at their sausages and pretended to drink the beer. Kasten had warned them to take it easy, as their stomachs would not be used to rich, decent food and the alcohol would go straight to their heads.[1] As usual, Kasten was thinking ahead.

Littell couldn't contain himself any longer, the constant suspicious glances from the air force officer were driving him to distraction. He leaned over and made to confess to Kasten, but he was interrupted by the waiter, who, smiling broadly, asked the group if there was anything else they wanted. The obvious lack of suspicion expressed by the waiter calmed Littell down, and he returned to nibbling at sausage and sipping beer.

"I think it's time we resumed our journey," announced Kasten in a low voice. Littell and Sinner nodded and made to leave. Kasten paid the waiter from his small stash of banknotes, then the trio stood and started to push through the crowd toward the tavern door. They had almost reached it when Kasten felt a hand grip hold of his shoulder. He turned in alarm. The Luftwaffe officer was standing behind him. His face was serious, his blue eyes searching.

"May I see your papers?" the German officer said in a friendly voice, a slight smile crossing his face.[2]

Several nearby patrons had stopped their conversations and turned to watch. Kasten stared back at the officer for a few seconds, and seemed to pull himself up to his full height. He glowered at the Luftwaffe officer.

"We don't have to show you anything," Kasten said, his voice irritated but confident.

Inside he was panicking. They had no papers, and in Nazi Germany everyone carried papers, whether German citizen or foreign worker.

But the Luftwaffe officer seemed unfazed by Kasten's attitude and smiled more broadly. "You are trying to find a room?" he enquired.[3]

Kasten glanced at his friends, then back at the German. He nodded curtly.

"The innkeeper down the street is a friend of mine," the officer said, smiling. "I think I can help you."[4]

With that, he pulled on his greatcoat and cap, and secured his belt around his waist. The three Americans all noted the heavy automatic inside the brown leather holster.

*

When they stepped out into the street, the cold air was like a slap in the face after the convivial warmth of the crowded bar. The Luftwaffe officer walked ahead of them, and like the pied piper, the three Americans dutifully followed. They had little choice in the matter, and could only hope that he would do what he had said he would—that there was no ulterior motive in his casual friendliness and solicitude.

Kasten and the others could see where the officer was leading them—back to the inn where they had first tried to obtain a room and been rebuffed due to overcrowding.

They went into the busy and noisy main dining room and took seats. It was as crowded, smoky, and dingy as the tavern. Kasten and his companions relaxed a little, but then the Luftwaffe officer stood before the table and outstretched his gloved right palm.

"May I see your papers?" he demanded once again.[5]

Kasten realized that in order to obtain a room, one had to sign the register and have identities checked. Kasten, his stomach roiling with nervous tension, decided to bluff. There was no other recourse at this point.

"We don't have to show you anything," repeated Kasten in a level tone.

The Luftwaffe officer's eyebrows went up and he withdrew his hand.

"If you want to see our papers," added Kasten, "why don't you call the police?"[6]

The officer smiled disarmingly and instead raised a hand to stay Kasten.

"A moment," he said in a friendly manner, "I will talk to the innkeeper." Then he disappeared into the crowd of drinkers.

Kasten turned to the others and breathed a sigh of relief—it appeared that their new friend was doing what he had promised. They were left alone at the table and started to relax a little. A while passed, with the Americans occasionally glancing about the room in the hope of seeing the Luftwaffe officer returning with good news. All they wanted now was to lie down in the warm.

It was Sinner who nudged Kasten's elbow. Kasten glanced at Sinner, whose eyes were wide with alarm, then he and Littell turned to see the Luftwaffe officer moving through the crowd toward them. But he was not alone. Behind him were two German policemen, their black helmets shiny from the snow outside, rifles strung over their shoulders. The drinkers parted for the police, and a sudden hush came upon the previously cheerful room as all eyes followed the policemen as they strode over to the Americans' table.[7]

"I'll handle this," whispered Kasten fiercely.

*

The two policemen were elderly. They stood before the Americans' table with slightly bored expressions on their lined faces. The Luftwaffe officer stood beside them, hands on his hips, a concerned look on his face. The three Americans swiveled in their chairs to face their inquisitors. The older of the policemen spoke.

"Please, gentlemen, may we see your papers?" he said in a tired tone.[8]

Kasten and his companions didn't know whether the police suspected them of being escaped prisoners of war. If they had, he doubted they would have been so casual. Probably they were checking if Kasten, Littell, and Sinner, who spoke excellent German, were deserters from the army or perhaps even absconded foreign workers.

Hans Kasten sighed and then replied. "Sorry, we have no papers."[9]

This was the worst possible response in Nazi Germany. Everybody possessed papers. In a nation as bureaucratic and suspicious as wartime Germany, no one was without identity documents, even the three million foreign forced laborers who existed uneasily alongside the German population.

The policemen glanced at each other in evident astonishment, as if a dog had suddenly spoken to them, before the more senior one responded.

"What! No papers!" he exclaimed. "That just won't do!" He quickly unslung the Mauser rifle from his shoulder, his colleague following suit, and they both pointed their weapons at Kasten. "Hands up!" he ordered in a guttural voice.[10]

The crowd of drinkers started to move away from the Americans' table, their eyes round with fascination. The raucous hubbub of conversation had almost ceased as everyone watched the exciting scene unfold.

Kasten, Sinner, and Littell reluctantly stood up and raised their hands above their heads. The Luftwaffe officer had also drawn his automatic, and was pointing it in their direction. They were trapped.

Turning to his comrade, the older policeman ordered him to search Kasten and his companions. Slinging his rifle back over his right shoulder, the policeman roughly patted the three Americans down while his boss kept them covered with his own rifle.

The policeman searched Kasten last. He murmured an exclamation as he felt some objects in the American's combat jacket. Thrusting a hand inside one, he pulled out some long red painted sticks. For a moment, he didn't know what he was looking at, but then the penny dropped. Kasten closed his eyes—he knew at that moment that he and his companions were finished.

*

"Dynamite!" yelled the policeman, holding the bars aloft in alarm. "Dynamite!" he repeated loudly, his hands shaking violently.

The effect on the onlookers was electric. People rushed for the main door or dived under tables. Within seconds the room had been almost emptied. Kasten, Littell, and Sinner stood still with their hands still raised while the older policeman, his rifle shaking violently, glanced at them and then at his colleague, who was holding the dynamite at arm's length, his hands also trembling.[11]

"Take them outside," hissed the older policeman, indicating with his head the sticks of dynamite. "Quick!"

The other policeman instantly obeyed, weaving his way through the tables toward the door, a sheen of sweat prominent on his forehead. Once this task was completed, he returned and covered the Americans with his rifle while the older policeman went for help. He left the room and then Kasten could hear his muted voice talking on a telephone in the tavern's entrance hall.

*

A short time later Kasten and his friends heard the sounds of cars pulling up in the street outside, their brakes squeaking, followed by the slamming of doors. The entrance to the room was flung open and five men came in. The first two were dressed in civilian suits, black leather trench coats, and fedora hats; while the other three were in field-gray uniforms and carrying MP40 machine pistols. The group's leader, a tall man with a hard face, marched up to the policeman who was guarding the Americans and opened his palm. Inside was a metal warrant disk emblazoned with a large Nazi eagle and a stamped serial number.

"Geheime Staatspolizei," announced the civilian without preamble. "I will take the prisoners now." The Gestapo had arrived. At this point, Kasten, Littell, and Sinner knew that they were in dire straits.

The Gestapo quickly handcuffed each of the Americans, their hands held in front of them, before one uniformed guard escorted each prisoner outside to where two black cars sat

228

by the curb. The rear doors were wrenched open and Kasten was placed in one car, while Littell and Sinner clambered awkwardly into the other. Then the Gestapo men piled in, machine pistols poking uncomfortably into the Americans' ribs. The cars roared away. The three Americans were driven to the local Gestapo Headquarters in Gera, a town twenty-five miles to the east.[12]

*

The Torhaus in Gera was a forbidding old prison built in 1874. The Gestapo had taken it over in 1933, and their headquarters was established in the administration wing. Even in March 1945, only five weeks before Gera would surrender to the advancing US Army, the prison housed a daily average of 154 inmates who were living in appalling conditions and subject to arbitrary torture and execution.[13] When Kasten and his comrades arrived at the prison, the inmates were nearly all Germans arrested as political opponents of the regime, Jews, or people suspected of defeatism or resistance to the Nazi state. The Gestapo was still shipping people out of Gera to concentration camps.[14]

Kasten, Littell, and Sinner were marched into the administration wing, the guards' boots ringing on the polished floor, the air heavy with the smell of disinfectant and misery. They were told to sit quietly on a hard wooden bench outside a closed office door and wait. Kasten knew that after escaping from a secret concentration camp, his life and those of his companions were probably already forfeit.

They sat and waited. Occasionally there was a faraway shriek or cry from some other part of the building, or the clang of a metal door, the ringing of a telephone, or the jangle of keys. Gestapo men stamped past with files in their hands, occasionally giving the trio baleful glances as they went about their work. Even the staccato sound of a typewriter down the hall sounded menacing. In hushed tones, they tried to decide what to do.

"We should tell them the truth," whispered Kasten. "We are escaped POWs, we have rights."

The other two agreed, but would the Gestapo listen?

"No talking," shouted the armed guard who was watching the Americans.

The trio fell into an uneasy silence as they waited for something to happen.

*

Quite suddenly, the office door opposite the bench was flung open. The sentry quickly grabbed Joe Littell and shoved him through the door into a well-lit room. Two German officers sat behind a long wooden desk. The sentry hastily unlocked and removed Littell's handcuffs.

One of the men behind the desk appeared to be the local Gestapo chief. He was in a field-gray SS uniform, with a brown shirt and black tie. His shoulder straps indicated a *Sturmbannführer*, or major. He was short and rotund and sported a bristly toothbrush moustache just like the Führer, whose portrait dominated the wall behind the desk. Littell was surprised to see an army colonel sitting beside the *Sturmbannführer*. He was slim and erect, middle-aged, and wearing rimless glasses that made him look rather like Heinrich Himmler. From the way that the army officer spoke to the Gestapo man, it was evident that he was in charge of the interrogation.[15] Having an army officer present was a good sign. Perhaps their identities as prisoners of war had already been established. After all, the alert had been posted from Berga camp.

"Take off your clothing," ordered the Gestapo chief, without introduction. Behind Littell stood the guard, his machine pistol leveled at the American's waist. Littell began to strip in the freezing room. As he removed each item of clothing the guard snatched it from his grasp and handed it to the *Sturmbannführer*, who searched it carefully.

"What are you three doing?" demanded the army colonel, his glare penetrating.

"Are you spies?" he continued. "Are you commandos dropped behind the German lines to disrupt communications? You'd better tell me exactly what you were doing or the very worst will happen to you."

It was all rather melodramatic, but for Littell, standing buck naked in the cold room inside Gestapo headquarters, it was nonetheless horribly real. These men meant business, and Littell realized that Kasten had made the mistake of his life when he had decided to bring along the sticks of dynamite. A charge of sabotage was clearly uppermost in the minds of the colonel and his Gestapo minion.

"We are American prisoners of war," replied Littell, holding the colonel's stare. "Two days ago we escaped from Work Camp 650 in Berga an der Elster. Our one, our *only*, objective was to find our way back to the American lines."

"Nonsense!" yelled the colonel, his face fierce. "If it was such a harmless little outing, as you assert, what was the dynamite for?"

Littell's stomach did a flip. What defense was there that he could plausibly make? Dynamite is highly explosive. The colonel's line of questioning was evidently moving toward a charge of attempted sabotage, a crime punishable by death. Littell's mind raced as he tried to think of a reply that would defuse the situation, but he couldn't think of anything convincing.

"We took a few sticks of dynamite along just in case of an

emergency," ventured Littell, his voice low and hesitant. "We never once discussed how or when we might use it."

The colonel's lip curled into what approximated to be a smile, but it looked more like the leer of a cat contemplating a particularly plump canary. He muttered something to the Gestapo chief, who was making notes on a pad in front of him.

"How did you escape from Berga?" asked the colonel, changing tack. A barrage of similar questions followed rapidly. He wanted to know how the Americans had managed to get out of the camp, what routes they had taken to reach Göschwitz, where they hoped to go next, who they had spoken to, and so on. Littell did his best to answer as truthfully as possible, as the trio had agreed. But it was evident that the colonel wasn't all that interested in the truth—he seemed to have another agenda entirely. It didn't take a genius to work out that these three American prisoners of war had escaped from a completely illegal work camp where they had been part of a top secret Nazi project. They knew exactly what was happening at Berga, which was in flagrant violation of the Geneva Conventions, placing the German Army in an awkward legal position. But the discovery of dynamite gave the Germans an out. Prisoners of war caught engaged in acts of sabotage could be legally executed under international law.

"Whatever the truth," the colonel warned Littell at the conclusion of the interrogation, "you three have created a very serious situation for yourselves." The colonel turned to the *Sturmbannführer*.

"Have him locked up for the night," ordered the colonel.

"*Jawohl*, Herr Oberst," replied the major obediently, before pointing at the pile of Littell's clothes with his pen. The guard quickly stepped forward and threw the garments at Littell's feet.

After hastily dressing, Littell was led out by the guard to

where his friends were waiting on the hard bench. Before he had a chance to speak to them, he was marched away down the corridor, then down a flight of steps to a basement cellblock. In the meantime, Kasten was marched into the office for a very similar interrogation, to be followed by Sinner. The questions were much the same, though in Kasten's case they concentrated on the dynamite.

*

Littell arrived outside a small cell. The door was opened and the guard unceremoniously shoved him inside. As the guard turned the large key in the lock he looked at Littell through the bars.

"You realize, of course," the guard said in a friendly, conversational tone, "that you will be shot."[16]

Littell stood in the freezing white cell, listening as the guard's footfalls echoed away down the corridor, and he had never felt so alone or frightened in his entire life.

CHAPTER 20

The End of the Line

A traitor is still a traitor, beard or no beard.
SS-Obersturmführer Willi Hack

Kasten, Littell, and Sinner passed a very uneasy night at Gestapo headquarters in Gera, locked into adjacent cells. The jailer shouted at them if they attempted to communicate. So they each spent a long night alone with only their own thoughts for company, sitting in a little white painted cell where a single lightbulb burned brightly, the combination of fear and light negating any meaningful sleep. As far as Joe Littell was concerned, it was his last night on earth. The guard's casual warning about his fate as he had locked the cell door had deeply unsettled him. He was convinced, as were Kasten and Sinner, that come the dawn they would be taken out into the prison courtyard, where three wooden posts had been cemented into the floor, and summarily executed by firing squad. What possible outcome could there be? They had escaped from a top secret concentration camp, had knowledge of a highly classified military project, and to cap it all off, they had been caught in possession of stolen explosives and detonators.

That night was true torture. The deathly silence of the cellblock was broken occasionally by the unfamiliar sounds of the prison, the faraway, echoing screech of some poor unfortunate person being tortured, the crack of jackboots on concrete floors, the distant ringing of a telephone on the floor above. None of the sounds was a comfort to the wretched Americans who crouched upon hard wooden bunks, shivering uncontrollably with cold and fright. Their minds took them home to parents and loved ones that they would never see again, to the sorrow of not being able to say good-bye, and the knowledge that their deaths would probably never be revealed to the American authorities, leaving their parents in the perpetual limbo of never knowing the true fates of their sons. And then the black square of window set high up in the cell wall began to lighten to gray—dawn was breaking. The last day of their lives was upon them.

*

Littell stiffened as he heard the steady tread of boots approaching his cell door. It was the sound of death coming to visit. He had pictured the scene a hundred times during the unending torture of the past night. The cell door would be unlocked and an SS man would enter, shackle his hands together with steel cuffs, and escort him the few steps to the yard door. Littell would be led through and toward one of the wooden posts, where two more SS men would lash him securely, before the light was forever extinguished by a blindfold tightly wrapped over his eyes. But before he lost his vision he would see a line of SS, each with a rifle, waiting for the order. And then...

Littell stood on shaking legs and prepared to face the end. The key jangled in the lock and the door swung open. In stepped an SS man, but instead of handcuffs and a blindfold he carried a tray of food. Breakfast! Without a word, the SS man set the meager breakfast on the wooden bed and withdrew, locking the door.[1]

Littell could scarcely believe what he had seen. But he knew one thing for certain—the Gestapo didn't feed condemned men breakfast. He could hear the guard unlocking Kasten's and Sinner's cells and the clatter of metal trays. They had all been spared. Reprieved! He glanced at the tray—it contained a slice of black bread and a cup of ersatz coffee. He stifled a nervous laugh, then he sat down hard. He found he had no appetite.[2]

*

Kasten, Littell, and Sinner were reunited at 1000 hours, when they were escorted back up the stairs to the Gestapo chief's office. The door was opened and the three Americans roughly shoved inside, where their jaws almost hit the floor. Standing in the center of the room was none other than Obersturmführer Hack. A malevolent grin was plastered across his face. Behind him stood two SS guards from the concentration camp at Berga. The Americans formed a line in front of him, but Hack's eyes were fixed on Hans Kasten, and Kasten alone.

"So!" shouted Hack, "you escaped! And Kasten, I see you have shaved your beard!"[3]

The Americans stood stock-still and waited. Hack was highly unpredictable, and they knew that their escape had been a humiliation for him. They also noticed that neither the Gera Gestapo chief nor the army colonel from yesterday's interrogations was present. Hack evidently had enough sway to see the Americans in private. It didn't bode well.

"Come, come now, Kasten," Hack said in a fake conversational tone, "you think you can deceive others by shaving it off? A traitor is still a traitor, beard or no beard."[4]

Kasten said nothing in reply, staring at a space a foot above Hack's left shoulder. Hack started to pace around in the room, like a tiger prowling impatiently inside a zoo cage.

"I have already given the order as to what shall be done with you," announced Hack. "No one will much care whether you have a beard or not after you and your two friends here have been shot."[5]

Kasten, Littell, and Sinner blanched. It was true after all—they were to be executed. The dawn firing squad had merely been postponed to allow Hack time to gloat over their recapture and deliver the news in person.

A cloud passed over Hack's face. Suddenly, he pushed Kasten hard in the chest. The American's head slammed into the wall behind him. Then Hack snatched up one of the SS guards' rifles, and struck Kasten viciously in the chest with the butt. As Kasten groaned breathlessly and crumpled down the wall, Hack and the two SS men attacked him with rifle butts and boots, beating him mercilessly until he passed into merciful unconsciousness.[6]

Hack, panting from the exertion, sweat running down his face, turned to Littell and Sinner, who flinched, expecting that he would now attack them. Instead, he pointed at the bleeding, motionless body of Kasten.

"Take this garbage back to his cell," he shouted, spittle flying from his mouth like a rabid dog. Then, seemingly once more in control of himself, he straightened up, smoothed down his uniform—now speckled with Kasten's blood—and left.

*

Littell and Sinner struggled to carry Kasten's unconscious body down the stairs, urged on by two SS guards. Kasten started to come around, and his comrades did what they could for him, using their clothes to wipe away some of the blood on his face. But the SS ordered them to put Kasten back into his cell, and they were forced to leave him on his bunk before returning to their own cells.

After a while, Littell and Sinner could hear Kasten moving around, groaning and coughing. They returned to considering their fates. It seemed clear that Hack meant what he said—they were to be executed. But would they be simply put to death, or would there be some kind of formal procedure beforehand? Littell and Sinner had no idea.

*

Two hours later, the three Americans were herded once more up the flight of stairs to the office. Kasten walked with difficulty, holding his ribs with one hand, one side of his face swollen and bruised, but he was at least conscious and aware of his surroundings. Littell and Sinner helped him to remain upright, as they could see he was in some pain.

Kasten and the others stood to attention before the desk, where the army colonel from the night before now sat with two junior officers. The colonel looked agitated and jumped to his feet, pacing the room, an angry expression on his face.

"Are you aware that on February thirteenth and fourteenth, American and British fliers slaughtered over fifty thousand innocent women and children in day-and-night bombings of Dresden? Do you know that?"[7]

The three Americans said nothing. What could they say? The colonel stomped over and stopped in front of Kasten, who visibly straightened, his defiance and pride obvious.

"*Do you know that*!?!" screamed the colonel into Kasten's bloody and bruised face.

Kasten said nothing. One eye was bloodshot and swollen, but he stared defiantly back at the German officer.

Suddenly, the colonel raised his right hand and slapped Kasten hard across the jaw. The sound was loud in the room. Kasten barely flinched, his eyes remaining locked on the German.

Then the colonel's left hand connected with the side of Kasten's face with another resounding whack. Still Kasten stared at the colonel with disdainful defiance written across his face. Littell thought he knew what Kasten's expression meant: *You can get me, and you can get my two buddies, but you can't get the Americans. They're coming. They're on the way. And believe me, buster, whatever you do to us, somehow, somewhere, sometime soon, you'll pay for it. Trust me.*[8] And he had an inkling that the colonel read Kasten's eyes as well.

The German started to pace the room again. He seemed to be considering his options. Hack was an SS officer, and he had announced two hours before that Kasten and his friends were to die. But the colonel outranked him and would share the responsibility for the Americans' deaths, since prisoners of war fell under army jurisdiction. The colonel knew better than most the dire state of Germany's defense; he must have known that the writing was already on the wall for Hitler's Germany. As with many people forced into a corner by circumstances, the colonel decided to pass the buck. He stopped pacing and turned to one of his aides.

"Take these three to Stalag Nine-C at Bad Sulza," he said curtly. "Solitary confinement."[9]

It seemed that Kasten, Littell, and Sinner would not die after all—at least not yet.

*

"Shame on you! Shame!" yelled a highly agitated old man into Hans Kasten's face.

Just feet away, a woman spat onto the cobbles in front of the three Americans, while other townspeople pelted the terrified prisoners with horse dung, screaming invectives and threats as they did so.[10] Kasten and his friends feared for their lives as they were jostled through the streets of Gera toward the railroad station, prior to beginning their journey to Bad Sulza. The commotion had begun when a man watching the three prisoners being escorted through the town decided that they were American airmen. The level of fury felt by ordinary Germans toward what the Nazi propaganda machine had labeled as "terror fliers" was immense, and more than a few shot-down Allied airmen had been lynched by enraged crowds or badly beaten by mobs. As city after city was reduced to smoldering ruins, their anger was understandable.

Within minutes of the man shouting out that Kasten's group were American airmen, a large and very hostile crowd of townspeople gathered to hurl abuse and excrement at them. Only two guards were escorting the Americans—just a lieutenant and a sergeant, who had a devil of a time trying to protect their prisoners from mob justice.

The lieutenant drew his automatic and bellowed at the top of his voice: "They aren't airmen—they are ground troops!"[11]

His shouts calmed the crowd, who ceased pushing, shoving, and throwing things. They drew back muttering and glaring balefully at the Americans, but the prisoners were allowed to continue their march to the station.

*

At Weimar, Kasten and his friends were escorted off the train and handed over to the Stalag IX-C authorities. Hustled outside into the freezing cold night, the prisoners were unshackled from each other and, still individually handcuffed, were placed in two field-gray-painted staff vehicles for the short drive to Bad Sulza.

The cars stopped at the camp's main gate, and Kasten peered out of a frosted-up car window at the all-too-familiar sight that greeted him—his third prison camp of the war. More wooden huts, tall guard towers, and probing searchlight beams, all so depressingly familiar.

Stalag IX-C was a large camp, divided between several different locations. The camp headquarters, where Kasten and his friends were taken, was located near the village of Bad Sulza, thirty-five miles northwest of Berga between Erfurt and Leipzig in Thuringia. It was also the location of the head-quarters of Landesschütz Battalion 621, providing the guards for several camps, including the platoon watching the Americans at Berga.[12]

Some three thousand POWs were housed at Bad Sulza, but this was a tiny fraction of the almost fifty thousand prisoners under the authority of Stalag IX-C. There were three branch camps. The first was at Mühlhausen and consisted of British and American prisoners laboring in potassium mines. The second was at Bad Langensalza, full of Red Army prisoners, and the third was at Molsdorf, holding Italians. In total, the prisoners were subdivided into 1,700 labor detachments working in salt mines, stone quarries, the aforementioned potassium mines, and a plywood factory, demonstrating just how valuable POW labor had become to the German war industry.[13]

The headquarters at Bad Sulza consisted of long wooden barrack huts, with 160 prisoners crammed into each one. Short of beds and mattresses, the prisoners slept in shifts. There were guard towers, a dry dike on the southern side of camp, and a rail-road line to the northwest; the camp was surrounded by farmers' fields and wooded hills, overlooked by Sonnenburg Castle. The prisoner population when the Americans arrived included 2,000 French, 500 Soviet, and 350 British.[14]

*

"*Aus, aus*," shouted the prisoner escort at Kasten, Littell, and Sinner. The three men shuffled with difficulty from the backseats of two German staff cars, their handcuffed hands making this simple task clumsy and slow. Impatient German guards grabbed each man by the arm or neck and dragged them to their feet.

"*Marsch!*" bellowed a German sergeant, and the three Americans were frog-marched toward a long, low fieldstone building in one corner of the camp, passing through an inner security gate.

Originally part of Buchenwald Concentration Camp, the Bad Sulza camp housed a *Haftbaracke*, or solitary confinement barrack, constructed of fieldstone and divided into forty small cells. Troublemakers and perpetual escapees were sent to solitary cells for set periods of punishment.[15] When Kasten and his friends arrived, the building housed six Frenchmen and eight Red Army POWs, all serving sentences for striking guards or trying to escape from other camps.

On arrival inside the dimly lit, freezing-cold building, the three Americans were formally handed over to the jailer, a short, fat, middle-aged corporal named Werner Quint. With a couple of assistants, Quint marched the prisoners down a long corridor, twenty stone cells with wrought iron bars along each side. Joe Littell looked as he passed several, and inside them he saw thin prisoners lying on hard wooden beds without mattresses under dim, hanging lightbulbs, curled up in fetal positions against the chill.[16] Before he or his companions had registered their surroundings, each was pushed into an identical cell and the door slammed and locked behind them. Littell, just before the door was closed, asked Corporal Quint how long he would be kept in the prison.

"Your sentence is for six months," replied Quint impatiently, before the door was shut with an echoing boom of finality.[17]

*

The German penal system had not finished yet with Hans Kasten. Of the three American prisoners deposited in the punishment barracks at Bad Sulza, Kasten was the one whose report sheet had been marked "Saboteur." For being found in possession of the sticks of dynamite, Kasten would pay dearly through not only imprisonment, but also repeated interrogations.

Littell and Sinner heard the authorities take Kasten from his cell three nights running. They also heard his screams intermingled with the sounds of violence as his interrogators tried to beat information out of him in a cell at the end of the barrack used for such grisly purposes.[18] But the interrogations turned up no new information because there was none to give. Kasten stuck to his story that he had taken the dynamite in case of some unforeseen emergency and had not intended to use it to sabotage anything in Hitler's crumbling Reich. But the Gestapo were thorough, and it took a lot to convince them. They smashed Kasten's teeth, cracked five of his vertebrae, and left him with permanently impaired hearing before they finally gave up.[19]

Kasten was tied to a chair, blood running down one side of his face from another vicious assault, when the mood of his tormentors abruptly changed. One of the two Gestapo men was in shirtsleeves, the other in full uniform. The senior man asked the questions while his well-built subordinate administered the blows to loosen Kasten's tongue. The senior officer suddenly held up his hand, stopping the abuse. He glanced impatiently at his wristwatch.

"Finish with it," he ordered. "Shoot him."[20]

Kasten's hanging head came up slowly, one good eye glaring at the Gestapo men, the other almost closed by an ugly purple bruise. Did they mean to carry out the execution this instant? No, the Germans were sticklers for order and paperwork. He would be added to the execution schedule. Kasten was dragged back to his cell by a couple of guards and thrown unceremoniously inside to recover.

Shortly afterward, Kasten was informed of his fate.

"You have been found guilty of sabotage against the Reich, Kasten," announced the senior interrogator without preamble; the jailer Corporal Quint stood nervously beside him, a large ring of keys in his hands.

"On the thirteenth of April, you will be shot." Then the Gestapo officer turned and stalked off, his jackboots ringing on the building's stone floor.[21]

Sitting on his wooden slat bed, Kasten said nothing in reply, but his eyes burned with hate. He had five days left to live. The finality was hard to take—knowing the date of one's own death was one final torture courtesy of the Gestapo. It looked as though Kasten's luck had finally deserted him. He was doomed.

CHAPTER 21

Deliver Us from Evil

Our joy was boundless—except for one unsolvable mystery.
Pfc. Joseph F. Littell

Now that Kasten's execution date had been set, there were no more interrogations or beatings. Instead, the solitary confinement barrack jailer, Corporal Quint, began to ingratiate himself with the American prisoners. He gave them good rations of food and brought them books to read. This largesse was not out of the goodness of his heart, but rather out of fear. Gen. George Patton's US Third Army was rapidly closing on the region, and Quint, like many uniformed Germans, was in a state of nervous tension about his fate. To be caught in charge of a punishment block, where prisoners had been starved and abused, would not endear him to the Americans—in fact, he might expect a dose of short, swift, and terminal punishment courtesy of liberating GIs or liberated inmates.

The camp commandant ordered Red Cross parcels distributed, including to Kasten's little group, and they devoured the contents with alacrity. It was their first proper food in weeks.[1]

*

Kasten, Littell, and Sinner could hear freedom long before they experienced it. It was the roar and drone of aircraft engines above the camp that first alerted them to the possibility of surviving the war. American P-51 Mustang and P-47 Thunderbolt fighters wheeled low over the camp and Bad Sulza in increasing numbers and with more regularity in the days since the Americans had arrived, and the planes shot up anything they saw moving on the ground. German planes attempted to intervene, and dogfights ensued. The noise was tremendous, and the looks of nervous tension on the faces of the Germans were even more pronounced than usual.

But each day that passed with no sign of American ground forces was one less day that Kasten had to live. The Germans were a thorough people, and Kasten knew that more than most. Though the war at Bad Sulza was nearly over, it was not beyond the realm of possibility that the Gestapo would still carry out Kasten's execution on April 13, or even remove him from the camp if they retreated. Each day dragged by, Kasten surviving hour to hour, the dread knot of tension in his stomach never leaving him for a second. Would the Germans leave any loose ends?[2]

The Germans were suddenly more amenable to sharing news. Already, three-quarters of the German staff had been evacuated to Bavaria, leaving a skeleton force of just fifty men to run the camp. Corporal Quint left with the column and was replaced by Corporal Columbus. Large numbers of civilians approached the camp and threw up shelters against the fences, hoping proximity to Allied POWs would save them from the worst of the aerial attacks. Tall columns of smoke rose from railway sidings and a station near the camp as American aircraft attacked anything that moved.

Kasten could only pace his tiny cell, fearful of every footstep in the corridor outside, every guttural shout that could bring his executioners hastening toward his cell to finish the job. Kasten willed the American armored force to make it to the camp before his appointed execution day.[3]

On April 10, another column of German staff cars, bicycles, and carts departed the camp.[4] Weimar, 12.5 miles southwest, was reported as being in American hands. *How much longer?* asked Kasten silently. A day or two at most? He was due to die in three days. Barely able to sleep or rest, Kasten waited, staring up at the tiny cell window, through which only a patch of gray sky was visible. But at noon on April 11, 1945, the sounds of far-away battle were unmistakable, coming from Bad Sulza village, 2.5 miles away. All the men inside their cells strained their ears and listened. The occasional crump of artillery or tank fire could be heard, and then the burble of machine guns. The Americans were close, very close. But the Germans still controlled the camp. Time continued to drag by, agonizingly slowly.

*

Then, at 1412 hours, a commotion of raised voices grew in intensity from the main camp. A chorus of shouting in the yard near the punishment barrack filled Kasten's cell with echoing sounds. Then came the grunt and rumble of heavy engines approaching.[5] Kasten heard a commotion, and the sounds of heavy footfalls approaching down the long stone corridor between the cells. He tensed, pressing himself against the back wall beneath the high-set window. The footfalls stopped outside his cell. A key turned noisily in the lock and the door was flung open. It was Corporal Columbus. Kasten's heart sank—other figures moved in the shadows behind the jailer. The Gestapo had not forgotten about the saboteur Kasten after all. Kasten tensed for the bullet. But then Columbus was shoved roughly aside and one of the figures moved into the light. Instead of the field-gray uniform of the Gestapo, the man wore the olive drab of the US Army. Standing there was a GI, an M1 helmet on his head, a carbine held across his chest, his fatigues dirty from combat.

"You American, buddy?" asked the young, strong-looking soldier.

Kasten croaked a reply, tears welling in his bruised eyes.

"Well, you're free," said the GI, before turning and moving to the next cell.

Kasten, Littell, and Sinner stumbled outside to find the camp in an uproar. An M4 Sherman tank, looking as big and solid as a house, had pushed through the camp's perimeter wire, pulling down several yards of fencing under its tracks. The tank was surrounded by cheering, laughing, and waving French, Soviet, and British prisoners, all of them delirious with joy at being liberated.[6] The crewmen stood in the turret waving, handing out smokes, chewing gum, and candy, and grinning as though they had just single-handedly won the war.

It didn't take long for Kasten and his friends to find out what had happened. Forward elements of the US Sixth Armored Division had entered Bad Sulza at noon.[7] They were heading for the heavily defended city of Leipzig. The Shermans of the Sixty-Ninth Tank Battalion had been the first to approach the camp after fighting off a few handfuls of diehard German troops who attempted to stop their advance with Panzerfaust antitank weapons and small arms. The Shermans had dealt with them, leaving the survivors to be mopped up by armored infantry teams. The commander of Company A, Sixty-Ninth Tank Battalion had ordered his driver to plunge through the camp's perimeter fence, liberating the camp.[8] The remaining German guards had either thrown down their rifles and thrown up their hands in surrender, or fled in panic.

Just outside the camp, a long line of Shermans, along with

jeeps and trucks, was driving slowly by in the direction of
Leipzig. Each vehicle was painted olive drab with big white
stars on its turret, doors, or hood, and loaded with young but
tough-looking American soldiers.

The Sixty-Ninth Tank Battalion would not linger long at Bad
Sulza—it was needed on point as the Sixth Armored Division
plunged on toward Leipzig.[9] But within the hour a US Army
medical unit arrived at the camp to begin sorting out the mess
of ill and emaciated former POWs of many nations, and to
evacuate the worst cases to hospital.

Kasten, Littell, and Sinner, as former inmates of the punishment barrack and Berga concentration camp, were given priority
treatment. They were issued fresh uniforms, which was a relief
after weeks in the same dirty, stained, and torn clothing they had
been wearing when captured in the Ardennes.[10]

"You're to be evacuated without delay," said an American
officer. "You're being flown to France!" he added with a big
smile. The three Americans didn't know what to say in reply.

"Don't wander off now," warned the officer from the medical
unit. "A jeep will take you to Weimar where you can board the
plane."[11]

The trio was told where to wait. But after a while Kasten, who
had been curiously quiet since his liberation, disappeared.

"Where's Hans?" Littell asked Sinner.

The yard was busy with people and vehicles. One minute
Kasten had been there, the next he was gone.

"I don't know," replied Sinner, looking around. "He was
just here."

Kasten never returned. When a jeep pulled up to collect
Littell and Sinner for the ride to Weimar, Kasten had not re-
joined them. His two friends hesitated and kept looking around,
searching the crowds for Kasten's familiar face.

"Hey, I can't wait here all day," said the young GI driver, somewhat impatiently. "Are you guys coming or what?"

Reluctantly, Littell and Sinner clambered aboard the jeep, which swung around and out the open main gate of the camp, past a fleet of US Army ambulances and other jeeps and a milling thong of medical staff and former POWs. They were soon racing through the German countryside toward Weimar. Littell couldn't stop thinking about Kasten, whose face was still swollen and bruised, courtesy of the Gestapo. It would be many months before he saw him again.[12]

*

As Littell and Sinner were speeding down the country road in one direction, Hans Kasten was walking painfully but determinedly toward the village of Bad Sulza, 2.5 miles from the camp. His new uniform clung to his emaciated frame, and the bruising and cuts to his face gave him a desperate and dangerous look. His mind was on only one thing—revenge. And he wasn't going to any airport until he had had a chance to find some. That revenge had a name—SS-Obersturmführer Willi Hack.[13]

*

When Kasten arrived in Bad Sulza, the village of neat wooden houses and churches was crammed with US Sixth Armored Division units, the roads choked with tanks, half-tracks, jeeps, and trucks, all moving east. It didn't take Kasten long to befriend some GIs and ask for help. He pointed at a gray-painted German staff car that was parked beside a building.

"You using this?" asked Kasten, walking over and opening the driver's side door.

"No," replied an American sergeant. "It ain't ours. Take it, Mac."

Kasten slipped behind the wheel and tried to start the engine. It started but the fuel gauge read almost zero.

"Can I get some gas?" asked Kasten.

"Sure thing, bud," said the sergeant, who quickly spoke to a couple of his men.

They went over to their jeeps and returned a few moments later with a couple of jerry cans of fuel. One of the privates quickly topped up the Mercedes's tank, and then loaded the other can in the car's trunk.

"You'd better take this as well," said the sergeant, placing a cardboard box of C rations on the car's backseat. "You look like you could do with feedin'."

Kasten and the sergeant spoke for a few more minutes. The sergeant gave him a map of the region marked with all the known POW cages where captured German troops were being held and processed.

"Thanks," muttered Kasten grimly, his thin, bruised face serious.

"No problem, bud," replied the sergeant cheerfully. "You got unfinished business?"

Kasten's blue eyes fixed the sergeant's eyes for a moment. It was the look of a wolf searching for its prey.

"Yes," hissed Kasten, "unfinished business."

The sergeant nodded uncomfortably and stood back as Kasten gunned the Mercedes engine and pulled away in a cloud of dust toward revenge.[14]

*

As Kasten hurtled down country roads inside his commandeered Mercedes, he was consumed with one thought only—finding Hack. He drove from town to town, to holding camp after holding camp marked on his map, an emaciated-looking man dressed in a brand-new American uniform. He was frequently in pain from the driving, his back aching from the torture he had endured. At each camp, he would climb out of the car and demand to speak to whomever was in charge, asking to search among the prisoners. When Kasten explained that he had been the Chief Man of Confidence at Bad Orb and Berga, they didn't argue. His appearance spoke volumes for what he had gone through. And the Allies were more than happy to apprehend suspected war criminals. Hack was already on a list prepared some months earlier by US intelligence, but having him fingered by a former inmate of one of his camps would be a boon.

Kasten would enter the camps with armed guards and walk around, through the throngs of German POWs who, dressed in tatty field-gray uniforms, squatted on the ground or stood around looking hungry and confused, their former arrogance now evaporated. The camps smelled of fear, mud, and human waste as tens of thousands of German soldiers were slowly processed and moved around to other more permanent facilities. Among the teenage conscripts and disillusioned veterans were war criminals who had shed their SS uniforms for plain army clothes and false identity papers, hoping to disappear into the sea of German POWs. These men lived in abject fear of identification and arrest, and Kasten hunted through each camp like a man possessed, looking for men of the same basic description as Hack, and then staring into their faces in the hope of a positive identification. But everywhere it was the same—no Hack.[15]

Kasten knew he couldn't check every camp and every inmate—the task was beyond one man—but he pushed himself as much as he dared, and in the end he pushed his body beyond human endurance. He collapsed and was taken to a hospital, his abused body no longer willing to be driven along by its revenge-fevered mind. Hack eluded him.[16]

*

Only later did Kasten learn some of the story of Willi Hack's movements before his disappearance. On March 1, 1945, the SS recorded a total of 1,837 prisoners still alive at Berga. Three hundred and fourteen had already perished on Project Swallow, the victims of accidents, beatings, and executions at the hands of the German camp authorities. Morton Goldstein, the Jewish Barrack Man of Confidence, had been executed on March 15, shot in the back of the head by Sergeant Kunz's replacement, a monster named Erwin Metz.[17] Goldstein had been caught after a failed escape attempt. Pvt. David Young had died soon after of injuries that he had sustained from a brutal beating by a German foreman with a shovel on February 20. In total, forty-seven American soldiers died at Berga.[18]

On April 4, Hack had issued orders that the camp was to prepare for evacuation. The project at Berga was to be abandoned. The remaining three hundred American prisoners left on the tenth, on what amounted to a death march toward Hof. The wretched survivors, now numbering 264 men, were liberated by US forces two and a half weeks later, after their guards abandoned them. Thirty-six had perished on the march alone. In total, Hack and his cronies had killed seventy-three American prisoners.[19]

The same day the Americans began their death march, April 10, Hack and the SS leadership staff relocated to Hallein near Salzburg, Austria. The concentration camp prisoners, always kept separate from the Americans, began their own horrific march on April 12, which resulted in a great many deaths.

Six days after Hack had left Berga, the town fell without a shot being fired to the US Eighty-Ninth Infantry Division. With the evidence from Kasten, Littell, and Sinner given after their liberation, plus the survivors from the death marches, an investigation was launched at the work site by US authorities. In June, they opened graves and exhumed around twenty-six corpses that were positively identified as American, and had these remains shipped back to the States for reburial with honor. But the investigation into the crimes at Berga were short-lived, for the whole area was within the Soviet occupation zone.[20] American forces evacuated Berga on June 12, and the Red Army arrived on July 1. The diggings at Berga began to return to nature; the camps were dismantled or fell into ruins. Just another tragically forgotten wartime atrocity.

As to what became of Willi Hack, the architect of American suffering at Berga, no one knew. He had simply disappeared into the chaos of Germany. Kasten's failure to find Hack would haunt him for the rest of his life. He was never given the opportunity to face his tormentor. Such again are the fortunes of war.

*

Hans Kasten spent some time at a medical clinic in Bonn before being transferred to Camp Lucky Strike in France. On arrival, after having survived everything World War II had to throw at him, Kasten weighed only ninety-six pounds. But he had survived, and that was the only important thing to him. He would now begin his life again, but he would be haunted for the rest of what would prove to be a very long life by Berga and the horrors he and his men had witnessed. It was how all the survivors of Berga felt. It marked them till the ends of their days.[21]

Epilogue

Willi Hack

Though Hans Kasten never managed to locate Hack after his liberation, justice eventually caught up with the erstwhile commander of Berga. Shortly after ordering the remaining prisoners at Berga on a death march, SS-Obersturmführer Hack slipped away on April 10, 1945, and disappeared into the chaos of the collapsing Third Reich. He lived openly under his own name in Weissensand near Reichenbach, Sachsen. In 1947, he was recognized in the town of Zwickau by one of the former Jewish concentration camp slaves from Berga who had worked along side the Americans. Zwickau was in the Soviet occupation zone, and Hack had been visiting an old girlfriend when his luck had run out.[1] He was arrested by the police and interrogated at Osterstein Castle, where he was placed on trial for his crimes. He was found guilty in 1949 and sentenced to death, but his lawyer lodged an appeal with the Superior Court in Dresden. This ultimately led to a retrial in Zwickau in 1951. His death sentence was confirmed on April 23, and Willi Hack was hanged in Dresden on July 26, 1952.[2] He was forty years old.

Richard Rohr

In 1974, the State Attorney's Office in Cologne, West Germany, investigated the role and culpability of SS-Hauptsturmführer Rohr and other known SS guards in crimes committed at Berga. Rohr had been commandant of the slave labor camp containing inmates from Buchenwald concentration camp. This investigation was halted on February 22, 1975. Rohr had already died several years earlier, on March 11, 1969, and many other former SS officials could not be identified or traced.

Ludwig Merz and Erwin Metz

Hauptmann Merz's unit provided the army guards for the American camp at Berga and, as commanding officer, Merz bore command responsibility for the brutalities meted out by his subordinates. Even though he was not based at the camp, he visited frequently and was fully aware of the conditions and regime in place that killed seventy-three American prisoners of war in nine weeks.

Merz had been captured by the US Army on the Bavarian-Czechoslovak border on April 23, 1945. In 1946, Merz was placed on trial by the United States at Dachau, along with his subordinate, Sgt. Erwin Metz, who had taken over after Feldwebel Kunz was dismissed following Kasten's escape. In a statement that he made to the court Merz said, "My hands were bound tightly by existing regulations and the chaotic circumstances of the last months of the war. I must state that I had the feeling, and this feeling is becoming greater to me all the time, that my superior authority left me holding the bag."[3]

Both men were found guilty. Merz and Metz, who had personally murdered Pfc. Morton Goldstein, were sentenced to death. This sentence was eventually overturned, and instead

Merz and Metz served a few years in the American prison for war criminals at Landsberg before being released.

Hans Kasten

One of the first things Kasten did after leaving the hospital was to compile a list of Berga guards who had beaten or killed American prisoners. He turned this list over to the US authorities. Kasten was awarded the Purple Heart for his multiple injuries—injuries so severe that he was left with permanent health problems for the rest of his life. The beatings that he had received while in German captivity left Kasten with 50 percent hearing loss, damaged eyesight, and damaged vertebrae that caused stiffness in his neck and headaches. Both of his legs were numbed from his feet midway to the knees, and his imprisonment resulted in chronic constipation for the rest of his life, requiring the daily use of laxatives.

The US government largely buried the story of the American POWs who slaved inside a German concentration camp, offering no benefits or compensation to the survivors. It was an embarrassment to the authorities, who probably feared censure over their failure to liberate the men earlier. Hans Kasten was not decorated, even though his personal sacrifices to try and protect Jewish American GIs from segregation and illegal treatment, and his battles to improve conditions at Stalag IX-B and at Berga, were valorous and worthy of recognition.

After the war, he worked for the US manufacturing company Muller & Phipps and was sent to the Philippines to set up their operations there. He settled permanently in the Philippines, married four times, and had several children. He was known as a patron of the arts.

Johann Kasten IV died in Mahati, Philippines, on August 9, 2007, just one week shy of his ninety-first birthday. His ashes were interred at Arlington National Cemetery in April 2008.

Joseph Littell

Littell arrived back in the States in late June 1945, still painfully underweight from his imprisonment. He was immediately sent to a special rest camp at Asheville, North Carolina, to recover and build up his weight before returning to his family. On September 1, 1945, Littell was discharged from the army after receiving the Purple Heart for the leg wound he suffered in the Ardennes.

Littell entered the publishing industry, and was executive editor at Macmillan's School Department for a decade, then editor in chief of Harper & Row's School Department. He co-founded McDougall, Littell & Co. His career often took him to Germany, to the Frankfurt Book Fair, but he never once re-visited Bad Orb, which was only a short drive from the city. He also hardly discussed his wartime experiences with his family.

Settling in Fallbrook, California, Joseph F. Littell published his autobiography, *A Lifetime in Every Moment*, in 1995. He passed away on August 14, 2018, during the writing of this book, at the age of ninety-three. He is survived by three daughters and four grandchildren.

*

Sadly, the author has not been able to discover the fate of Ernesto Sinner, who survived the war and returned to the United States.

Acknowledgments

This book was only possible because of the generous assistance of so many individuals and institutions from all over the world.

Firstly, I wish to extend my cordial thanks to the veterans and their families that assisted me: Pfc. Bob Pope, 590th Field Artillery Battalion, 106th Infantry Division for kindly sharing with me his memories of combat and capture in the Ardennes and imprisonment in Germany, 1944–1945; Pfc. Richard Lockhart, 106th Infantry Division, and his son David Lockhart, for sending me fascinating information about imprisonment at Stalag IX-B; Julia Littell, daughter of Pfc. Joseph F. Littell, for kind permission to use her father's memoir and for providing photographs.

My great thanks to the following individuals for research assistance: James D. West, webmaster of the 106th Infantry Division Association, for permission to use extensive veterans' and photographic materials from IndianaMilitary.org; John R. Schaffner, historian of the 106th Infantry Division Association; Tracey Diehl of the Battle of the Bulge Association; Sgt. Damian Smith, US Army, for research assistance; Gwenne Underwood of the Twenty-Eighth Infantry Division Association; Megan Harris of the Veterans' History Project,

Library of Congress, Washington, DC; and the staff of the National Archives (Public Record Office), Kew, London; the National Archives and Records Administration, College Park, Maryland.

My thanks also to Pamela Whissel, membership director, American Atheists, Inc., for permission to use an extensive article on Hans Kasten; Leah Petrakis of Houghton Mifflin Harcourt, Orlando, Florida, for putting me in touch with the Littell family; and Ron Hussey of Houghton Mifflin Harcourt, New York City, for assistance in tracking down Joseph Littell.

Thanks also to Sabiner Stein of Buchenwald Concentration Camp archives, Germany; Daniel Schneider of the Military Archive at the Bundesarchiv, Freiburg, Germany; Lutz Möser of the Bundesarchiv, Berlin; and the Photographic Archive at the United States Holocaust Memorial Museum, Washington, DC.

My publishers have been marvelous—many thanks to Jaime Coyne, my editor at Center Street, New York City, and to Duncan Heath at Icon Books, London. A great many thanks to my literary agent, Andrew Lownie, for his support and enthusiasm during the course of writing this book.

Finally, many thanks to my wife, Fang Fang, for her assistance during field research in Belgium, Luxembourg, and Germany, and for her unfailing enthusiasm, support, encouragement, advice, and love.

Bibliography

Archival Sources

Library of Congress, Washington DC

"The Story of the War Experience of J. C. F. Kasten IV (Hans) During World War II," Experiencing War, Veterans History Project.
"Roster of Interpreters, MPs, and Leaders Among the Men of Stalag IX B."
"Letter to the International Red Cross Concerning the Fates of Men Interned in M-Stammlager IX B, Bad Orb, Germany," January 16, 1945.
Congressional Record—Senate, April 26, 2001.

The National Archives and Records Administration (NARA),

College Park, Maryland

"Rules and Regulations for the Operations of German Prisoner of War Camps," March 11, 1942.
"Personnel Card of Lt. Col. Albert Wodarg, Deputy Commander of Stalag IX B," November 16, 1943.
"Personnel Card of Col. Karl Sieber, Commander of Stalag IX B," January 2, 1945.
"Hans Kasten (Chief Man of Confidence) to the International Red Cross Concerning the Fates of Men Interned in M-Stammlager IX B, Bad Orb, Germany," January 16, 1945.
"Red Cross Report, Stalag IX-B," January 24, 1945.
"List of Men Shipped on 8 February 1945," Seventieth Infantry Division Records, Stalag IX-B Reports.

"Camp Reports: Dulag Luft to Ilag, Report on Stalag IXB—Bad Orb," March 23, 1945.

"Report of the Main Camp IX B Physician, Dr. Jaitner, Concerning the Health of the Prisoners of War and the General and Food Conditions at Stalag IX B," March 29, 1945.

"Report to Secretary of State, Washington from US Embassy, Bern, 2054 Seventh: American Interests, Germany," April 7, 1945.

"American Prisoners of War in Germany," Military Intelligence Service, War Department, November 1, 1945.

"Berga an Elster (Subcamp of Buchenwald Concentration Camp—Afro-American and Jewish-American POWs Sent There to Work in Mines)," 1945.

United States vs. Erwin Metz, et al., Deputy Judge Advocate's Office, 7708 War Crimes Group, European Command, September 15, 1947.

The National Archives (Public Record Office), Kew, London

"Stalag IXB Bad Orb—War Office: IRC and Protecting Powers (Geneva): Reports Concerning POW Camps in Europe and the Far East. Stalag IXB Bad Orb," WO 224/30, 1 March 1944–31 March 1945.

"War Office: Dept. of the Permanent Undersecretary of State: Casualties (L) Branch: Enquiries in Missing Personnel, 1939–45 War. POWs, Germany: Stalag IXB, Bad Orb, Report in Conditions, Captain T. C. N. Gibbens, RAMC," WO 361/1877, 1 June 1945–31 July 1945.

"War Office: JAG Office, BAOR War Crimes Group (NW Europe) and Predecessors: Registered Files (BAOR and Other Series). Bad Sulza and Ziegenhain, Germany: Killing and Ill-Treatment of Allied Nationals," WO 309/1186, 1 May 1947–28 February 1948.

Books

Bard, Mitchell G., *Forgotten Victims: The Abandonment of Americans in Hitler's Camps*, Boulder, CO: Westview Press, 1996.

Beevor, Antony, *Ardennes 1944: Hitler's Last Gamble*, London: Viking, 2015.

Caddick-Adams, Peter, *Snow & Steel: The Battle of the Bulge 1944–45*, London: Arrow Books, 2014.

Cohen, Roger, *Soldiers and Slaves: American POWs Trapped by the Nazis' Final Gamble*, New York: Alfred A. Knopf, 2005.

Drooz, Daniel B., *American Prisoners of War in German Death, Concentration, and Slave Labor Camps: Germany's Lethal Policy in the Second World War*, Lewiston, NY: Edwin Mellen Press, 2004.

Eisenhower, John S. D., *The Bitter Woods: The Battle of the Bulge*, Edinburgh, UK: Birlinn, 2001.

Frenkel, Paul N., *Life Reclaimed: Rural Transylvania, Nazi Camps, and the American Dream*, Bloomington, IN: iUniverse, 2013.

Gragg, Rod, *My Brother's Keeper: Christians Who Risked All to Protect Jewish Targets of the Nazi Holocaust*, London: Hachette Books, 2016.

Hackett, David A., *The Buchenwald Report*, Boulder, CO: Westview Press, 1997.

Hastings, Max, *Armageddon: The Battle for Germany, 1944–1945*, New York: Vintage Books, 2005.

Hirsh, Michael, *The Liberators: America's Witnesses to the Holocaust*, New York: Random House, 2010.

Kurowski, Franz, *Hitler's Last Bastion: The Final Battles for the Reich 1944–1945*, Atglen, PA: Schiffer Military History, 1998.

LaCroix, Hal, and Jorg Meyer, *Journey out of Darkness: The Real Story of American Heroes in Hitler's POW Camps—An Oral History*, Westport, CT: Praeger Security International, 2007.

Littell, Joseph F., *A Lifetime in Every Moment*, New York: Houghton Mifflin, 1995.

Middlebrook, Martin, and Chris Everitt, *The Bomber Command War Diaries: An Operational Reference Book, 1939–1945*, Barnsley, UK: Pen & Sword Aviation, 2014.

Mollo, Andrew, *The Armed Forces of World War II: Uniforms, Insignia and Organization*, London: Black Cat, 1987.

Moore, Deborah Dash, *G.I. Jews: How World War II Changed a Generation*, Cambridge, MA: Harvard University Press, 2009.

Pope, Bob, *My Nine Lives*, Lincoln, MA: Personal History Press, 2017.

Spiller, Harry, *American POWs in World War II: Twelve Personal Accounts of Captivity by Germany and Japan*, Jefferson, NC: McFarland & Company, 2009.

Swedberg, Claire E., *In Enemy Hands*, Mechanicsburg, PA: Stackpole Books, 1998.

Thomas, Nigel, *The German Army 1939–45 (5): Western Front 1943–45*, Oxford: Osprey, 2009.

Toland, John, *The Last 100 Days*, London, Phoenix, 1996.

Whitlock, Flint, *Given Up for Dead: American G.I.'s in the Nazi Concentration Camp at Berga*, Cambridge, MA: Westview Press, 2005

Wistrich, Robert S., *Who's Who in Nazi Germany*, London: Routledge, 2001.

Zaloga, Steven J., *Downfall 1945: The Fall of Hitler's Third Reich*, Oxford: Osprey, 2016.

Magazines and Newspapers

American Atheist
New York Times

Online Resources

IndianaMilitary.org

Veteran Accounts

Brown, Raymond, "Diary of Raymond Brown, Leeds, Utah," 106th Infantry Division.

Cavanaugh, Father Paul W., S.J., "Pro Deo et Patria (For God and Country)," 106th Infantry Division. This document contains Fr. Cavanaugh's original manuscript, "American Priest in a Nazi Prison."

Frampton, D. B., Jr., "Ich Bin Ein Kriegsgefangener: A Rather Loose Narrative by a Foot Soldier Who Got Caught in the Battle of the Bulge—December 1944."

Hannon, Philip A., "One Man's Story," 106th Infantry Division.

House, Pete, "Life in Stalag IX-B: Story of an American Held in a German POW Camp."

Kimmel, Troy H., "Troy H. Kimmel," 106th Infantry Division.

Klingman, Myron "Mike," "German Prisoner No. 25708."

Reinfenrath, John W., An American Slave in Nazi Germany: My Story of Combat, Capture, and Slave Labor," 106th Infantry Division.

Rosenberg, Theodore, "My Story as a Prisoner of Germany," 106th Infantry Division.

Vermont, Ernest B. [Ernest Valmont], "Summation of Service and Prison Experiences of Ernest Valmont, 106th Infantry Division."

Other Websites

"Gedenk- und Begegnungsstätte im Torhaus der Politischen Haftanstalt von 1933 bis 1945 und 1945 bis 1989," http://www.torhaus-gera.de.

"Germany Campaign 10 March to 16 April 1945," chap. 6 of *Combat History of the Super Sixth*, Sixth Armored Division, http://www.super6th.org/cmbthist/cmbgrmny.htm.

"Mannschafts-Stammlager (Stalag) IX B," *The Holocaust Encyclopedia*, The United States Holocaust Memorial Museum, https://www.ushmm.org.

Milmeister, Jean, "Identifying the Clervaux Castle Sherman," Diorama-Clervaux by Claude Joachim (website), http://www.diorama-clervaux.com/indexsherman.html.

Endnotes

1. Hold the Line!

1 Peter Caddick-Adams, *Snow & Steel: The Battle of the Bulge 1944–45* (London: Arrow Books, 2014), 284.
2 Roger Cohen, *Soldiers and Slaves: American POWs Trapped by the Nazis' Final Gamble* (New York: Alfred A. Knopf, 2005), 75.
3 Francesca L. Ortigas, "People You Should Know in Manila: A Profile in Courage," indianamilitary.org. http://www.indianamilitary.org%2FGerman%2520PW%2520Camps%2FPrisoner%2520of%2520War%2FPW%2520Camps%2FStalag%2520IX B%2520Bad%2520Orb%2FUnused%2FHans%2520Kasten.rtf.
4 Ibid.
5 Conrad F. Goeringer, "Hans Kasten IV: Foxhole Atheist, American Hero," *American Atheist*, Vol. 44, No. 7, October 2006.
6 Cohen, *Soldiers and Slaves*, 76.
7 Ibid.
8 Goeringer, "Hans Kasten IV."
9 Ibid.
10 Caddick-Adams, *Snow & Steel*, 284.
11 Goeringer, "Hans Kasten IV."
12 Joseph F. Littell, *A Lifetime in Every Moment* (New York: Houghton Mifflin, 1995), 19.
13 Ibid., 76.
14 Ibid., 117.
15 Ibid.
16 John S. D. Eisenhower, *The Bitter Woods: The Battle of the Bulge* (Edinburgh: Birlinn, 2001), 159.
17 Flint Whitlock, *Given Up for Dead: American GI's in the Nazi Concentration Camp at Berga* (Cambridge, MA: Westview Press, 2005), 44.

2. Surrounded!

1 Joseph F. Littell, *A Lifetime in Every Moment* (New York: Houghton Mifflin, 1995), 117.
2 Peter Caddick-Adams, *Snow & Steel: The Battle of the Bulge 1944–45* (London: Arrow Books, 2014), 324.
3 Conrad F. Goeringer, "Hans Kasten IV: Foxhole Atheist, American Hero," *American Atheist*, Vol. 44, No. 7, October 2006.
4 Caddick-Adams, *Snow & Steel*, 331.
5 Ibid., 308.
6 Littell, *Lifetime*, 117.
7 Ibid.
8 Ibid.
9 Ibid., 120.
10 Ibid., 117.
11 Ibid.
12 Ibid., 120.
13 John S. D. Eisenhower, *The Bitter Woods: The Battle of the Bulge* (Edinburgh: Birlinn, 2001), 204–206.
14 Goeringer, "Hans Kasten IV."
15 Ibid.
16 Flint Whitlock, *Given Up for Dead: American GI's in the Nazi Concentration Camp at Berga* (Cambridge, MA: Westview Press, 2005), 56.
17 Caddick-Adams, *Snow & Steel*, 531.
18 Ibid., 533.
19 Goeringer, "Hans Kasten IV."

3. Go West!

1 Conrad F. Goeringer, "Hans Kasten IV: Foxhole Atheist, American Hero," *American Atheist*, Vol. 44, No. 7, October 2006.
2 Peter Caddick-Adams, *Snow & Steel: The Battle of the Bulge 1944–45* (London: Arrow Books, 2014), 332.
3 Ibid., 333.
4 Goeringer, "Hans Kasten IV."
5 Ibid.
6 Roger Cohen, *Soldiers and Slaves: American POWs Trapped by the Nazis' Final Gamble* (New York: Alfred A. Knopf, 2005), 77.
7 Goeringer, "Hans Kasten IV."
8 Ibid.
9 Caddick-Adams, *Snow & Steel*, 525.
10 Ibid., 451.
11 Jean Milmeister, "Identifying the Clervaux Castle Sherman," Diorama-Clervaux by Claude Joachim (website), http://www.diorama-clervaux.com/indexsherman.html, accessed June 6, 2018.
12 Cohen, *Soldiers and Slaves*, 77.

13 Caddick-Adams, *Snow & Steel*, 528.
14 Antony Beevor, *Ardennes 1944: Hitler's Last Gamble* (London: Viking, 2015), 152.
15 Milmeister, "Identifying the Clervaux Castle Sherman."
16 Ibid.
17 Ibid.

4. The Alamo

1 Jean Milmeister, "Identifying the Clervaux Castle Sherman," Diorama-Clervaux by Claude Joachim (website), http://www.diorama-clervaux .com/indexsherman.html, accessed June 6, 2018.
2 Ibid.
3 John S. D. Eisenhower, *The Bitter Woods: The Battle of the Bulge* (Edinburgh, Birlinn, 2001), 226–227.
4 Milmeister, "Identifying the Clervaux Castle Sherman."
5 Flint Whitlock, *Given Up for Dead: American GI's in the Nazi Concentration Camp at Berga* (Cambridge, MA: Westview Press, 2005), 56.
6 John Toland, *Battle: The Story of the Bulge* (New York: Bison Books, 1999), 89.
7 Antony Beevor, *Ardennes 1944: Hitler's Last Gamble* (London: Viking, 2015), 153.
8 Roger Cohen, *Soldiers and Slaves: American POWs Trapped by the Nazis' Final Gamble* (New York: Alfred A. Knopf, 2005), 21.
9 147 Cong. Rec. 6407 (2001).
10 Cohen, *Soldiers and Slaves*, 35.
11 Whitlock, *Given Up for Dead*, 56.
12 Peter Caddick-Adams, *Snow & Steel: The Battle of the Bulge 1944–45* (London: Arrow Books, 2014), 534.
13 Milmeister, "Identifying the Clervaux Castle Sherman."
14 Conrad F. Goeringer, "Hans Kasten IV: Foxhole Atheist, American Hero," *American Atheist*, Vol. 44, No. 7, October 2006.
15 Milmeister, "Identifying the Clervaux Castle Sherman."
16 Joseph F. Littell, *A Lifetime in Every Moment* (New York: Houghton Mifflin, 1995), 120.

5. Give Us This Day Our Daily Bread

1 Antony Beevor, *Ardennes 1944: Hitler's Last Gamble* (London: Viking, 2015), 141.
2 Ernest B. Vermont [*sic*], "Summation of Service and Prison Experiences of Ernest Valmont, 106th Infantry Division," Indiana Military Org, http://www.indianamilitary.org/German%20PW%20Camps/Prisoner%20of %20War/PW%20Camps/Stalag%20IX-B%20Bad%20Orb/ErnestVer mont/ErnestValmont.htm.
3 Peter Caddick-Adams, *Snow & Steel: The Battle of the Bulge 1944–45* (London: Arrow Books, 2014), 526.

4 Conrad F. Goeringer, "Hans Kasten IV: Foxhole Atheist, American Hero," *American Atheist*, Vol. 44, No. 7, October 2006.

5 Ibid.

6 Ibid.

7 Ibid.

8 Beevor, *Ardennes 1944*, 141.

9 Goeringer, "Hans Kasten IV."

10 Roger Cohen, *Soldiers and Slaves: American POWs Trapped by the Nazis' Final Gamble* (New York: Alfred A. Knopf, 2005), 77.

11 Goeringer, "Hans Kasten IV."

12 Ibid.

13 Ibid.

14 Caddick-Adams, *Snow & Steel*, 526.

15 "Summation of Service."

16 Beevor, *Ardennes 1944*, 185–186.

17 Joseph F. Littell, *A Lifetime in Every Moment* (New York: Houghton Mifflin, 1995), 121.

18 Ibid.

19 Ibid.

20 Ibid.

21 Flint Whitlock, *Given Up for Dead: American GI's in the Nazi Concentration Camp at Berga* (Cambridge, MA: Westview Press, 2005), 61.

22 Ibid., 64.

23 Pete House, "Life in Stalag IX-B: Story of an American Held in a German POW Camp," Indiana Military Org, http://www.indianamilitary.org /German%20PW%20Camps/Prisoner%20of%20War/PW%20Camps /Stalag%20IX-B%20Bad%20Orb/Pete%20House/Life/House-Pete-Life .pdf.

24 Littell, *A Lifetime in Every Moment*, 121.

25 Ibid., 122.

26 Caddick-Adams, *Snow & Steel*, 530.

27 Ibid.

6. The Long March

1 Pete House, "Life in Stalag IX-B: Story of an American Held in a German POW Camp," Indiana Military Org, http://www.indianamilitary.org /German%20PW%20Camps/Prisoner%20of%20War/PW%20Camps /Stalag%20IX-B%20Bad%20Orb/Pete%20House/Life/House-Pete-Life .pdf.

2 Ibid.

3 Ernest B. Vermont [*sic*], "Summation of Service and Prison Experiences of Ernest Valmont, 106th Infantry Division," Indiana Military Org, http:// www.indianamilitary.org/German%20PW%20Camps/Prisoner%20of %20War/PW%20Camps/Stalag%20IX-B%20Bad%20Orb/ErnestVer mont/ErnestValmont.htm.

4 Ibid.

5   Joseph F. Littell, *A Lifetime in Every Moment* (New York: Houghton Mifflin, 1995), 122.
6   Ibid., 123.
7   Ibid.
8   Vermont [*sic*], "Summation of Service."
9   House, "Life in Stalag IX-B."
10 Ibid.
11 "Troy H. Kimmel," Indiana Military Org, http://www.indianamilitary.org/German%20PW%20Camps/Prisoner%20of%20War/PW%20Camps/Stalag%20IX-B%20Bad%20Orb/TroyKimmel/TroyKimmel.htm.
12 Ibid.
13 House, "Life in Stalag IX-B."
14 Littell, *A Lifetime in Every Moment*, 124.
15 House, "Life in Stalag IX-B."
16 Ibid.
17 John W. Reinfenrath, "An American Slave in Nazi Germany: My Story of Combat, Capture, and Slave Labor," Indiana Military Org, http://www.indianamilitary.org/German%20PW%20Camps/Prisoner%20of%20War/PW%20Camps/Berga/JohnReinfenrath/JohnReinfenrath.htm.
18 Conrad F. Goeringer, "Hans Kasten IV: Foxhole Atheist, American Hero," *American Atheist*, Vol. 44, No. 7, October 2006.
19 Ibid.
20 Ibid.
21 Ibid.
22 "Troy H. Kimmel."
23 Ibid.
24 Flint Whitlock, *Given Up for Dead: American GI's in the Nazi Concentration Camp at Berga* (Cambridge, MA: Westview Press, 2005), 78.
25 Vermont [*sic*], "Summation of Service."
26 House, "Life in Stalag IX-B."

7. Friendly Fire

1   Joseph F. Littell, *A Lifetime in Every Moment* (New York: Houghton Mifflin, 1995), 126.
2   Pete House, "Life in Stalag IX-B: Story of an American Held in a German POW Camp," Indiana Military Org, http://www.indianamilitary.org/German%20PW%20Camps/Prisoner%20of%20War/PW%20Camps/Stalag%20IX-B%20Bad%20Orb/Pete%20House/Life/House-Pete-Life.pdf.
3   John W. Reinfenrath, "An American Slave in Nazi Germany: My Story of Combat, Capture, and Slave Labor," Indiana Military Org, http://www.indianamilitary.org/German%20PW%20Camps/Prisoner%20of%20War/PW%20Camps/Berga/JohnReinfenrath/JohnReinfenrath.htm.
4   Theodore Rosenberg, "My Story as a Prisoner of Germany," Indiana Military Org, http://www.indianamilitary.org/German%20PW%20Camps/Prisoner%20of%20War/PW%20Camps/Berga/TheodoreRosenberg/TheodoreRosenberg.htm.

5   House, "Life in Stalag IX-B."

6   Reinfenrath, "An American Slave in Nazi Germany."

7   "Troy H. Kimmel," Indiana Military Org, http://www.indianamilitary
    .org/German%20PW%20Camps/Prisoner%20of%20War/PW%20
    Camps/Stalag%20IX-B%20Bad%20Orb/TroyKimmel/TroyKimmel
    .htm.

8   Theodore Rosenberg, "My Story as a Prisoner of Germany," Indiana Military
    Org, http://www.indianamilitary.org/German%20PW%20Camps/Prisoner
    %20of%20War/PW%20Camps/Berga/TheodoreRosenberg/Theodore
    Rosenberg.htm.

9   House, "Life in Stalag IX-B."

10 Reinfenrath, "An American Slave in Nazi Germany."

11 Conrad F. Goeringer, "Hans Kasten IV: Foxhole Atheist, American Hero," *American Atheist*, Vol. 44, No. 7, October 2006.

12 Ibid.

13 Littell, *A Lifetime in Every Moment*, 126.

14 Reinfenrath, "An American Slave in Nazi Germany."

15 "Troy H. Kimmel."

16 Reinfenrath, "An American Slave in Nazi Germany."

17 Ibid.

18 Ibid.

19 "Troy H. Kimmel."

20 Martin Middlebrook and Chris Everitt, *The Bomber Command War Diaries: An Operational Reference Book, 1939–1945* (Barnsley, UK: Pen & Sword Aviation, 2014), 98.

21 Fr. Paul W. Cavanaugh, S.J., "Pro Deo et Patria (For God and Country)," available at Indiana Military Org, http://www.indianamilitary.org /German%20PW%20Camps/Prisoner%20of%20War/PW%20Camps/ Oflag%20XIII-B/FrPaulCavanaugh/Fr.%20Cavanaugh.DOC.doc. This document contains Fr. Cavanaugh's original manuscript, "American Priest in a Nazi Prison."

22 Ibid.

8. A Christmas Story

1   Fr. Paul W. Cavanaugh, S.J., "Pro Deo et Patria (For God and Country)," available at Indiana Military Org, http://www.indianamilitary.org/German %20PW%20Camps/Prisoner%20of%20War/PW%20Camps/Oflag%20 XIII-B/FrPaulCavanaugh/Fr.%20Cavanaugh.DOC.doc. This document contains Fr. Cavanaugh's original manuscript, "American Priest in a Nazi Prison."

2   Ibid.

3   Conrad F. Goeringer, "Hans Kasten IV: Foxhole Atheist, American Hero," *American Atheist*, Vol. 44, No. 7, October 2006.

4   Martin Middlebrook and Chris Everitt, *The Bomber Command War Diaries: An Operational Reference Book, 1939–1945* (Barnsley, UK: Pen & Sword Aviation, 2014), 98.

5 "Hans Kasten (Chief Man of Confidence) to the International Red Cross Concerning the Fates of Men Interned in M-Stammlager IX B, Bad Orb, Germany, 16 January 1945," National Archives and Records Administration (NARA), College Park, Maryland.

6 Cavanaugh, "Pro Deo et Patria."

7 Goeringer, "Hans Kasten IV."

8 Theodore Rosenberg, "My Story as a Prisoner of Germany," Indiana Military Org, http://www.indianamilitary.org/German%20PW%20Camps/Prisoner%20of%20War/PW%20Camps/Berga/TheodoreRosenberg/TheodoreRosenberg.htm.

9 Flint Whitlock, *Given Up for Dead: American GI's in the Nazi Concentration Camp at Berga* (Cambridge, MA: Westview Press, 2005), 84.

10 Rosenberg, "My Story as a Prisoner of Germany."

11 Cavanaugh, "Pro Deo et Patria."

12 Rosenberg, "My Story as a Prisoner of Germany."

13 Cavanaugh, "Pro Deo et Patria."

14 Rosenberg, "My Story as a Prisoner of Germany."

15 Cavanaugh, "Pro Deo et Patria."

16 Ibid.

17 John W. Reinfenrath, "An American Slave in Nazi Germany: My Story of Combat, Capture, and Slave Labor," Indiana Military Org, http://www.indianamilitary.org/German%20PW%20Camps/Prisoner%20of%20War/PW%20Camps/Berga/JohnReinfenrath/JohnReinfenrath.htm.

18 Goeringer, "Hans Kasten IV."

19 Pete House, "Life in Stalag IX-B: Story of an American Held in a German POW Camp," Indiana Military Org, http://www.indianamilitary.org/German%20PW%20Camps/Prisoner%20of%20War/PW%20Camps/Stalag%20IX-B%20Bad%20Orb/Pete%20House/Life/House-Pete-Life.pdf.

20 Ibid.

21 Pfc. Philip A. Hannon, "One Man's Story," Indiana Military Org, http://www.indianamilitary.org/German%20PW%20Camps/Prisoner%20of%20War/PW%20Camps/Stalag%20IX-B%20Bad%20Orb/Philip%20Hannon/Philip%20Hannon.htm

22 "Camp Reports: Dulag Luft to Ilag, report on Stalag IXB—Bad Orb," March 23, 1945, National Archives and Records Administration (NARA), College Park, Maryland.

23 "Troy H. Kimmel," Indiana Military Org, http://www.indianamilitary.org/German%20PW%20Camps/Prisoner%20of%20War/PW%20Camps/Stalag%20IX-B%20Bad%20Orb/TroyKimmel/TroyKimmel.htm.

9. Abandon Hope

1 D. B. Frampton Jr., "Ich Bin Ein Kriegsgefangener und Still Singing the Praises of General George S. Patton, USA: A Rather Loose Narrative by a Foot Soldier Who Got Caught in the Battle of the Bulge—December 1944," Indiana Military Org, http://www.indianamilitary.org/German%20PW%20Camps/Prisoner%20of%20War/PW%20Camps/Stalag

%20IX-A%20Ziegenhain/D%20B%20Frampton/Frampton-D-B.pdf.

2   Conrad F. Goeringer, "Hans Kasten IV: Foxhole Atheist, American Hero," *American Atheist*, Vol. 44, No. 7, October 2006.

3   Frampton, "Ich Bin Ein Kriegsgefangener."

4   Goeringer, "Hans Kasten IV."

5   "Stalag IXB Bad Orb—War Office: IRC and Protecting Powers (Geneva): Reports Concerning POW Camps in Europe and the Far East. Stalag IXB Bad Orb, WO 224/30, 1 Mar 1944—31 Mar 1945," The National Archives (Public Record Office), Kew, London, UK.

6   Pete House, "Life in Stalag IX-B: Story of an American Held in a German POW Camp," Indiana Military Org, http://www.indianamilitary.org/German%20PW%20Camps/Prisoner%20of%20War/PW%20Camps/Stalag%20IX-B%20Bad%20Orb/Pete%20House/Life/House-Pete-Life.pdf.

7   "Camp Reports: Dulag Luft to Ilag, Report on Stalag IXB—Bad Orb," March 23, 1945, National Archives and Records Administration (NARA), College Park, Maryland.

8   Ibid.

9   "Personnel Card of Karl Sieber, Commander of Stalag IX B, 2 January 1945," National Archives and Records Administration (NARA), College Park, Maryland.

10 "Stalag IXB Bad Orb."

11 "Personnel Card of Albert Wodarg, Deputy Commander of Stalag IX B, 16 November 1943," National Archives and Records Administration (NARA), College Park, Maryland.

12 House, "Life in Stalag IX-B."

13 Ibid.

14 Ibid.

15 Ibid.

16 Pfc. Philip A. Hannon, "One Man's Story," Indiana Military Org, http://www.indianamilitary.org/German%20PW%20Camps/Prisoner%20of%20War/PW%20Camps/Stalag%20IX-B%20Bad%20Orb/Philip%20Hannon/Philip%20Hannon.htm.

17 Ibid.

18 Ibid.

19 Ibid.

20 Ibid.

21 "Diary of Raymond Brown, Leeds, Utah," Indiana Military Org, http://www.indianamilitary.org/German%20PW%20Camps/Prisoner%20of%20War/PW%20Camps/Stalag%20IX-B%20Bad%20Orb/Raymond%20Brown/Raymond%20Brown.htm.

22 "Camp Reports: Dulag Luft to Ilag."

23 House, "Life in Stalag IX-B."

24 Goeringer, "Hans Kasten IV."

25 Ibid.

26 Ibid.

10. Chief Man of Confidence

1 "Roster of Interpreters, MPs, and Leaders Among the Men of Stalag IX B," Experiencing War, Veterans History Project, Library of Congress, Washington, DC, https://memory.loc.gov/diglib/vhp-stories/loc.natlib .afc2001001.12002/pageturner?ID=pm0005001.

2 Conrad F. Goeringer, "Hans Kasten IV: Foxhole Atheist, American Hero," *American Atheist*, Vol. 44, No. 7, October 2006.

3 "Stalag IX-B, German Prisoner of War Camp, Bad Orb, Germany, History," Indiana Military Org, http://www.indianamilitary.org/German %20PW%20Camps/Prisoner%20of%20War/PW%20Camps/Stalag%2 0IX-B%20Bad%20Orb/History.htm

4 Joseph F. Littell, *A Lifetime in Every Moment* (New York: Houghton Mifflin, 1995), 129–131.

5 "Stalag IXB Bad Orb—War Office: IRC and Protecting Powers (Geneva): Reports Concerning POW Camps in Europe and the Far East. Stalag IXB Bad Orb, WO 224/30, 1 Mar 1944—31 Mar 1945," The National Archives (Public Record Office), Kew, London, UK.

6 Littell, *A Lifetime in Every Moment*, 129.

7 Roger Cohen, *Soldiers and Slaves: American POWs Trapped by the Nazis' Final Gamble* (New York: Alfred A. Knopf, 2005), 82.

8 Pete House, "Life in Stalag IX-B: Story of an American Held in a German POW Camp," Indiana Military Org, http://www.indianamilitary.org/Ger man%20PW%20Camps/Prisoner%20of%20War/PW%20 Camps/Stalag%20IX-B%20Bad%20Orb/Pete%20House/Life/House -Pete-Life.pdf.

9 "Roster of Interpreters."

10 House, "Life in Stalag IX-B."

11 Ibid.

12 "Stalag IX-B, German Prisoner of War Camp."

13 "Camp Reports: Dulag Luft to Ilag, Report on Stalag IXB—Bad Orb," March 23, 1945, National Archives and Records Administration (NARA), College Park, Maryland.

14 House, "Life in Stalag IX-B."

15 Goeringer, "Hans Kasten IV."

16 Littell, *A Lifetime in Every Moment*, 131.

17 Ibid.

11. Herr Buchmuller Recommends

1 Conrad F. Goeringer, "Hans Kasten IV: Foxhole Atheist, American Hero," *American Atheist*, Vol. 44, No. 7, October 2006.

2 "Red Cross Report, Stalag IX-B," January 24, 1945, National Archives and Records Administration (NARA), College Park, Maryland.

3 Goeringer, "Hans Kasten IV."

4 "Red Cross Report, Stalag IX-B."

5 Ibid.
6 Ibid.
7 Ibid.
8 Ibid.
9 Ibid.
10 Goeringer, "Hans Kasten IV."
11 "Red Cross Report, Stalag IX-B."
12 Ibid.
13 Ibid.
14 Pete House, "Life in Stalag IX-B: Story of an American Held in a German POW Camp," Indiana Military Org, http://www.indianamilitary.org /German%20PW%20Camps/Prisoner%20of%20War/PW%20Camps /Stalag%20IX-B%20Bad%20Orb/Pete%20House/Life/House-Pete-Life .pdf.

12. The Reprisal

1 Pete House, "Life in Stalag IX-B: Story of an American Held in a German POW Camp," Indiana Military Org, http://www.indianamilitary.org /German%20PW%20Camps/Prisoner%20of%20War/PW%20Camps /Stalag%20IX-B%20Bad%20Orb/Pete%20House/Life/House-Pete-Life .pdf.
2 Conrad F. Goeringer, "Hans Kasten IV: Foxhole Atheist, American Hero," *American Atheist*, Vol. 44, No. 7, October 2006.
3 Ibid.
4 "Rules and Regulations for the Operations of German Prisoner of War Camps," March 11, 1942, National Archives and Records Administration (NARA), College Park, Maryland.
5 Goeringer, "Hans Kasten IV."
6 Ibid.
7 Ibid.
8 House, "Life in Stalag IX-B."
9 Goeringer, "Hans Kasten IV."
10 Ibid.
11 Ibid.
12 Ibid.

13. Blue Sunday

1 John W. Reinfenrath, "An American Slave in Nazi Germany: My Story of Combat, Capture, and Slave Labor," Indiana Military Org, http://www.indianamilitary.org/German%20PW%20Camps/Prisoner %20of%20War/PW%20Camps/Berga/JohnReinfenrath/JohnReinfen rath.htm.
2 Theodore Rosenberg, "My Story as a Prisoner of Germany," Indiana Military Org, http://www.indianamilitary.org/German%20PW%20Camps/

Prisoner%20of%20War/PW%20Camps/Berga/TheodoreRosenberg/
TheodoreRosenberg.htm.

3 Myron "Mike" Klingman, "German Prisoner No. 25708," Indiana Military Org, http://www.indianamilitary.org/German%20PW%20Camps/
Prisoner%20of%20War/PW%20Camps/Stalag%20IX-B%20Bad%20
Orb/Myron%20Klinkman/Klingman-Myron.pdf.

4 Reinfenrath, "An American Slave in Nazi Germany."

5 Ibid.

6 Ibid.

7 Pete House, "Life in Stalag IX-B: Story of an American Held in a German POW Camp," Indiana Military Org, http://www.indianamilitary.org
/German%20PW%20Camps/Prisoner%20of%20War/PW%20Camps
/Stalag%20IX-B%20Bad%20Orb/Pete%20House/Life/House-Pete
-Life.pdf.

8 Ibid.

9 Ibid.

10 Klingman, "German Prisoner No. 25708."

11 Johann Kasten, "Detailed Report on an Assault on a Guard by American POWs at Stalag IX B," January 29, 1945, Veterans History Project, Library of Congress, Washington, DC, http://memory.loc.gov/diglib/vhp/
story/loc.natlib.afc2001001.12002/pageturner?ID=pm0004001.

12 "Diary of Raymond Brown, Leeds, Utah," Indiana Military Org, http://
www.indianamilitary.org/German%20PW%20Camps/Prisoner%20of%
20War/PW%20Camps/Stalag%20IX-B%20Bad%20Orb/Raymond%20
Brown/Raymond%20Brown.htm.

13 Kasten, "Detailed Report on an Assault."

14 Ibid.

15 Ibid.

16 Ibid.

17 Ibid.

18 Rosenberg, "My Story as a Prisoner of Germany."

19 "Diary of Raymond Brown."

20 United States vs. Erwin Metz, et al, Deputy Judge Advocate's Office, 7708 War Crimes Group, European Command, September 15, 1947, National Archives and Records Administration (NARA), College Park, Maryland.

21 Ibid.

22 Ibid.

23 "Diary of Raymond Brown."

24 Ibid.

25 Ibid.

26 House, "Life in Stalag IX-B."

27 "Diary of Raymond Brown."

28 Ibid.

29 Pfc. Philip A. Hannon, "One Man's Story," Indiana Military Org,
http://www.indianamilitary.org/German%20PW%20Camps/Prisoner%
20of%20War/PW%20Camps/Stalag%20IX-B%20Bad%20Orb/Philip%
20Hannon/Philip%20Hannon.htm.

30 Rosenberg, "My Story as a Prisoner of Germany."

31 Ibid.
32 Ibid.
33 Ibid.

14. Berga

1 John W. Reinfenrath, "An American Slave in Nazi Germany: My Story of Combat, Capture, and Slave Labor," Indiana Military Org, http://www .indianamilitary.org/German%20PW%20Camps/Prisoner%20of%20War/PW%20Camps/Berga/JohnReinfenrath/JohnReinfenrath.htm.
2 Ibid.
3 Ibid.
4 Conrad F. Goeringer, "Hans Kasten IV: Foxhole Atheist, American Hero," *American Atheist*, Vol. 44, No. 7, October 2006.
5 Reinfenrath, "An American Slave in Nazi Germany."
6 Theodore Rosenberg, "My Story as a Prisoner of Germany," Indiana Military Org, http://www.indianamilitary.org/German%20PW%20Camps/Prisoner%20of%20War/PW%20Camps/Berga/TheodoreRosenberg/TheodoreRosenberg.htm.
7 Goeringer, "Hans Kasten IV."
8 "Red Cross Report, Stalag IX-B," January 24, 1945, National Archives and Records Administration (NARA), College Park, Maryland.
9 Rosenberg, "My Story as a Prisoner of Germany."
10 Goeringer, "Hans Kasten IV."
11 Ibid.
12 "Berga an Elster (Subcamp of Buchenwald Concentration Camp—Afro-American and Jewish-American POWs Sent There to Work in Mines)," 1945, National Archives and Records Administration (NARA), College Park, Maryland.
13 Ibid.

15. The Devil's Mountain

1 "Mannschafts-Stammlager (Stalag) IX B," The Holocaust Encyclopedia, The United States Holocaust Memorial Museum, https://encyclopedia.ushmm .org/content/en/article/mannschafts-stammlager-stalag-ix-b, accessed November 20, 2018.
2 Ibid.
3 "Berga an Elster (Subcamp of Buchenwald Concentration Camp—Afro-American and Jewish-American POWs Sent There to Work in Mines)," 1945, National Archives and Records Administration (NARA), College Park, Maryland.
4 Ibid.
5 Ibid.
6 Theodore Rosenberg, "My Story as a Prisoner of Germany," Indiana Military Org, http://www.indianamilitary.org/German%20PW%20Camps/

Prisoner%20of%20War/PW%20Camps/Berga/TheodoreRosenberg/
TheodoreRosenberg.htm.

7 Ibid.
8 Roger Cohen, *Soldiers and Slaves: American POWs Trapped by the Nazis'
   Final Gamble* (New York: Alfred A. Knopf, 2005), 136.
9 Rosenberg, "My Story as a Prisoner of Germany."
10 John W. Reinfenrath, "An American Slave in Nazi Germany: My Story of
   Combat, Capture, and Slave Labor," Indiana Military Org, http://www
   .indianamilitary.org/German%20PW%20Camps/Prisoner%20of%20
   War/PW%20Camps/Berga/JohnReinfenrath/JohnReinfenrath.htm.

16. Mutiny

1 "Berga an Elster (Subcamp of Buchenwald Concentration Camp—
   Afro-American and Jewish-American POWs Sent There to Work in
   Mines)," 1945, National Archives and Records Administration (NARA),
   College Park, Maryland.
2 Joseph F. Littell, *A Lifetime in Every Moment* (New York: Houghton Mifflin, 1995), 135.
3 Ibid.
4 Ibid.
5 Conrad F. Goeringer, "Hans Kasten IV: Foxhole Atheist, American Hero,"
   American Atheist, Vol. 44, No. 7, October 2006.
6 Littell, *A Lifetime in Every Moment*, 135.
7 Ibid.
8 Ibid.
9 Ibid.
10 Flint Whitlock, *Given Up for Dead: American GI's in the Nazi Concentration
   Camp at Berga* (Cambridge, MA: Westview Press, 2005), 137.
11 Ibid.
12 Roger Cohen, *Soldiers and Slaves: American POWs Trapped by the Nazis'
   Final Gamble* (New York: Alfred A. Knopf, 2005), 141.
13 Ibid.
14 Littell, *A Lifetime in Every Moment*, 136.

17. The Dogs of War

1 Conrad F. Goeringer, "Hans Kasten IV: Foxhole Atheist, American Hero,"
   American Atheist, Vol. 44, No. 7, October 2006.
2 Ibid.
3 Ibid.
4 Ibid.
5 Joseph F. Littell, *A Lifetime in Every Moment* (New York: Houghton Mifflin, 1995), 137.
6 Ibid.
7 Ibid.

8   Goeringer, "Hans Kasten IV."
9   Littell, *A Lifetime in Every Moment*, 137.
10 Goeringer, "Hans Kasten IV."
11 Ibid.
12 Ibid.
13 Littell, *A Lifetime in Every Moment*, 138.
14 Ibid.
15 Goeringer, "Hans Kasten IV."
16 Littell, *A Lifetime in Every Moment*, 138.
17 Goeringer, "Hans Kasten IV."

18. Breakout

1   Joseph F. Littell, *A Lifetime in Every Moment* (New York: Houghton Mifflin, 1995), 138.
2   Conrad F. Goeringer, "Hans Kasten IV: Foxhole Atheist, American Hero," *American Atheist*, Vol. 44, No. 7, October 2006.
3   Littell, *A Lifetime in Every Moment*, 138–139.
4   Ibid., 138.
5   Goeringer, "Hans Kasten IV."
6   Littell, *A Lifetime in Every Moment*, 139.
7   Goeringer, "Hans Kasten IV."
8   "Berga an Elster (Subcamp of Buchenwald Concentration Camp—Afro-American and Jewish-American POWs Sent There to Work in Mines)," 1945, National Archives and Records Administration (NARA), College Park, Maryland.
9   Ibid.
10 Littell, *A Lifetime in Every Moment*, 139.
11 Ibid.
12 Ibid.
13 Ibid.
14 Goeringer, "Hans Kasten IV."
15 Littell, *A Lifetime in Every Moment*, 139.
16 Ibid.
17 Goeringer, "Hans Kasten IV."
18 Littell, *A Lifetime in Every Moment*, 140.

19. Forgive Us Our Trespasses

1   Joseph F. Littell, *A Lifetime in Every Moment* (New York: Houghton Mifflin, 1995), 140.
2   Ibid.
3   Conrad F. Goeringer, "Hans Kasten IV: Foxhole Atheist, American Hero," *American Atheist*, Vol. 44, No. 7, October 2006.
4   Littell, *A Lifetime in Every Moment* 141.
5   Goeringer, "Hans Kasten IV."

6   Littell, *A Lifetime in Every Moment*, 141.
7   Goeringer, "Hans Kasten IV."
8   Littell, *A Lifetime in Every Moment*, 141.
9   Goeringer, "Hans Kasten IV."
10 Ibid.
11 Ibid.
12 Littell, *A Lifetime in Every Moment*, 141.
13 "Gedenk- und Begegnungsstätte im Torhaus der Politischen Haftanstalt von 1933 bis 1945 und 1945 bis 1989," http://www.torhaus-gera.de, accessed September 12, 2018.
14 Ibid.
15 Littell, *A Lifetime in Every Moment*, 142.
16 Ibid., 143.

20. The End of the Line

1   Joseph F. Littell, *A Lifetime in Every Moment* (New York: Houghton Mifflin, 1995), 143.
2   Ibid., 144.
3   Conrad F. Goeringer, "Hans Kasten IV: Foxhole Atheist, American Hero," *American Atheist*, Vol. 44, No. 7, October 2006.
4   Ibid.
5   Littell, *A Lifetime in Every Moment*, 144.
6   Goeringer, "Hans Kasten IV."
7   Littell, *A Lifetime in Every Moment*, 144.
8   Ibid., 145.
9   Ibid.
10 Goeringer, "Hans Kasten IV."
11 Littell, *A Lifetime in Every Moment*, 146.
12 "War Office: JAG Office, BAOR War Crimes Group (NW Europe) and Predecessors: Registered Files (BAOR and other series). Bad Sulza and Ziegenhain, Germany: Killing and Ill Treatment of Allied Nationals," WO 309/1186, 1 May 1947–28 Feb. 1948.
13 Ibid.
14 Ibid.
15 Ibid.
16 Littell, *A Lifetime in Every Moment*, 146.
17 Ibid., 147.
18 Goeringer, "Hans Kasten IV."
19 Ibid.
20 Ibid.
21 Ibid.

21. Deliver Us from Evil

1 Joseph F. Littell, *A Lifetime in Every Moment* (New York: Houghton Mifflin, 1995), 150.
2 Conrad F. Goeringer, "Hans Kasten IV: Foxhole Atheist, American Hero," *American Atheist*, Vol. 44, No. 7, October 2006.
3 Ibid.
4 "War Office: JAG Office, BAOR War Crimes Group (NW Europe) and Predecessors: Registered Files (BAOR and Other Series). Bad Sulza and Ziegenhain, Germany: Killing and Ill-Treatment of Allied Nationals," WO 309/1186, 1 May 1947–28 Feb. 1948.
5 Littell, *A Lifetime in Every Moment*, 153.
6 Goeringer, "Hans Kasten IV."
7 "Chapter VI: Germany Campaign 10 March 1945 to 16 April 1945," *Combat History of the Super Sixth*, Super Sixth: The Story of Patton's 6th Armored Division in WW II (website), http://www.super6th.org/cmbthist/cmbgrmny.htm, accessed December 11, 2018.
8 Ibid.
9 Ibid.
10 Goeringer, "Hans Kasten IV."
11 Littell, *A Lifetime in Every Moment*, 153.
12 Ibid., 154.
13 Goeringer, "Hans Kasten IV."
14 Ibid.
15 Ibid.
16 Ibid.
17 "Berga an Elster (Subcamp of Buchenwald Concentration Camp—Afro-American and Jewish-American POWs Sent There to Work in Mines)," 1945, National Archives and Records Administration (NARA), College Park, Maryland.
18 Ibid.
19 Ibid.
20 Ibid.
21 Goeringer, "Hans Kasten IV."

Epilogue

1 Paul N. Frenkel, *Life Reclaimed: Rural Transylvania, Nazi Camps, and the American Dream* (Bloomington, IN: iUniverse, 2013), 160.
2 Ibid.
3 Roger Cohen, *Soldiers and Slaves: American POWs Trapped by the Nazis' Final Gamble* (New York: Alfred A. Knopf, 2005), 242.

Index

About the Author

MARK FELTON is a well-known British historian whose many books include *Zero Night* ('a thundering good read' – *History of War* magazine) and *Castle of the Eagles* ('an extraordinary and largely forgotten wartime story, brought back to life in this Boy's Own account' – *Daily Mail*). He writes regularly for publications including *Military History Monthly* and *World War II* and has appeared as a historical expert on television programmes for Netflix, the History Channel and the Discovery Channel.

www.markfelton.co.uk

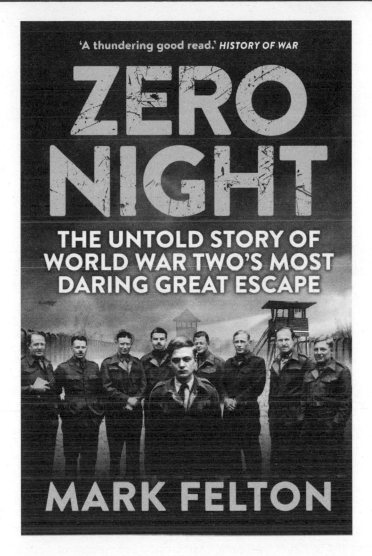

Staged in August 1942, the 'Warburg Wire Job' was the first Great Escape of World War Two. Months of meticulous planning hung in the balance during three minutes of mayhem as prisoners charged the camp's double perimeter fences and climbed to freedom using ingenious wooden scaling contraptions. Mark Felton recounts the extraordinary escape itself, and the adventures of the fugitives in enemy territory. Will any of the prisoners make it home?

ISBN 9781848318472 (paperback) / 9781848317321 (ebook)

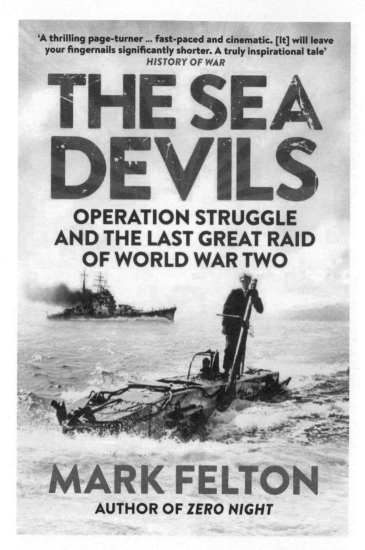

'A thrilling page-turner ... fast-paced and cinematic. [It] will leave
your fingernails significantly shorter. A truly inspirational tale'
HISTORY OF WAR

THE SEA DEVILS

OPERATION STRUGGLE
AND THE LAST GREAT RAID
OF WORLD WAR TWO

MARK FELTON
AUTHOR OF *ZERO NIGHT*

July 1945. Eighteen young men from a top-secret underwater
warfare unit prepare to undertake three audacious missions
against the Japanese. Using XE-craft midget submarines,
the raiders will creep deep behind enemy lines to sink two
huge warships and sever vital undersea communications
cables. Can the Sea Devils overcome Japanese defences,
mechanical failures, oxygen poisoning and submarine
disasters to fulfil their missions? Mark Felton tells
the true story of the last great raid of World War Two.

ISBN 9781785780493 (paperback) / 9781848319097 (ebook)

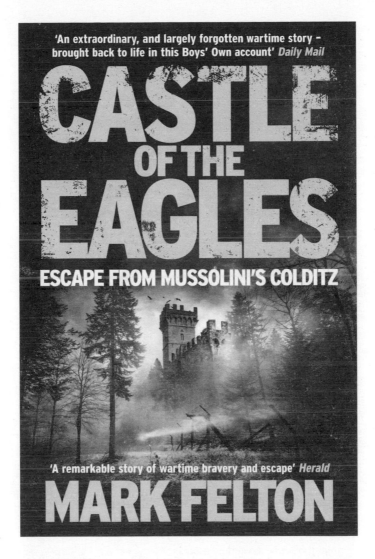

'An extraordinary, and largely forgotten wartime story – brought back to life in this Boys' Own account' *Daily Mail*

CASTLE OF THE EAGLES

ESCAPE FROM MUSSOLINI'S COLDITZ

'A remarkable story of wartime bravery and escape' *Herald*

MARK FELTON

In a POW camp high in the Tuscan hills – an elaborate medieval castle converted on Mussolini's personal orders – a dozen senior Allied officers sit plotting their escape. A series of daring getaway attempts culminates in a complex tunnel deep beneath the castle, and one rainswept night, six men burst from the earth beyond the curtain wall and slip away. Historian Mark Felton tells the thrilling true story of how they will attempt to negotiate the treacherous 200-mile journey to Switzerland – and freedom.

ISBN 9781785782824 (paperback) / 9781785781193 (ebook)

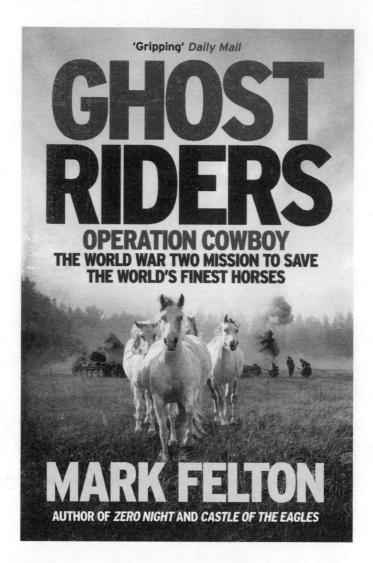

'Gripping' *Daily Mail*

GHOST RIDERS

OPERATION COWBOY
THE WORLD WAR TWO MISSION TO SAVE THE WORLD'S FINEST HORSES

MARK FELTON

AUTHOR OF *ZERO NIGHT* AND *CASTLE OF THE EAGLES*

Alerted to the fact that the world's finest horses are in danger, the US Army launches Operation Cowboy, the greatest World War Two story that has never been fully told. GIs will join forces with a cadre of disillusioned Wehrmacht in a bid to save the famous Lipizzaner stallions of Vienna – but faced with fanatical SS and the ruthless Red Army in the increasingly lawless last days of the war, will they live to tell the tale?

ISBN 9781785785092 (paperback) / 9781785784033 (ebook)